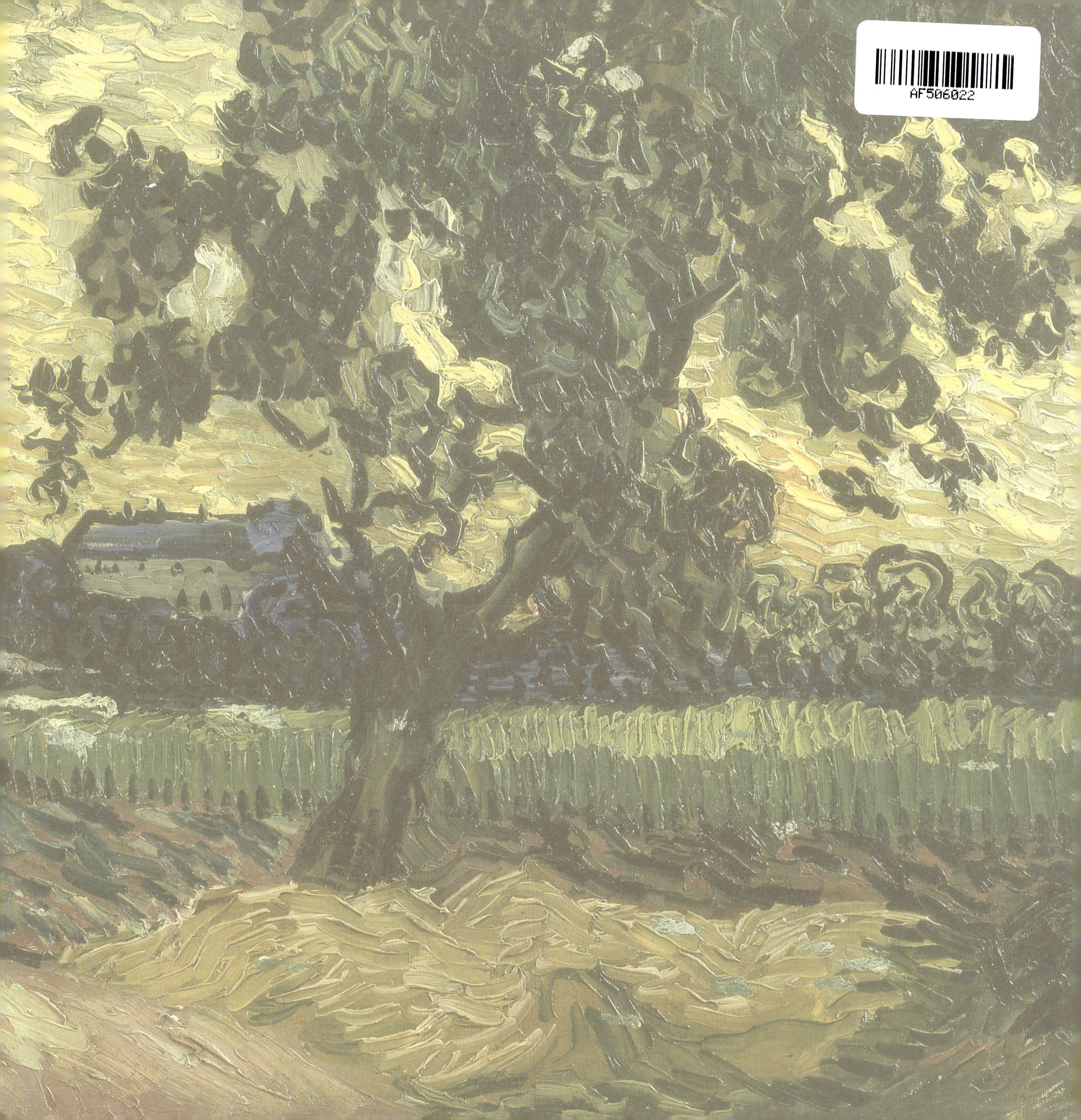
AF506022

Van Gogh

Art and Emotion

Debra N. Mancoff, Ph.D.

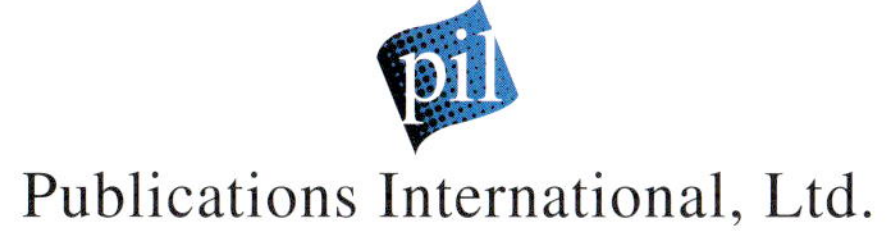

Publications International, Ltd.

CONTENTS

VINCENT VAN GOGH: A BRIEF LIFE IN ART

"It is not the language of painters but the language of nature which one should listen to."

VINCENT TO THEO, JULY 1882, FROM THE HAGUE

EARLY IN NOVEMBER 1883, Vincent van Gogh (1853–1890) wrote a consoling letter to his younger brother Theo (1857–1891), an up-and-coming art dealer worried about his future. Sharing the insight of his own experiences, Vincent reflected on the unpredictability of an existence in which a calm morning could suddenly be transformed by a violent gale. He warned Theo that unexpected twists and turns could leave him shaken and questioning the direction his life had taken. However, Vincent also reassured him that as brothers they would always support one another and that misfortune might have the unexpected result of bringing them even closer together. Vincent himself had passed through years of similar frustrations and indecision during which he embarked on several paths—as an art dealer, as a teacher, as a lay minister—hoping to find a vocation that would engage his heart and his mind. But he found neither contentment nor success, and now, with single-minded determination, he was teaching himself to paint. He suggested that Theo leave the gallery and take up the brush as well and closed his letter with the telling declaration: "So it seems to me that we must concentrate our whole energy on painting with the utmost single-ness of purpose—it being the raft that will take us safely to shore after the shipwreck." Theo rejected his brother's advice and stayed in his profession. But Vincent's words proved true for his own destiny, a brief life in which art served as his sole consolation.

Vincent van Gogh's career as a painter spanned a scant decade. Although short in duration, his life as an artist proved productive and powerful, leaving a legacy of works that bear the unmistakable

Irises (1890). Vincent's fascination with color prompted him to paint bouquets of flowers throughout his career. The iris, along with the sunflower, was his favorite. He had painted the bold blue-violet petals and flamelike leaves many times during the years he lived in Provençe. The vibrant contrast he attained by setting the blue flowers against the yellow background became a hallmark of his expressive use of color.

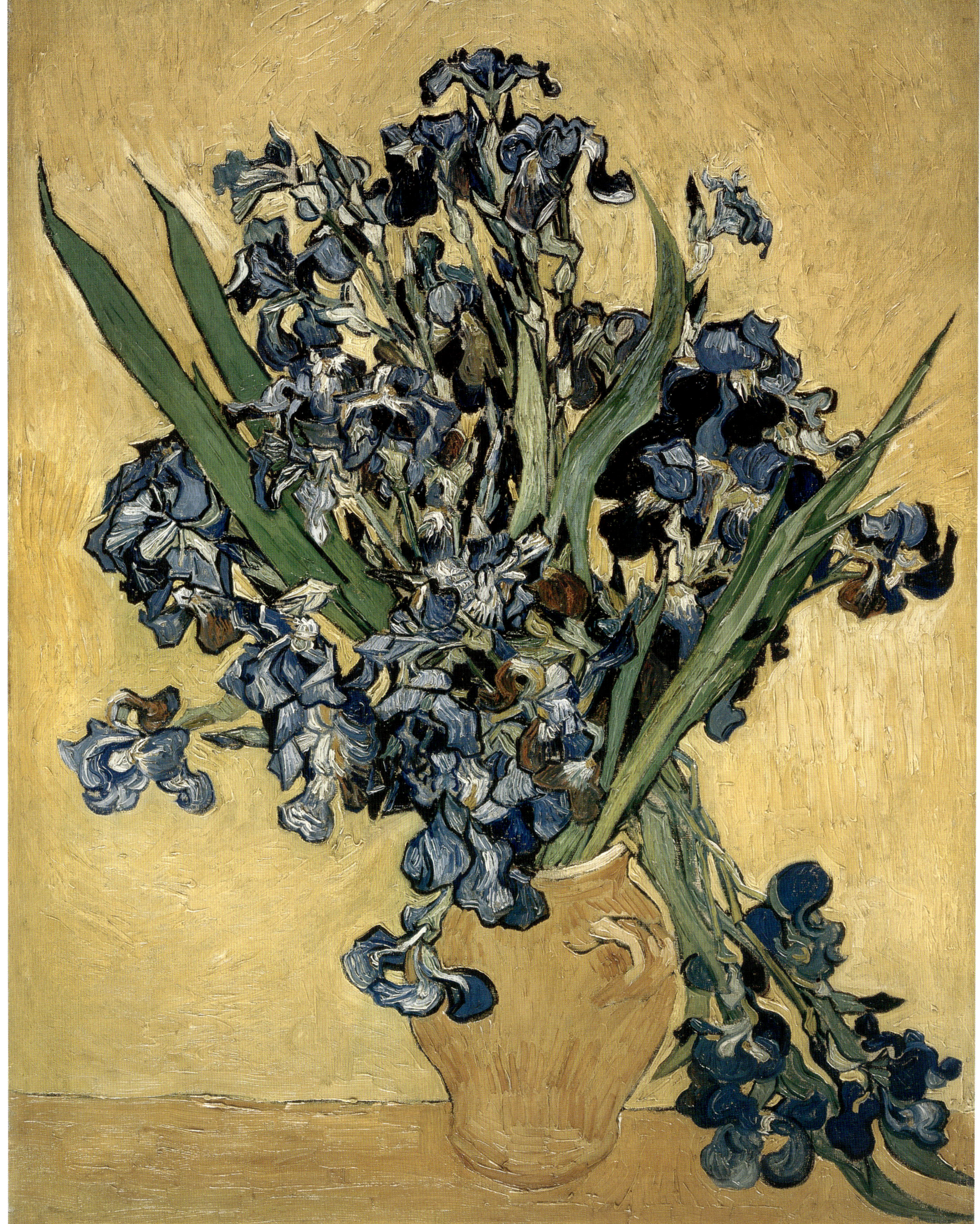

A Brief Life

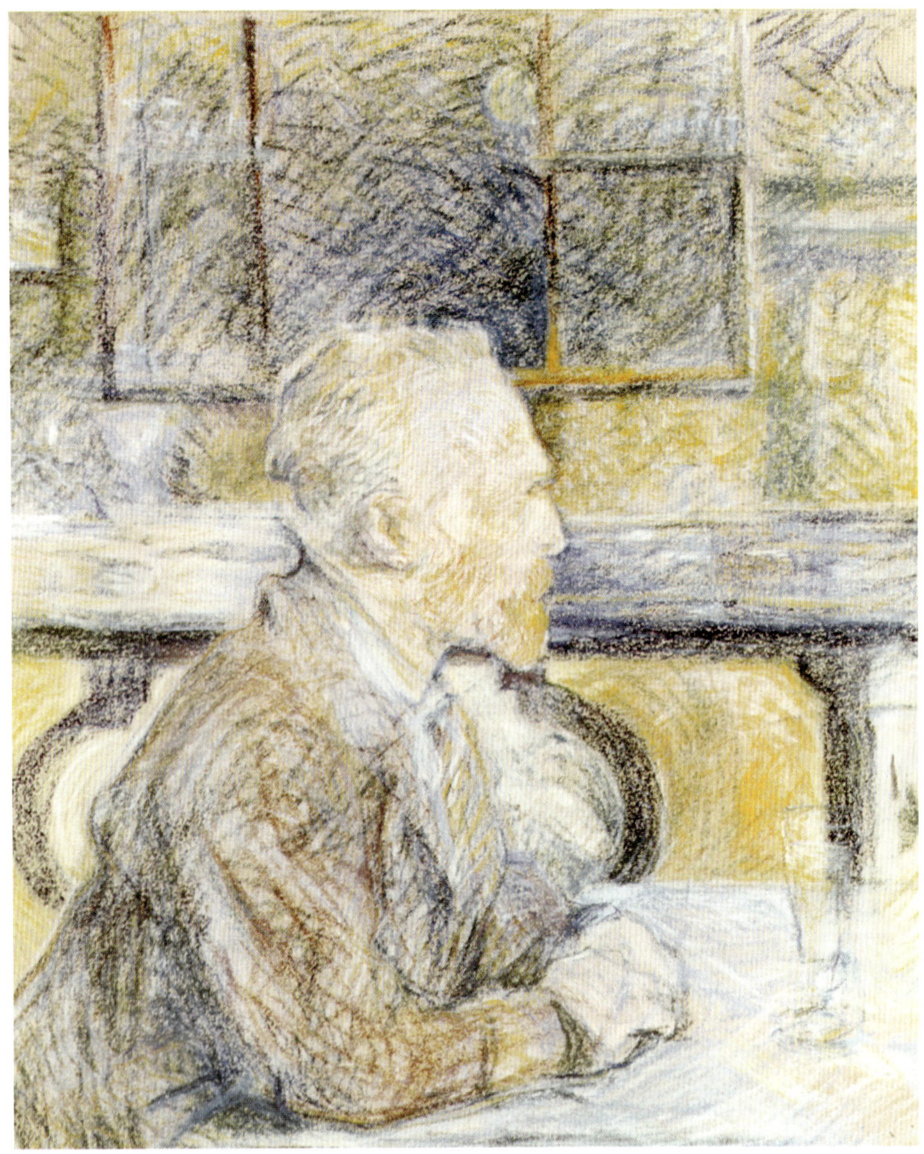

HENRI DE TOULOUSE-LAUTREC, Portrait of Vincent van Gogh in a Cafe *(1887). When he moved to Paris, Vincent found himself in the center of the art capital of Europe. He attended gallery exhibitions and visited artists in their studios. He briefly enrolled in classes at an atelier (training studio) where he met other aspiring artists, including Toulouse-Lautrec.*

VAN GOGH MUSEUM, AMSTERDAM. PASTEL (21¼×17¾ INCHES).

stamp of his deep passion and his highly charged imagination. In his life, he yearned to attain the status of a serious, successful painter whose work could provide an anodyne to the sorrow and stresses of the modern condition. He signed his works "Vincent," striking an element of intimacy and openness with his viewers. As an artist, he had a singular goal that he defined at the start of his career. He wrote to his brother, "I want to do drawings which touch some people." The force of his empathy and his emotions can be sensed in his signature works: panoramic landscapes, unflinching self-portraits, radiant sunflowers. But less than his choice of subject, Vincent's message was conveyed in a palette of strong, startling color applied with a brush stroke that transformed the act of applying pigment to canvas into an intense relationship between the artist and his art. In his time—and even in ours—the turbulence of his life overshadowed the intentions that he had for his art. But in his last letter to Theo, who did indeed support him through every misfortune, Vincent stated his enduring conviction, "the truth is, we can only make our pictures speak."

Born on March 30, 1853, in the village of Groot-Zundert in the Brabant province in the Netherlands, Vincent Willem van Gogh was the oldest surviving child of Theodorus and Anna van Gogh. His father, descended from a comfortable bourgeois family, was a pastor in the Dutch Reformed Church, and his mother, an amateur botanist, painted in watercolor. He had two brothers and three sisters, and there was little in Vincent's youth to indicate any talent in the arts. A competent student, Vincent excelled at languages and read in English and French, as well as in Dutch. At 16, Vincent moved to The Hague, where his uncle Vincent (called "Cent"), an art dealer for the Paris-based firm Goupil and Company, gave him a post as an assistant in a gallery. The firm specialized in contemporary art, and Vincent readily developed an interest in the work

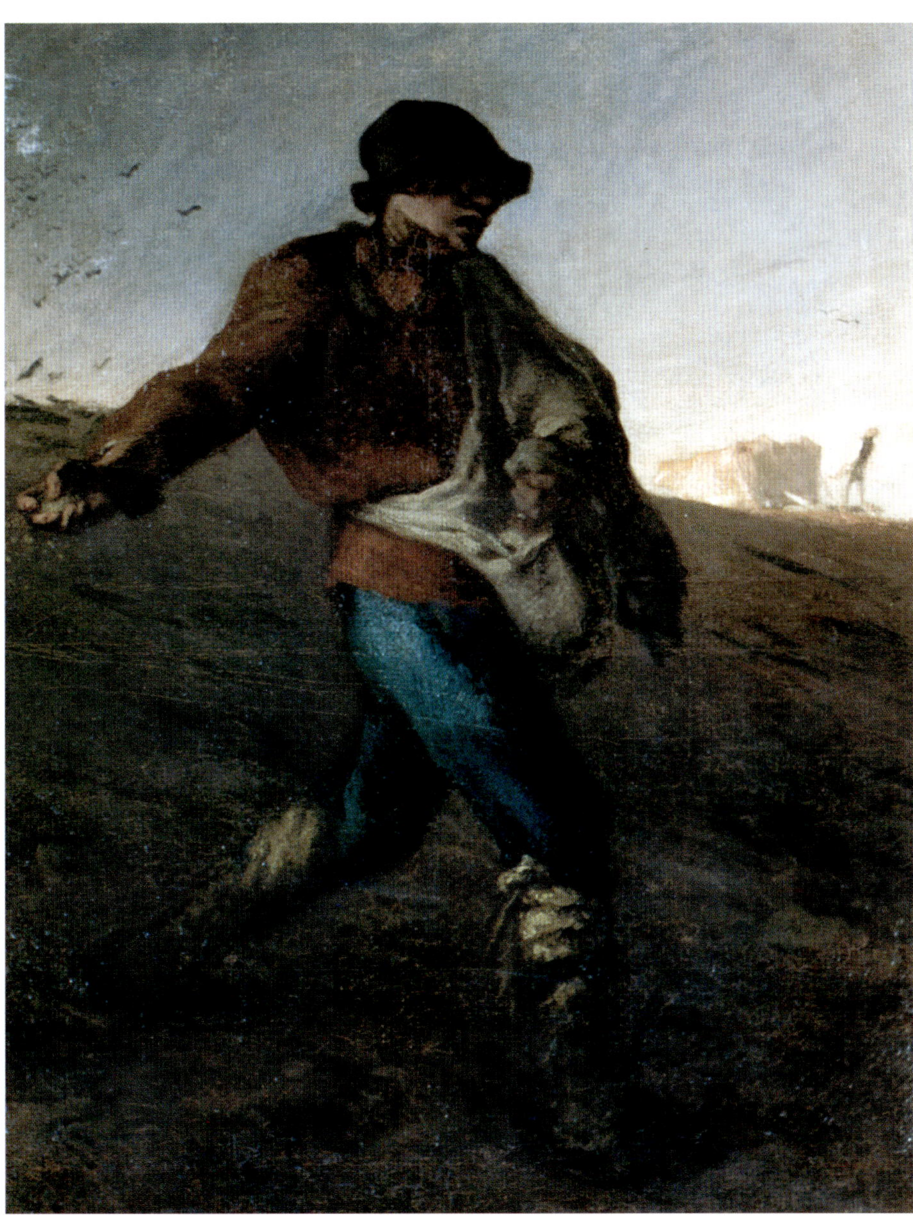

of the French rural naturalists such as Jean-François Millet. Vincent remained with Goupil and Company for seven years, working in branch galleries in London and Paris. His younger brother Theo followed him into the business, filling his position in The Hague and then moving on to Paris. Always close, the brothers maintained a lively correspondence, and over the years Vincent shared his most personal thoughts with Theo, relying upon his brother's full understanding, financial help, and sympathetic support. Vincent failed to fulfill his initial promise as an

art dealer, and he was dismissed in April 1876. He moved back to England, where he served as an assistant to a school master, giving lessons in French and German. He became active in a parish in Isleworth, and when given the opportunity to preach a sermon, he fixed his ambitions on a clerical career. In 1877, again with the help of Uncle Cent, Vincent moved to Dordrecht and then to Amsterdam to prepare for the entrance examinations required for a university course in theology. But he neglected his studies, preferring to devote his time to eccentric projects—drawing meticulous maps of the Holy Land and composing a multilingual translation of the Bible. In July 1878, Vincent began a training program for an evangelical ministry, but after three months' probationary work, he was denied a post. With his family's help, he moved to the Borinage, an impoverished mining region in Belgium, where he became a lay minister. His now fanatical devotion led to the intervention of his superiors, and by July 1879, Vincent was barred from preaching. He stayed in the Borinage for another year, living in extreme poverty. In 1880, he wrote to Theo that he was "homesick for that land of pictures" and, with the fervor that fueled his religious calling, he embraced the mission of art.

At Vincent's request, Theo sent his brother art materials and instructional manuals, as well as a set of prints after Millet's *Labors of the Field*. As an art dealer, Vincent had admired Millet's por-

A Brief Life

trayal of the dignity of agricultural toil in such works as *The Sower* (1850), and he intended to copy the pieces as part of his training. Over the next few years, Vincent restlessly pursued his new vocation. In 1880, he went to Brussels to study at the academy, but by 1881, he was living with his parents, who had moved to Etten. Early in 1882, he returned to The Hague, where he rented a studio and studied briefly with the painter Anton Mauve, a relative by marriage. Mauve encouraged Vincent to work in color, and he also experimented with plein air (open air) painting, setting up his easel outdoors under natural light. In the autumn of 1883, Vincent moved again, this time to the picturesque region of Drenthe, where he planned to paint peasants at their labor. But by

the end of the year, short of money and lonely for company, he again joined his parents, who had now settled in the rural village of Nuenen.

While in Nuenen, Vincent sketched the field workers at their labors, intent on painting a large and important picture to send to Paris to launch his career. In his letters to Theo, written in the early months of 1885, he described his desire to paint peasants as if he were one of them, to "rouse serious thoughts in those who think seriously about art and about life." He completed *The Potato Eaters* that April, and the rough treatment and dark palette he used were meant to convey the true spirit of those whose toil sustained life. At the same time, Vincent was mourning the death of his father. In recent years, the pair had become estranged; Theodorus was convinced that his eldest son was chasing a capricious dream. In *Still Life with Bible* (1885), painted a few months after his father's death, Vincent juxtaposes his father's beliefs with his own, perhaps putting their differences to rest.

In the autumn of 1885, Vincent moved again, this time to Antwerp to enroll in the academy to study life drawing.

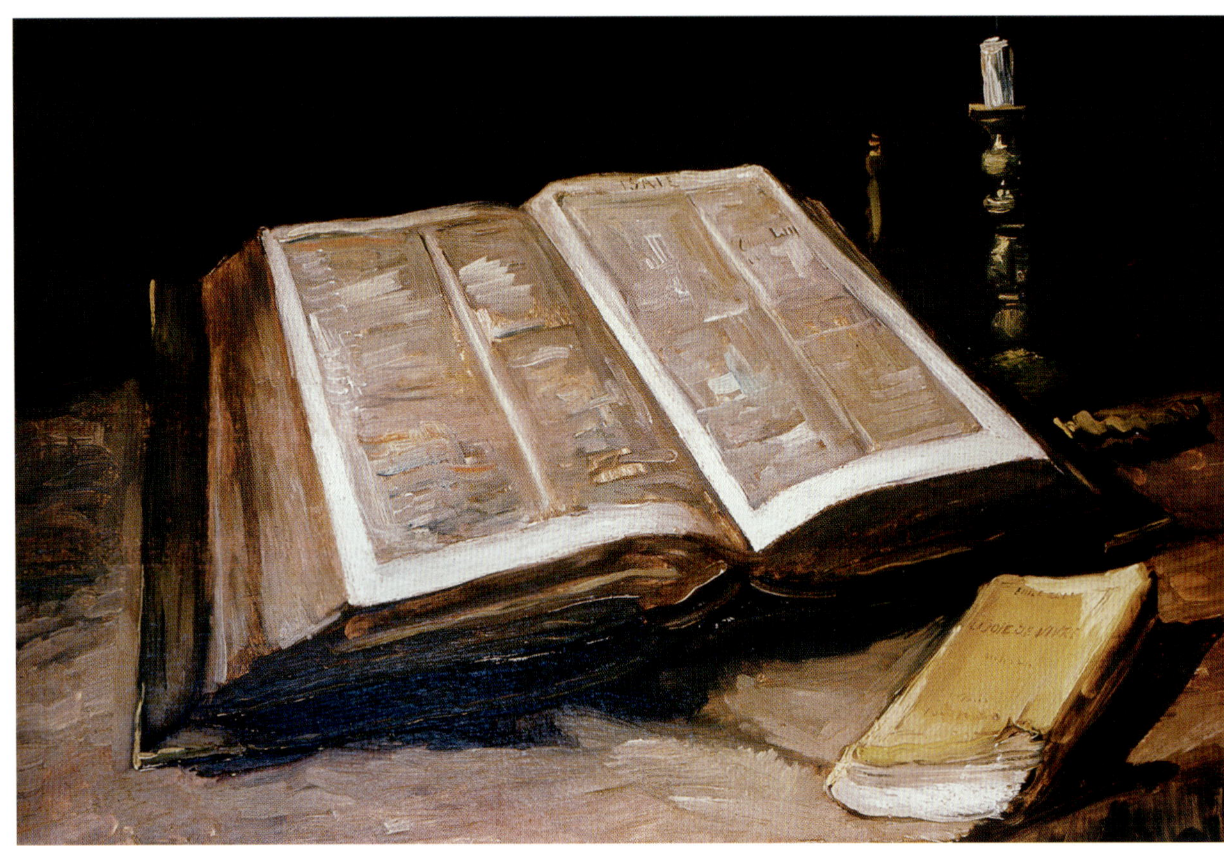

Still Life with Bible *(1885). Vincent painted this still life shortly after his father's death. The Bible and the extinguished candle represent not only his father, who had been a clergyman, but the old truths of religion. Émile Zola's novel, recognizable by its yellow cover, indicates Vincent's belief that contemporary art and literature could fulfill modern society's need for guidance and consolation.*

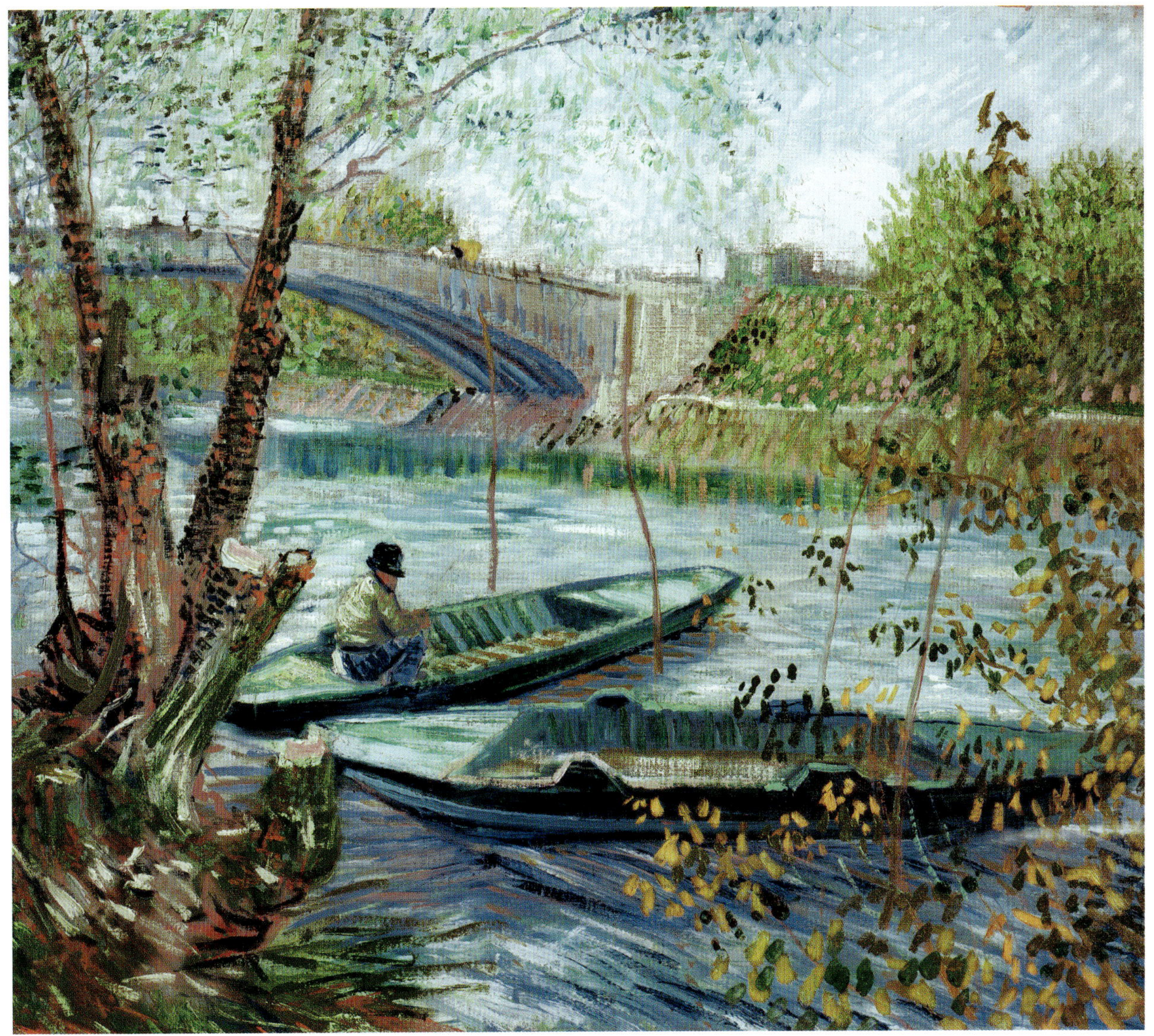

Vincent made regular trips to the museum, where the works of Peter Paul Rubens convinced him that his own palette was too dark and too dull. He began to investigate color theory by reading Éugene Delacroix's reflections on the use of color. But he found the academy curriculum—most notably its examinations and competitions—constricting, and by January 1886, Vincent wanted to move to Paris. Theo urged him to wait until June. By that time, he could secure a large apartment and arrange for Vincent to have some instruction and studio space. But in March, Theo received a note while at work announcing his brother's unexpected arrival: "Do not be cross with me for having come all at once like this; I have thought about it so much."

Once settled in his brother's apartment in Paris, Vincent seemed intent upon self-improvement. For years, he had neglected his health and his appearance. Now he trimmed his beard, visited a dentist, and bought new clothes. Theo described the transformation in a letter to their mother, claiming that she would not recognize her eldest son. Vincent made the rounds of the galleries and art exhibitions, and that spring he attended the eighth and final Impressionist exhibition. There he saw Georges Seurat's *A Sunday on La*

A Brief Life

Grande Jatte (1884–1886), in which the juxtaposition of dots of pure pigment prompted the eye—rather than the painter's hand—to mix the tones. He frequented Fernand Cormon's *Atelier Libre* (Free Studio), where the curriculum was unstructured and the other students shared his interest in the innovative developments in contemporary art. With Theo's connections, he visited the studios of artists whose work he had admired from a distance. He wrote to Horace Levens, an English painter he had met in Antwerp just a few short months ago, "I did not even know what the impressionists were, now I have seen them." Most significantly, Vincent acquired a circle of friends, including aspiring painters such as Henri de Toulouse-Lautrec, Émile Bernard, and Paul Signac, with whom he could exchange ideas, share experiences, and debate issues.

To advance his own development, Vincent experimented with new techniques. He worked in fresh, high-keyed color, painting en plein air to master the spontaneous approach of the Impressionists. He adopted a pointillist brush stroke, using dots, dabs, and dashes to explore the theories of Neo-Impressionism. He shed his gloomy Nuenen palette, as seen in *Fishing in the Spring, the Pont de Clichy* (Asnières) (1887), a sun-drenched image of boating on the Seine. Vincent acquired more confidence in his color by painting bouquets. Flowers were readily available at the market, and with a bouquet he could work alone in his studio without having to hire a model. Over the course of two years in Paris, Vincent painted more than 30 floral still lifes, varying the blossoms for color effects and seeking to purge the dark tones from his palette. He described his work to his friend Levens: "I have made a series of color studies in painting, simply flowers.... Trying to render intense color and not a grey harmony."

Vincent also made copies of Japanese prints. For many artists of Vincent's generation, the Japanese

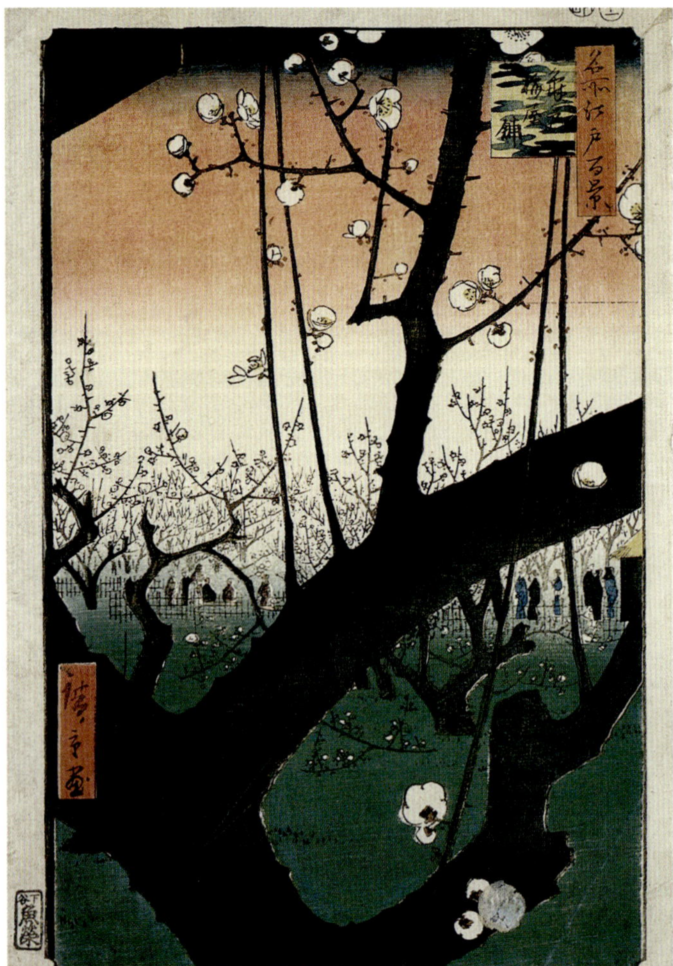

UTAGAWA HIROSHIGE, The Plum Tree Teahouse at Kameido *(1857). Like many artists of his generation, Vincent collected Japanese prints. This work by the* ukiyo-e *master displays the distinctive aesthetic elements that attracted him: visual strength and simplicity, asymmetrical spatial organization, clear bright color, and a subject based in nature.*

VAN GOGH MUSEUM, AMSTERDAM. PASTEL (21¼×17¾ INCHES).

prints that were available in European markets offered an intriguing aesthetic alternative to western conventions of space, composition, and color. Vincent first purchased Japanese prints in Antwerp, where he pinned them up on his walls for decoration. In Paris, there were many shops where he could browse through large selections and buy prints at reasonable prices. In 1887, he made three meticulous copies of prints, two by Utagawa Hiroshige and one by Keisai Eisen. Replicating the color and the formal structure in his own medium of oil convinced him that elements of Japanese art could be transferred to western compositions. He wished as well to replicate his sense of how artists lived in Japan. Vincent based his idealistic vision on what the prints portrayed: a neat, orderly world of broad, tranquil vistas where men and women carried out their daily tasks with grace and purpose. He came to believe that the balanced beauty of Japanese art reflected a similar balance of life and nature in Japan. Vincent, in fact, was beginning to tire of Paris. He had found little recognition in the fiercely competitive art world, and the pace of Parisian life had drained him. During the last months of 1887, an early, harsh winter descended on Paris, and Vincent yearned for sun and a more moderate climate, as well as the easy

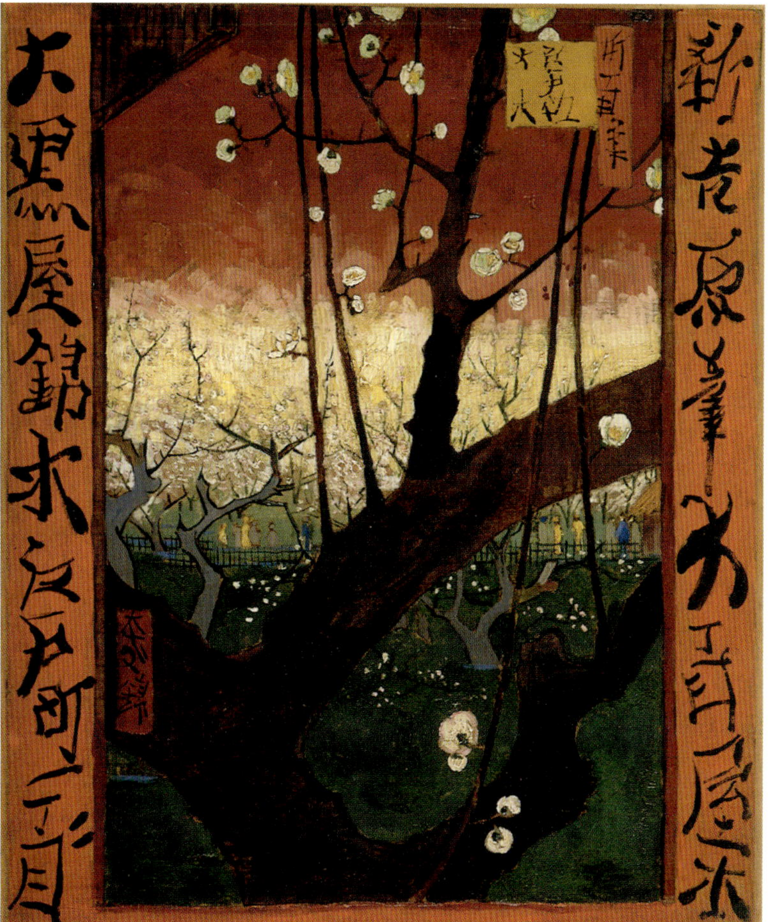

Flowering Plum Tree (After Hiroshige) *(1887). Vincent made oil replicas of* ukiyo-e *prints to better understand the subtle elegance of Japanese art. This is believed to be the earliest of his studies. He modulated the tones in the background to match the gradations of the printing ink, and he copied the characters on either side of his composition from a notice advertising an exhibition of Japanese prints.*

Van Gogh Museum, Amsterdam. Oil on canvas (21½×18 inches).

rhythm of rural life. In February, he boarded a train headed south for Provence. His destination was Arles; he had never been there, but he imagined it as calm, quiet, and tranquil, a French counterpart to his idealized vision of Japan.

Snow covered the ground when Vincent arrived in Arles, but within a few weeks the fruit trees began to bud and flower, and he took his easel out into the orchards to paint. Well aware that the spectacle of trees in flower was transient, he worked with speed and intensity, writing to Theo that "there is nothing like striking when the iron is hot." He kept as many as 9 canvases in progress at the same time, and by late April, as the blossoms fell and the fruit burgeoned, he had completed more than 20 paintings. Theo met his

A Brief Life

constant needs for more paint and canvases and also sent him money for living expenses. In return, Vincent shipped his paintings to Paris, hoping that Theo could sell them, writing, "I must reach the point where my pictures will cover my expenses." As spring warmth gave way to summer heat, Vincent changed his subjects, first painting the meadows of irises and then setting his easel up in the fields to capture the first June harvest. As the sun gained intensity his palette became more brilliant, reflecting the vibrant contrast of the golden fields seen against the cerulean skies. He explained to Theo that he often exaggerated the saturation of his tones for striking juxtapositions and powerful effects: "Instead of trying to reproduce exactly what I have before my eyes, I use color more arbitrarily, in order to express myself forcibly."

Lacking a like-minded circle of companions in Arles, Vincent confessed to Theo that he was lonely. Although he claimed that his work diminished his need for company, he expressed the desire to create a community of artists who would live and paint together under the high colors and hot sun of Provence. He enlisted Theo's help to bring his vision of the "Studio of the South" into being, arguing that shared expenses would reduce the cost of living in Arles. In the company of other artists, Vincent could

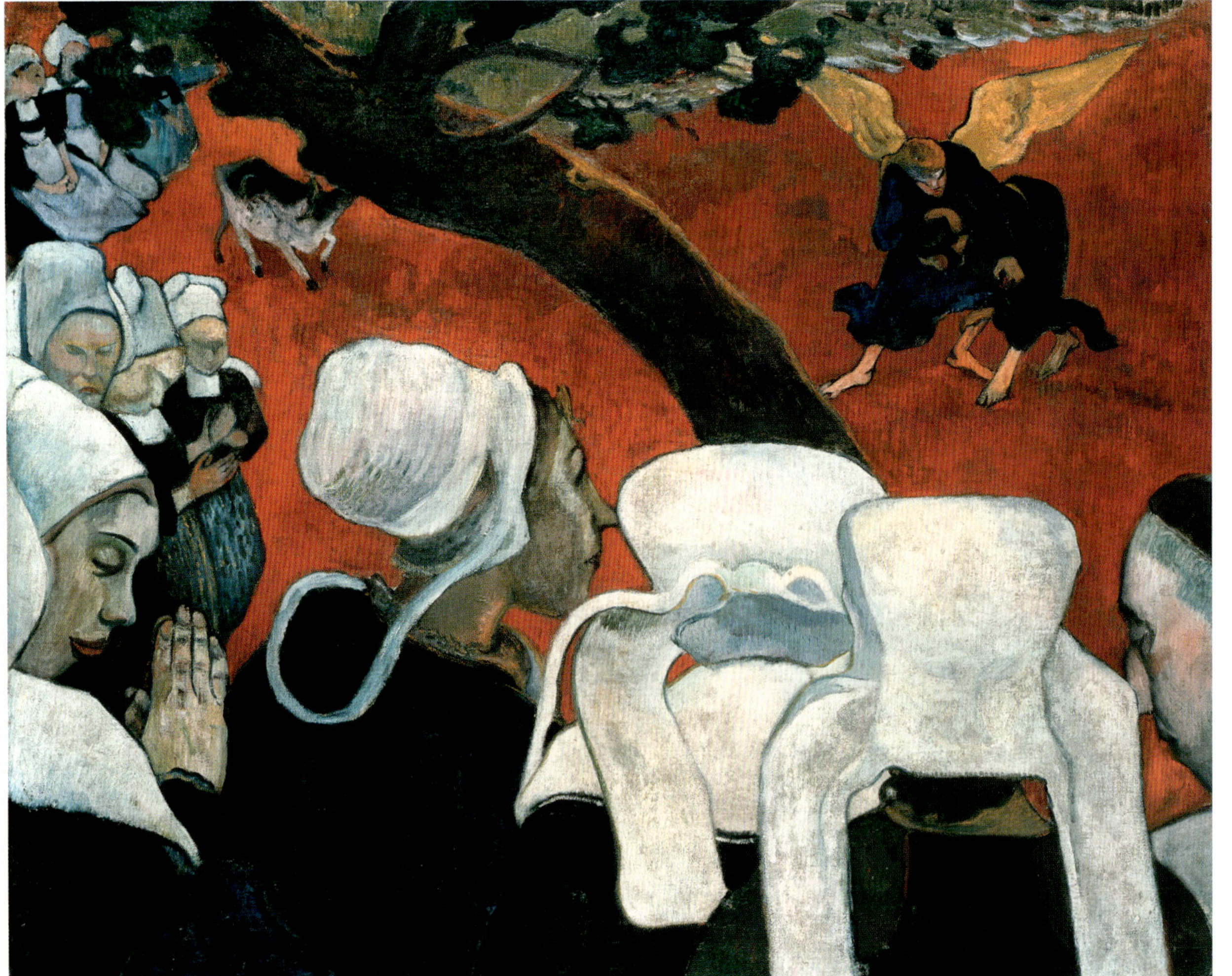

PAUL GAUGIN, Vision After the Sermon *(1888). Vincent admired Gauguin for his defiance of artistic and social conventions. This work, painted in Brittany before Gauguin stayed with Vincent in Arles, bridges the gulf between perceived reality and visionary imagination. The jutting tree trunk that divides the composition recalls the spatial organization of Japanese prints, and the pure, bold use of red is in accord with Vincent's belief that color could be used arbitrarily to convey emotional force.*

reap the benefits of mutual encouragement and criticism, and he confessed to Theo, "I wish everybody would come south like me." In July, Uncle Cent died, naming Theo as his main heir. In his typical generosity, Theo shared his windfall with his brother, and Vincent

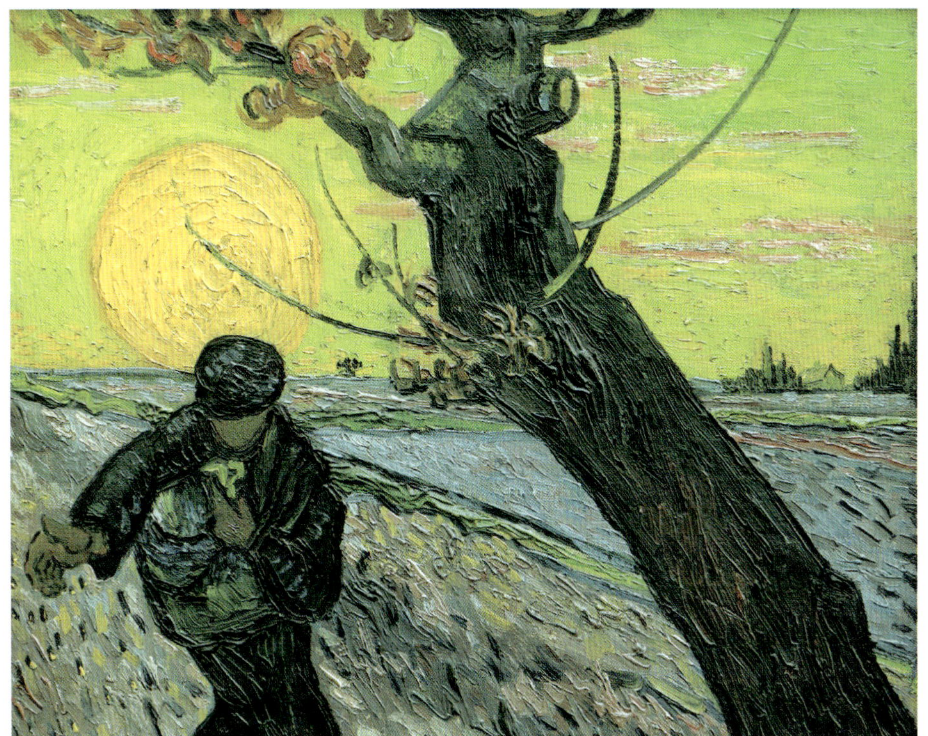

The Sower *(1888).* *Vincent recorded that he was inspired to return to Millet's subject of a man sowing during a walk with Gauguin on an autumn evening in Arles. Their exchange of ideas, though often heated, inspired Vincent to greater daring in spatial composition and color choices. The motif had the special significance in evocation of new birth whether in nature's cycle or the artistic imagination.*

used the money to convert the space that he had been renting for studio and storage into an inviting residence. With an exterior painted the color of fresh butter, the "Yellow House" had whitewashed interior walls and four rooms: two on the ground floor to be used for a studio and a kitchen and two above to provide a bedroom for Vincent and room for a guest.

Vincent hoped his first guest would be Paul Gauguin, whom he had met in Paris the previous November, when he and Theo visited the painter's studio. Both van Gogh brothers had been impressed with Gauguin's paintings from a recent trip to Martinique. Theo took several on consignment, and Vincent persuaded Gauguin to trade one of his tropical landscapes with figures for two of his own studies of sunflowers. Now Gauguin was living in Brittany, where he worked in a bold, unorthodox manner that depended as much upon imagination as observation. He had already approached Theo for financial help, and Vincent had a solution: Give Gauguin a train ticket and encourage him to move to Arles. While Gauguin did not reject Vincent's invitation, he repeatedly postponed his travel plans. His ambivalence did not deter Vincent, who quickly immersed himself in preparing the Yellow House for Gauguin's arrival, decorating the guest room with fine furnishings and his recent paintings of radiant sunflower bouquets.

Throughout the summer and into the early autumn, Gauguin and Vincent exchanged letters, sharing their ideas and descriptions of their current work. But, as Gauguin delayed his visit, Vincent's anxiety rose. By the end of October, when Gauguin finally arrived in Arles, Vincent was overwrought with anticipation. At first Gauguin proved a calming presence, taking over the house-

A Brief Life

hold chores, cooking nourishing meals, and fascinating Vincent with tales of his travels with the merchant marines. Vincent took Gauguin to his favorite painting sites in Arles where they worked together. Gauguin's powerful image of spirituality in Brittany, *Vision After the Sermon* (1888), inspired Vincent to be even bolder in his color and his composition, as seen in his reinterpretation of *The Sower,* a longstanding favorite motif.

As the weeks passed, and inclement weather forced them to work more often in the cramped confines of the Yellow House, their different views often led to heated debates. Gauguin urged Vincent to rely more on his memory and imagination, but Vincent remained firmly committed to working in the open air, in front of his model. In his letters to Theo, Vincent described his struggle to incorporate Gauguin's suggestions into his method. Gauguin was more blunt, writing to their mutual friend Bernard that Arles fell short of his expectations, and that he and Vincent did not see eye to eye. In December, Gauguin painted a portrait of Vincent painting a sunflower bouquet, reflecting his sympathy with

Vincent's endeavors, but whenever he raised the topic of departure, Vincent would become agitated. According to Gauguin's account, on the evening of December 23, 1888, Vincent confronted him with a razor, demanding to know if he intended to leave Arles. Gauguin's confirmation further upset Vincent, who turned and fled. Disturbed by his companion's irrational behavior, Gauguin spent the night in a hotel. The following morning when Gauguin returned to the Yellow House, he was shocked to find it spattered with blood. Taken into custody by the police for interrogation, he discovered that Vincent had returned home after their confrontation and mutilated his left ear. Bleeding profusely, he went to a brothel and was then taken to a hospital. Upon release from the authorities, Gauguin

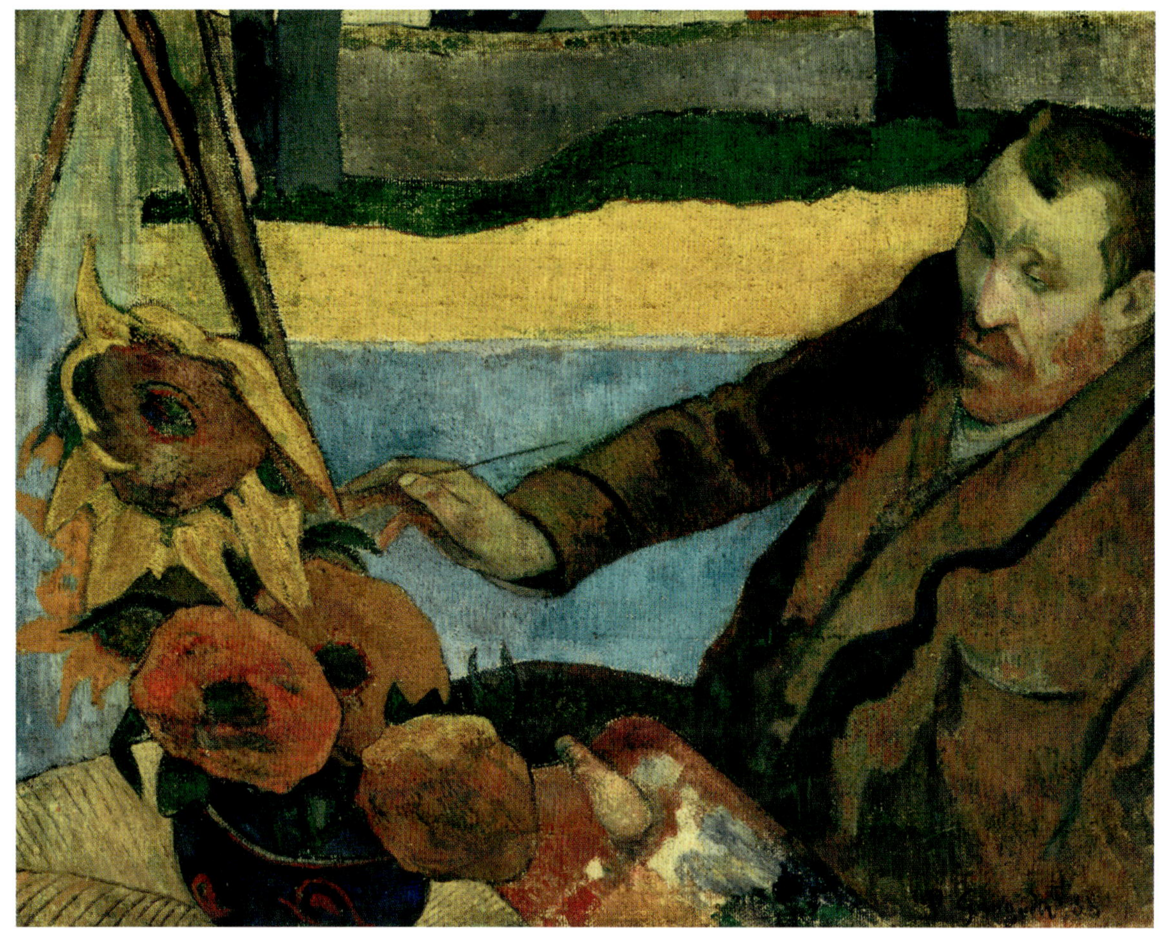

Paul Gaugin, Van Gogh Painting Sunflowers *(1888). Gauguin painted this portrait during the time he resided with Vincent in the Yellow House in Arles. He depicts Vincent absorbed in his work, painting the sunflowers that became a signature motif in his art. Vincent took great pride in his sunflower bouquets, stating "the sunflower is mine in a way."*

Van Gogh Museum, Amsterdam. Oil on canvas (28¾×35¾ inches).

telegraphed Theo, who arrived on the next morning's train. Convinced that his brother's condition was stable, Theo took the night train back to Paris. Gauguin rode with him, and Vincent never saw him again.

In the hospital, Vincent was treated for blood loss and was released in the first week of January 1889. He returned to the Yellow House where he resumed painting familiar motifs such as still-life arrangements and sunflower bouquets. He wrote to his brother, "Since it is still winter…let me go quietly on with my work." But in mid-January he suffered a hallucinatory incident that required a brief hospitalization. Late in February, his erratic behavior so alarmed his neighbors that they petitioned the mayor to either have him readmitted to the hospital or returned to his family. Vincent entered the hospital, where he was allowed to paint on the premises, but the Yellow House was closed. Acknowledging that the danger of another psychomotor seizure made it impossible for him to live on his own, Vincent voluntarily entered Saint-Paul-de-Mausole, a psychiatric asylum in nearby Saint-Rémy-de-Provence. There, his condition was diagnosed as a form of epilepsy, and Theo convinced his doctors to allow him to paint. At first, Vincent was required to remain indoors under observation, so Theo secured a ground-floor room with a garden view that he could use as his studio. The window of his hospital room on a floor above overlooked groves of olive and cypress trees, the cluster of buildings around the town church, and the Alpilles hills rising in the distance. The view inspired his painting *The Starry Night* (1889) in which gleaming stars and trailing comets illuminate a tumultuous sky.

Self-Portrait with Bandaged Ear *(1889). After Vincent left the hospital, he returned to painting by taking up familiar motifs. He portrayed himself bundled up in his winter coat and hat while his ear was still bandaged. He was firmly convinced that he would be well if he kept working, and if he could work he could prove he was not insane.*

By late June, Vincent was allowed to work under supervision in the fields near the asylum. During the first week of July, while painting a reaper swinging his sickle in a vast wheat field, Vincent suddenly went into a severe seizure. The attendant with him later reported that Vincent drank turpentine and tried to eat his paint. Debilitated for more than five weeks, Vincent was tormented by nightmares and his swollen throat made it difficult to eat. By September, he was again able to write to Theo and resume his painting, but since he was confined to the asylum, he painted

A Brief Life

his own portrait and copied prints that he had in his possession, including reproductions of paintings by Millet and Delacroix. With his enduring conviction that painting outdoors before nature would restore his health, he now planned to leave the asylum and move to Auvers-sur-Oise, a village north of Paris. Although he informed Theo that "I could almost believe that I have a new period of lucidity before me," he realized that further seizures were likely. His spirits were buoyed by increasing recognition. *Starry Night over the Rhône* (1888) was well received at the autumn exhibition of the *Société des Artistes Indépendants,* and he was invited to present his work in Brussels in February at an exhibition organized by the Symbolist circle *Les Vingt.* In January 1890, the young critic G.-Albert Aurier published an appreciation of his work in the popular journal *Mercure de France.* Theo, who had married Johanna Bonger the previous April, became a father on January 30 and named his son Vincent Willem. But a series of attacks—in December and again in January and February—forced Vincent to remain in the asylum until his condition was stable. On May 16, Vincent checked himself out of the asylum in Saint-Rémy and traveled by train to Auvers-sur-Oise.

Cautious but optimistic, Vincent found a congenial environment in Auvers-sur-Oise. Following the advice of the painter Camille Pissarro, he introduced himself to Paul Gachet, a local homeopathic physician as well as an enthusiastic and knowledgeable collector of contemporary art who was willing to offer his supportive supervision. In a letter to Theo and Johanna, Vincent described the region as "lush" and far enough from Paris to be "the real country." Gachet found him a room in an inn, and Vincent rapidly adopted a regular routine, spending his days

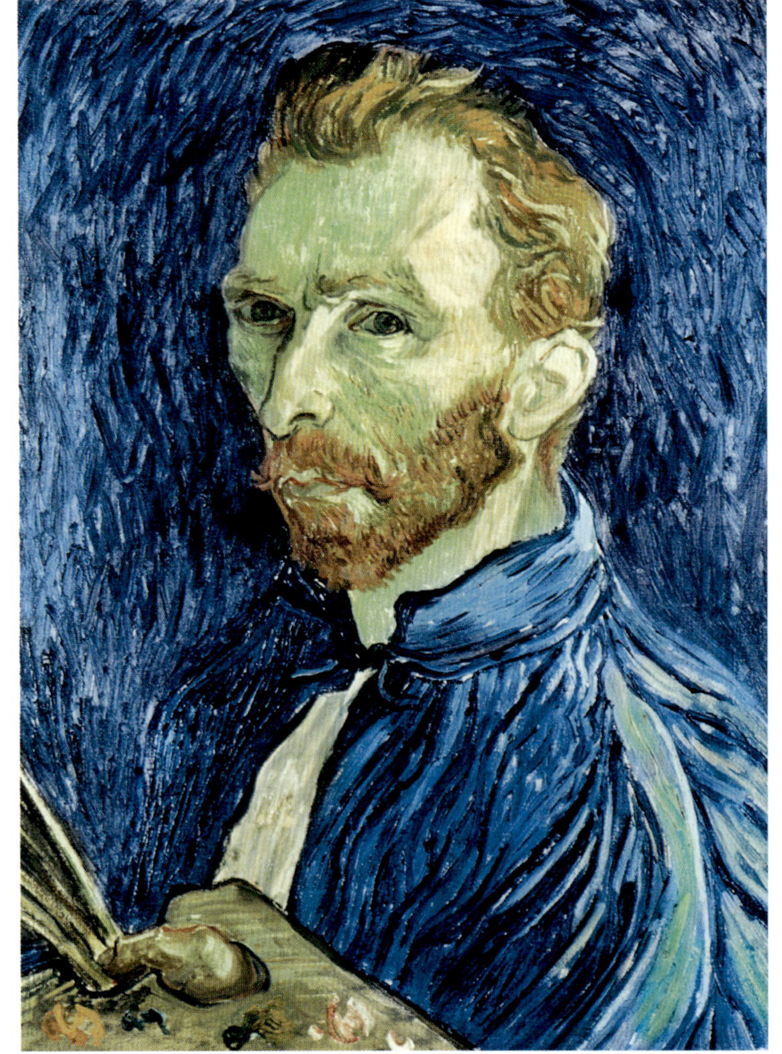

Self-Portrait (1889). The severe attack Vincent suffered in the summer disabled him for weeks. He resumed painting early in September, returning to familiar subjects to regain confidence and seek consolation. He painted two self-portraits in his signature color combination of blue and yellow. Here, he identifies himself as a painter with his palette and has turned to hide his damaged ear.

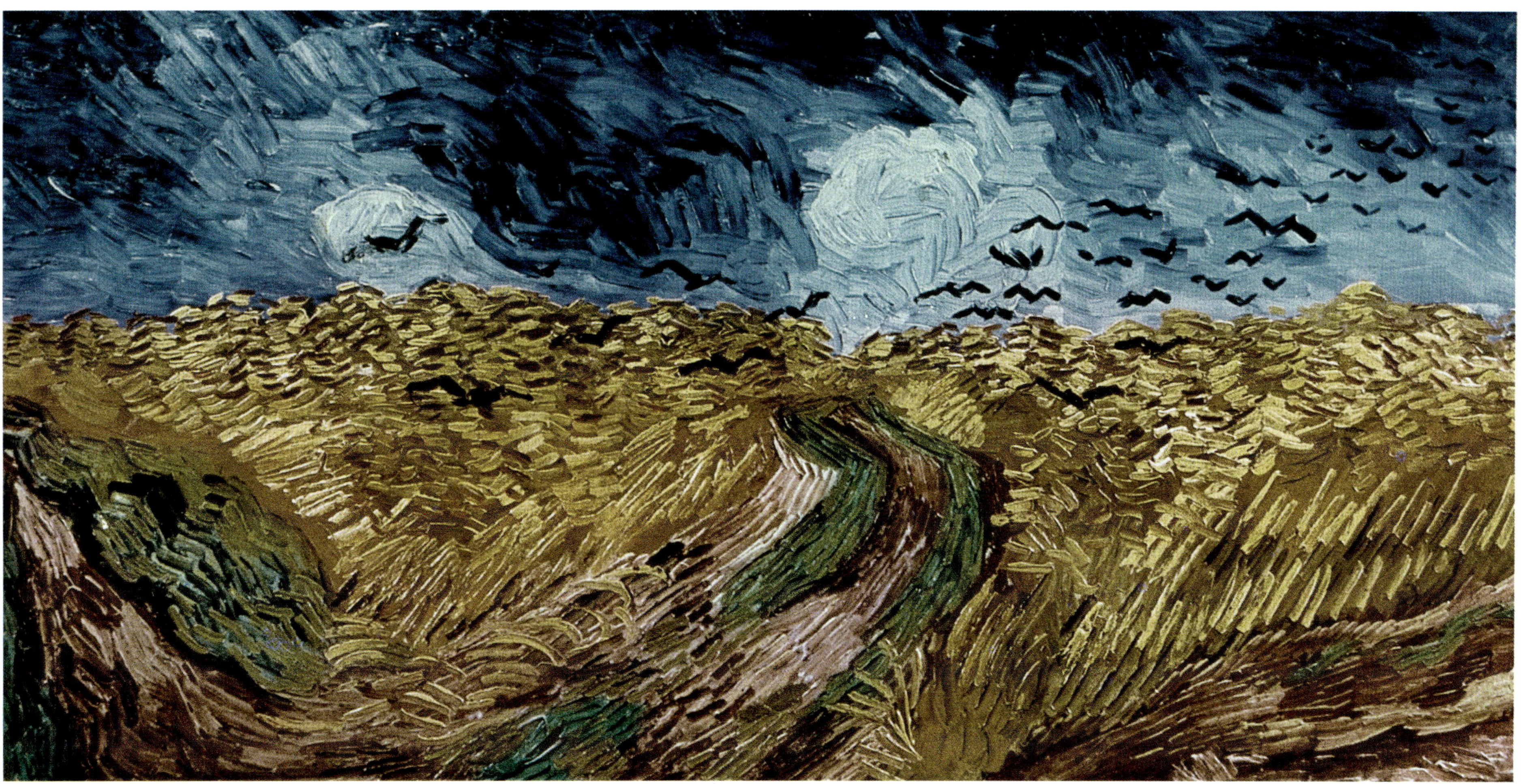

painting in the countryside. Theo and his family visited in June, and Vincent made a brief trip to Paris in July. When he returned, he gave his full attention to a new subject, which he described in his last letter to his mother and his sister Wil as "the immense plain of wheatfields against the hills, boundless as the sea." He worked quickly in strong, pure color, laying down his pigment with thick impasto that preserved the direction of every stroke.

On July 25, Theo received a letter from his brother that seemed to him to be incomprehensible. Two days later, Vincent shot himself in the wheat field where he had been painting. Theo came immediately and was at his brother's side when Vincent died on July 29. A quiet funeral was held in Auvers-sur-Oise with Theo, Gachet, and a few friends from Paris paying their respects. In a letter to the critic G.-Albert Aurier, Bernard noted that Vincent's recent canvases were displayed on the wall above his coffin and that the coffin itself was covered with yellow dahlias and sunflowers. This, he observed, was an appropriate tribute, writing, "It was his favorite color, if you remember, symbol of the light that he dreamed of finding in hearts as in artworks." Vincent's paints and easel were placed on the floor in front of the coffin. Gachet offered a few words of consolation, reminding the mourners that Vincent gave his whole being to art and humanity and sagely observing, "It is the art that he cherished above all else that will ensure he lives on."

Wheatfield with Crows (1890). In his last letters to his family, Vincent mentions that he was painting in the wheat fields that surrounded Auvers-sur-Oise. He worked on several paintings at the same time, so it is impossible to determine which was his last. But this work, with its distinctive blue and yellow pigment applied in heavy impasto, reveals all that he achieved by making the elements of his painting—color and brush stroke—express his understanding of life.

Van Gogh Museum, Amsterdam. Oil on canvas (20×40½ inches).

HOMESICK FOR THE LAND OF PICTURES

"When I was in other surroundings, in the surroundings of pictures and works of art, you know how I had a violent passion for them, reaching the highest pitch of enthusiasm. And I am not sorry about it, for even now, far from that land, I am often homesick for that land of pictures."

VINCENT TO THEO, JULY 1880, FROM THE BORINAGE

AT THE AGE OF 27, Vincent wrote to his brother Theo of his burning desire to change the course of his life. He had spent his youth in the pursuit of a rewarding vocation, but every one of his attempts met with failure. He admitted that he was a "man of passions, capable of and subject to doing more or less foolish things," but he was determined to put those passions to good use. Recalling the enthusiasm for paintings that he had enjoyed during his years as an art dealer, he confessed, "I am often homesick for that land of pictures." But rather than return to the profession that would once again surround him with works of art, he now planned to rely upon his own initiative and become a painter.

Throughout the summer of 1880, Vincent remained in the poor mining district of the Borinage, copying reproductions of the works of Jean-François Millet and studying art manuals such as Karl Robert's *Le fusain sans maître (Sketching Without a Master)*. That autumn he moved to Brussels to enroll in an art academy, but he left in April of 1881 to join his parents in Etten. He continued to draw, and later in the year, he visited The Hague, where his mother's relative, the painter Anton Mauve, gave him informal instructions. Mauve encouraged Vincent to paint as well as draw. Motivated by this encouragement, Vincent moved to The Hague in January 1882. He rented a small studio and

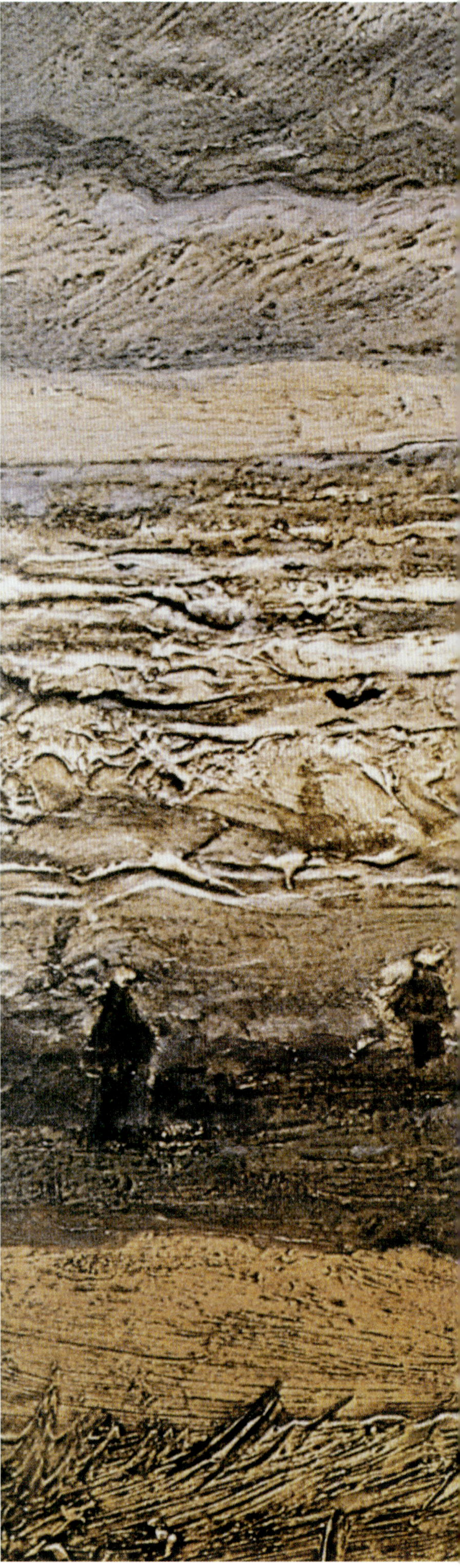

View of the Sea at Scheveningen (1882). While living in The Hague, Vincent made regular trips to Scheveningen, a nearby fishing village. He had begun to experiment with oil paint, and he set up his easel on the bleak stretch of beach and worked directly on his canvas in the windblown sand. His strong and bold approach to the composition, using broad horizontal zones to delineate sand, water, and sky, was matched by his thick and expressive application of pigment. His compulsion to capture his observations on the spot reflects his awareness of contemporary Impressionism.

VAN GOGH MUSEUM, AMSTERDAM. OIL ON CANVAS (13½×20 INCHES).

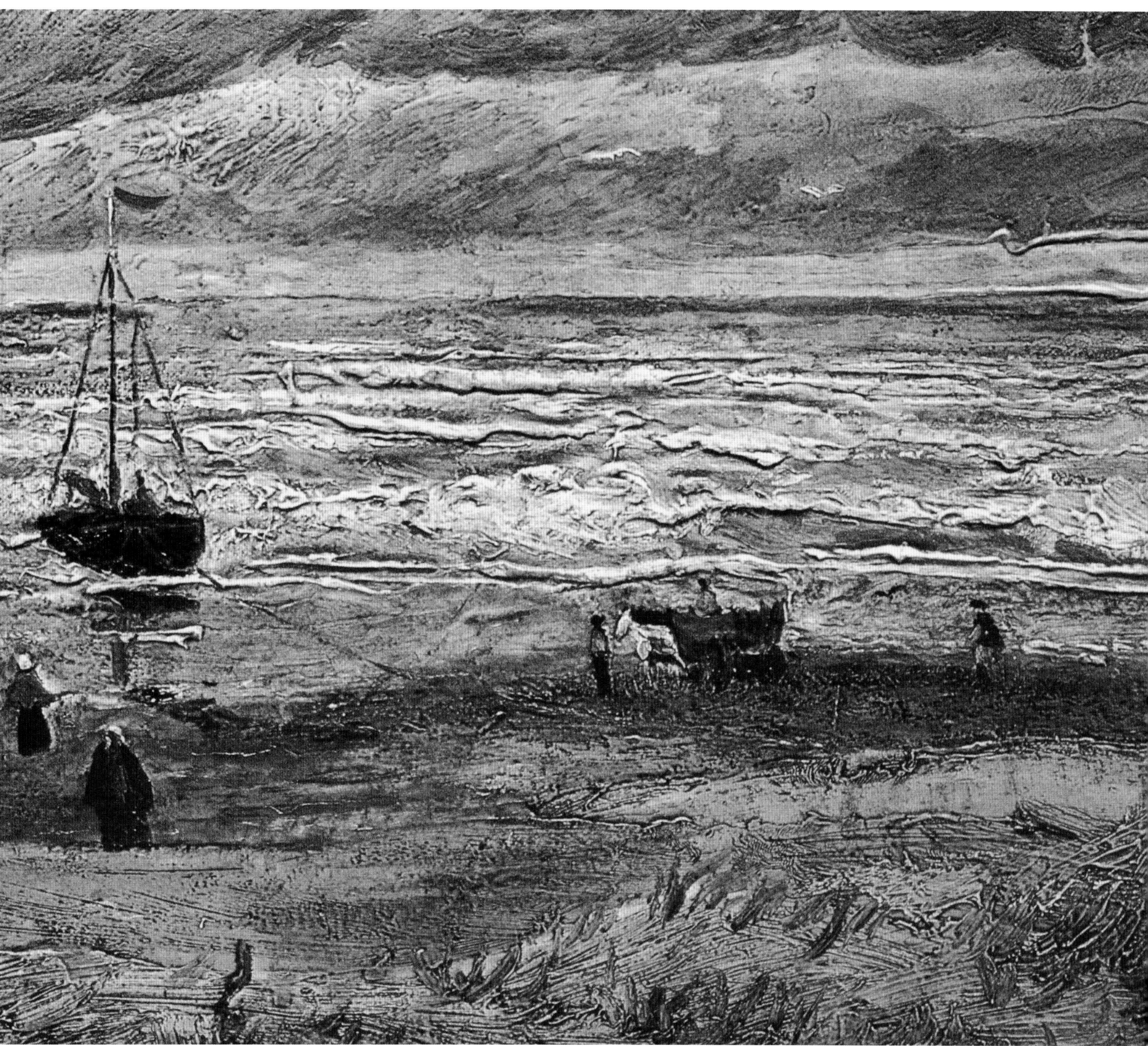

LAND OF PICTURES

Carpenter's Yard and Laundry *(1882). Vincent recorded the view out of his studio window in a meticulous and innately skillful rendering. Work-ing with pencil, pen, and brush, he demonstrated a precise hand and an exacting eye. He created a deep and credible spatial recession through the structure of the architectural elements, but his handling of the figures was less certain, as seen in the proportions of the man pushing the wheelbarrow along the road on the right.*

KRÖLLER-MÜLLER MUSEUM, OTTERLO, NETHERLANDS. PENCIL, PEN, BRUSH, HEIGHTENED WITH WHITE (11¼ × 18½ INCHES).

continued his regimen of disciplined drawing. As seen in *Carpenter's Yard and Laundry* (1882), a meticulously rendered ink drawing on tinted paper heightened with white, he had developed a keen eye and a sure hand through self-discipline and intense effort.

By the summer he was painting in oil, and in August 1882, he set up his easel on the coast near Scheveningen, a local fishing village. As an art dealer, Vincent had become acquainted with the work of the Barbizon School, a loose association of painters who lived in the French village of Barbizon near the Forest of Fontainebleau. They used portable easels and premixed pigments in tubes so that they could paint landscapes in the open air rather than in the studio. Impressionists, such as Claude Monet and Camille Pissarro, also

practiced plein air painting to capture the fleeting effects of natural light and atmosphere. To paint *View of the Sea at Scheveningen* (1882), Vincent endured a sudden squall to observe and record the choppy waters and the volatile sky. Despite his initial difficulties, Vincent continued to work outdoors. Throughout his career, he always preferred to paint directly from his subject rather than from memory. Vincent rapidly acquired a command of color, as seen in his depiction of *Flower Beds in Holland* (1883). But by autumn, he had tired of The Hague and moved on to the rural province of Drenthe, where he painted the cottage tradespeople and the farm laborers in the spirit of Millet's depictions of weary peasants.

At the end of 1883, Vincent once again joined his parents, who were now living in Nuenen. Over the next two years, he struggled to find his identity as an artist, living on his family's generosity and enduring his father's disapproval of the direction he had taken his life. Vincent's desire to teach, and then to enter the ministry, had been in part motivated by his profound identification with the poor. In Nuenen, as in Drenthe, he painted impoverished farm laborers, admiring the way their work sustained life. Late in 1884, Vincent

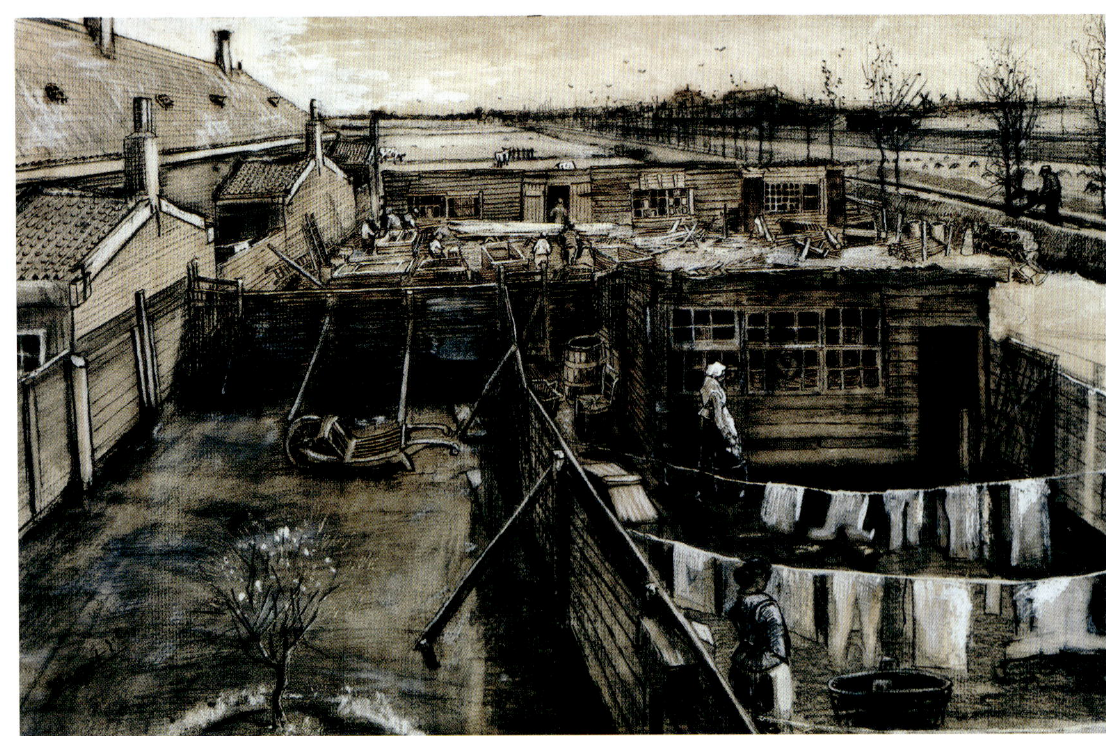

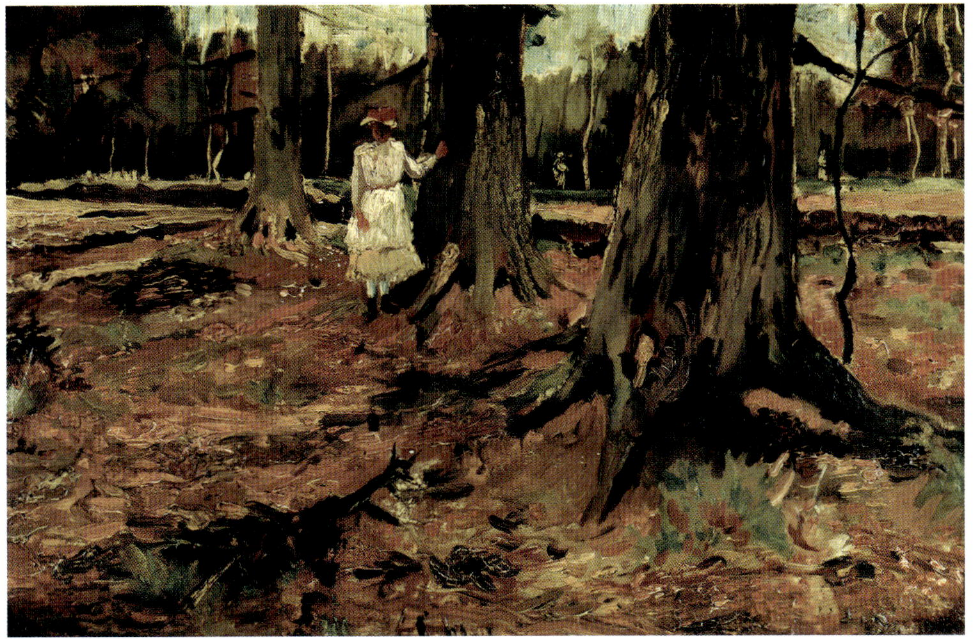

Young Girl in a Wood *(1882). While living in The Hague, Vincent sought informal instruction with painter Anton Mauve, who worked with him on drawing and color theory. As his confidence grew, Vincent loosened his stroke and adopted a more daring approach to color, as seen in the warm palette of this woodland scene. He explained his development as intuitive, writing to Theo, "I know for sure that I have an instinct for color."*

concentrated on the mundane activities of peasant life, and in the following year, he painted portraits of unidentified sitters—local farm workers with weather-beaten faces, careworn expressions, and work-hardened hands. He wrote to Theo in April 1885 that painting peasant life was a deeply serious endeavor that demanded the artist understand his subjects' thoughts and feelings. Intending to "make pictures that rouse serious thoughts in those who think seriously about art and life," Vincent was working on a painting that he hoped would launch—as well as define—his career. In *The Potato Eaters* (1885), Vincent portrayed a family gathered around the table for their evening meal. Their simple repast of boiled potatoes is a tribute to their life. Vincent wrote: "I have tried to emphasize that those people, eating their potatoes in the lamp light, have dug the earth with the very hands they put in the dish, and so it speaks of manual labor, and how they have honestly earned their food." Vin-

cent expressed this idea not only through his subject, but also through color, using a limited range of earthy browns as his palette.

In November 1885, in hopes of resuming his art training, Vincent left Nuenen for Antwerp. He found new stimulation working in the city. He visited museums and galleries and sought out urban entertainments. He set up his easel on the docks to paint the porters at labor. Vincent developed new interests in the arts, studying the works of the Baroque master Peter Paul Rubens, reading the color theory of the French romantic painter Eugène Delacroix, and collecting colorful prints by the Japanese practitioners of the *ukiyo-e* (prints of the *Floating World*). These new examples prompted him to reconsider the dark palette he had developed in Nuenen, and he began to experiment with richer and warmer tonalities. His enrollment in the Académie Royale des Beaux-Arts was brief. He signed up for the winter course to study life drawing in January, and he informed Theo, who was now his sole financial support, that with his fellow students he found "the friction of ideas" that allowed him to "get a fresh look at [his] own work." But by February, he was losing interest in the restricted curriculum and proposed to join Theo in Paris. Theo encouraged him to wait a few months, but early in March, a railway porter gave Theo a note scrawled in black crayon in his brother's hand. Unexpectedly, Vincent had arrived in Paris.

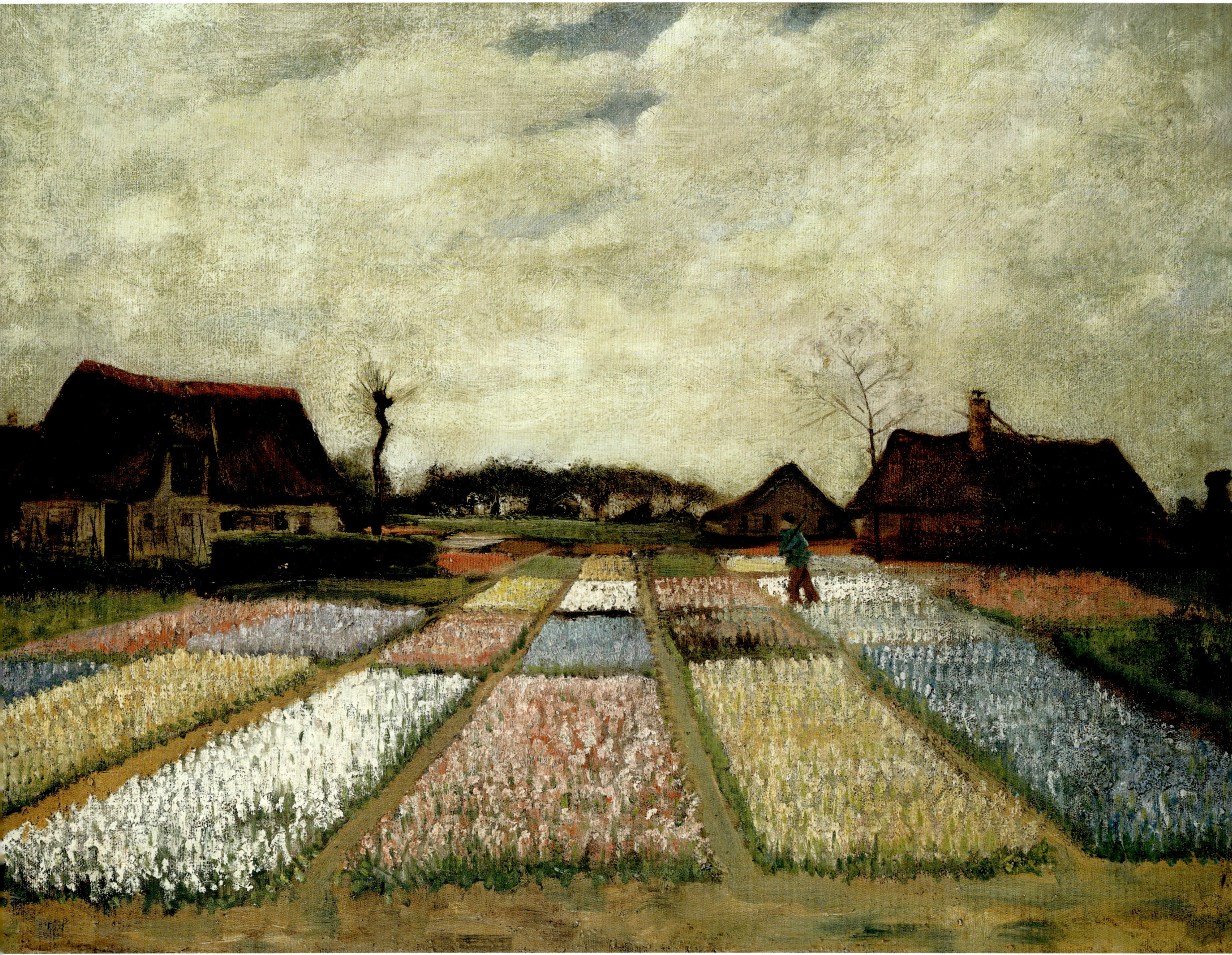

Flower Beds in Holland *(1883). During his second year in The Hague, Vincent painted this small but luminous view of tulip fields in blossom. The foreground of his composition, observed from a low position, seems to rise sharply, accentuating the low horizon in a panoramic effect. The thatched cottages and bare tree trunks in the distance are engulfed in somber shadow, a striking contrast to the bright colors of the flower beds. These elements—raked perspective and tonal contrast—persisted in Vincent's conception of landscape painting.*

NATIONAL GALLERY OF ART, WASHINGTON, D.C. COLLECTION OF MR. AND MRS. PAUL MELLON. OIL ON CANVAS MOUNTED ON WOOD (19¼×26 INCHES).

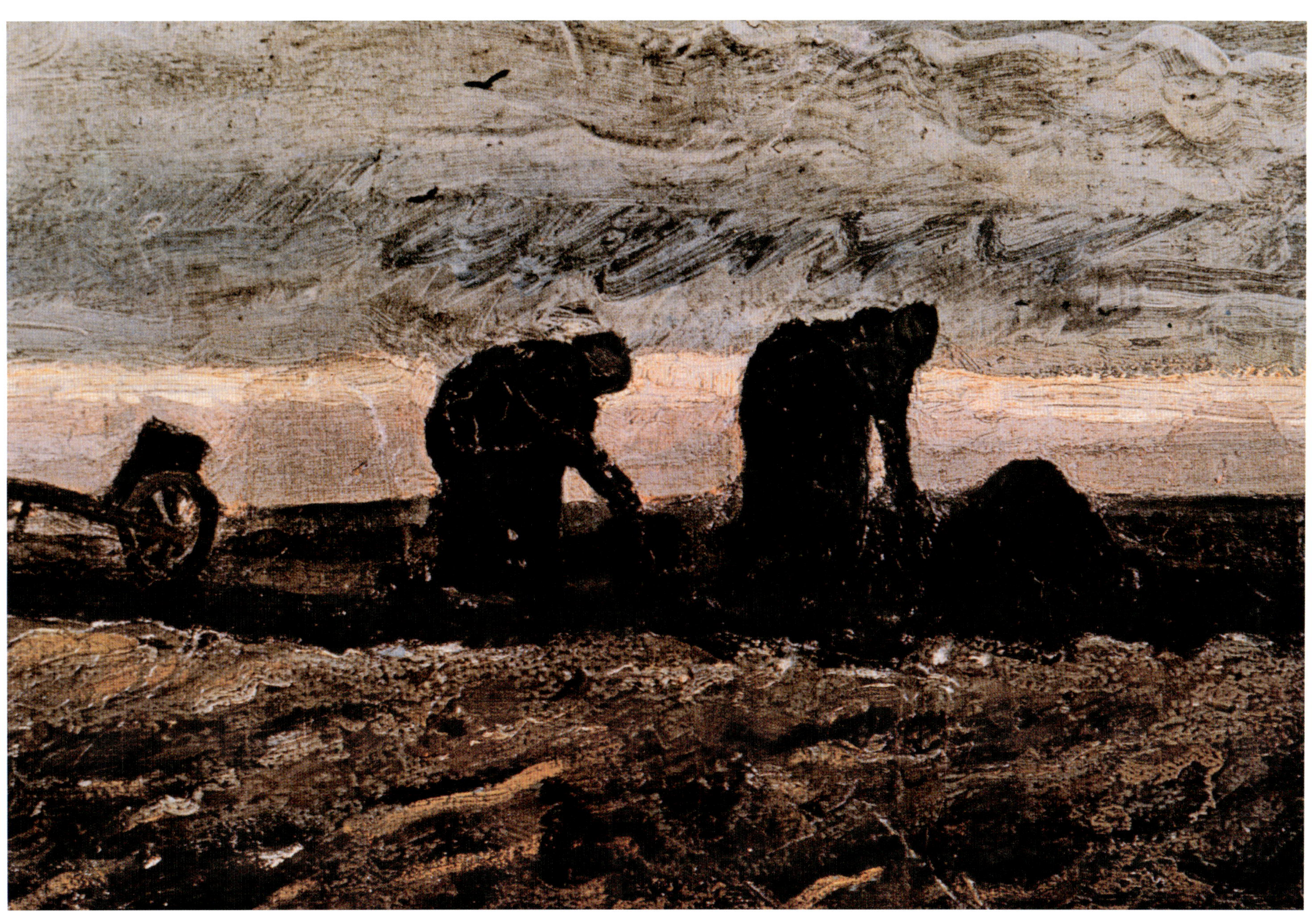

Peat Field *(1883). In the autumn of 1883, Vincent moved to the picturesque province of Drenthe, focusing again on the subject of agricultural labor. The heavy, bent forms of the women working in the field, reduced almost to silhouette, recalls the monumental solidity of the figures in Millet's* The Gleaners *(1857). But the daring handling of the sky, in striations of green, orange, and gold, is Vincent's own bold concept.*

Van Gogh Museum, Amsterdam. Oil on canvas (10¾×14¼ inches).

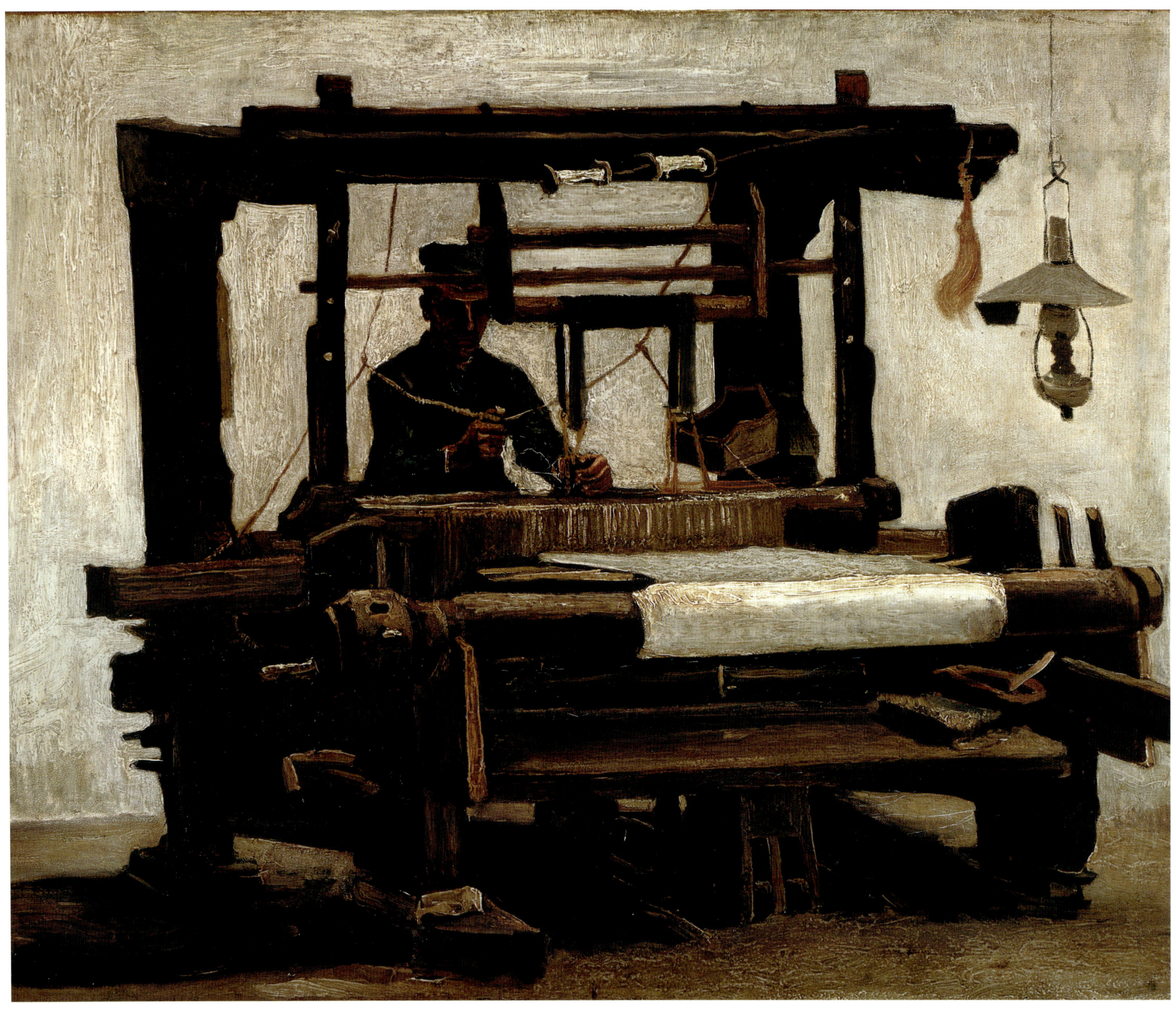

The Loom *(1884). Living in Drenthe, Vincent quickly ran through his limited resources for art supplies. Early in the new year, he moved to Nuenen, where his father had relocated the family to a new parsonage. He sought his subjects, such as this weaver, whom he paid a small fee to pose, among the working poor. The confining structure of the large loom displays the weaver fully absorbed in his task, and Vincent sensed a parallel intensity in his own endeavors.*

KRÖLLER-MÜLLER MUSEUM, OTTERLO, NETHERLANDS. OIL ON CANVAS (27½×33½ INCHES).

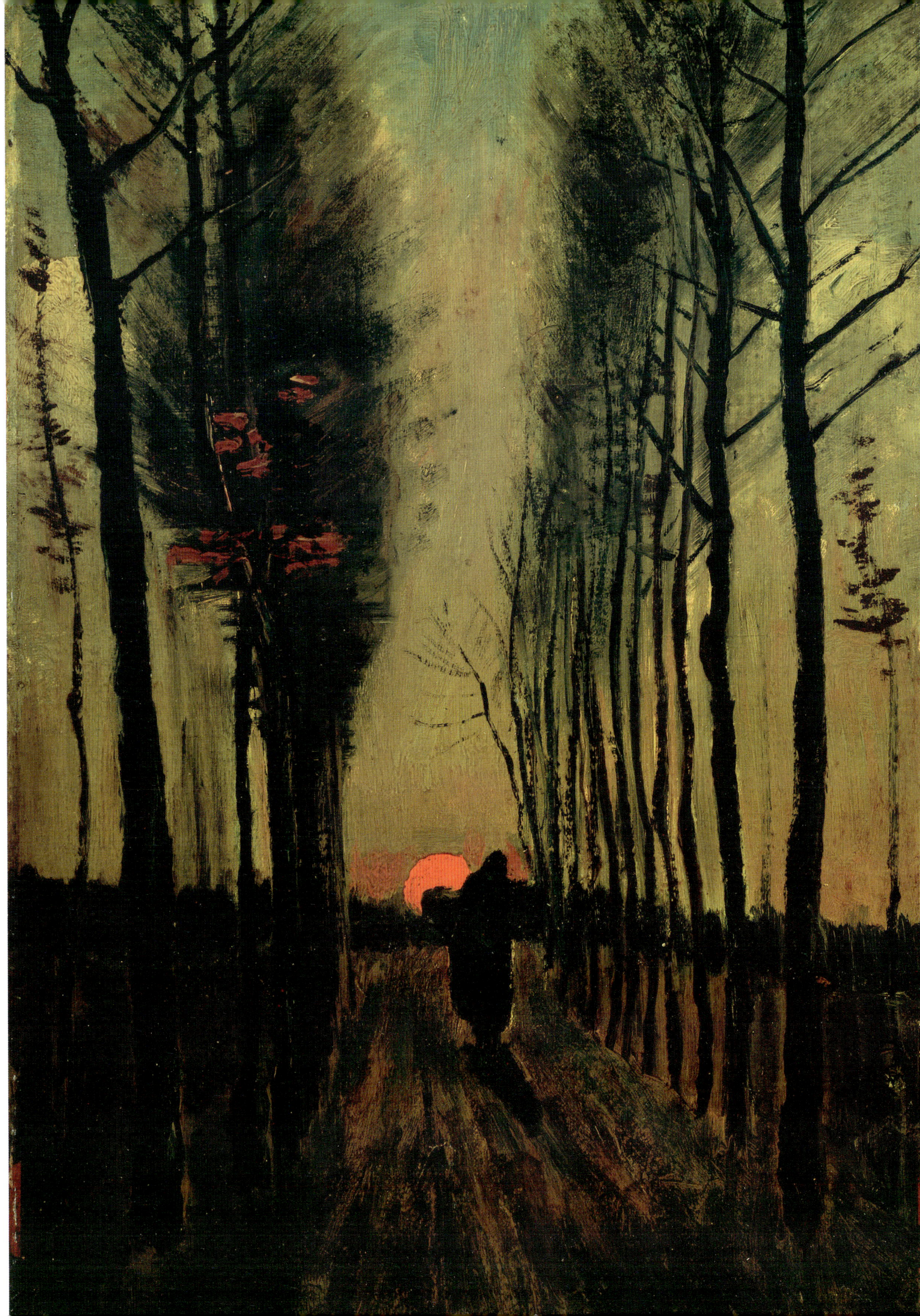

Lane of Poplars at Sunset *(1884). Vincent continued to paint landscapes, seeking to capture the natural effects of seasonal change through color. The flame-red foliage of the stands of poplar gain intensity from the low angle of the setting sun. Flanking the path, they cast red-brown shadows, but where the sun breaks through, the ground takes on an orange glow. The chill in the air is expressed in the way the woman on the path gathers her shawl around her to protect against the cold.*

LAND OF PICTURES

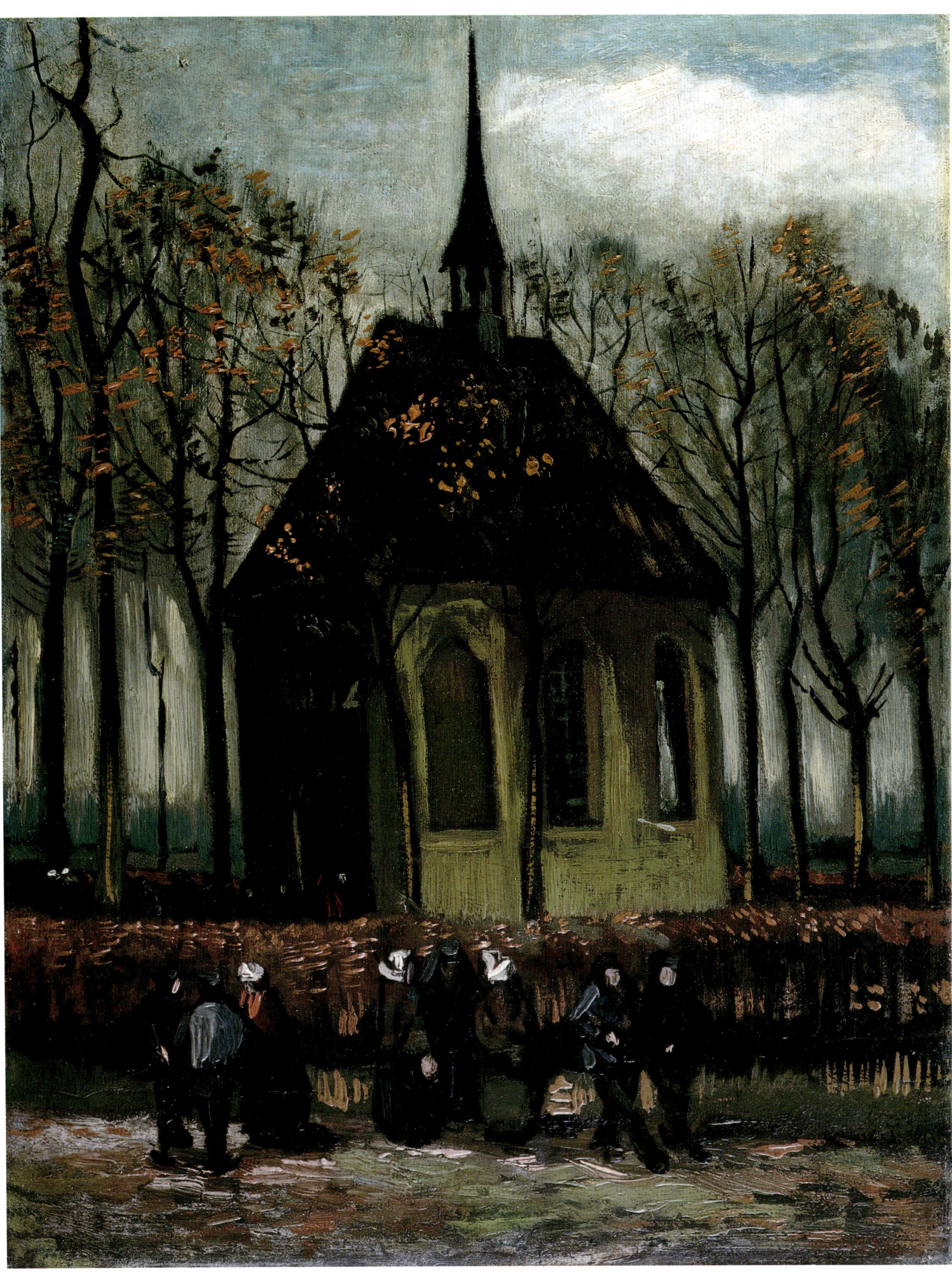

Congregation Leaving the Reformed Church in Nuenen *(1884). The solid form of the chapel with its high, pointed spire anchors this composition. The stone building topped by its dark roof rises in front of a bright blue sky filled with soft white clouds. In the foreground, Vincent has roughed in the townspeople with a few quick strokes. His varied brush stroke—cross-hatched on the chapel, feathery for the dry leaves on the bare branches, thick on the garments of the figures—adds expressive force to a straightforward subject.*

Van Gogh Museum, Amsterdam. Oil on canvas (16¼×12½ inches).

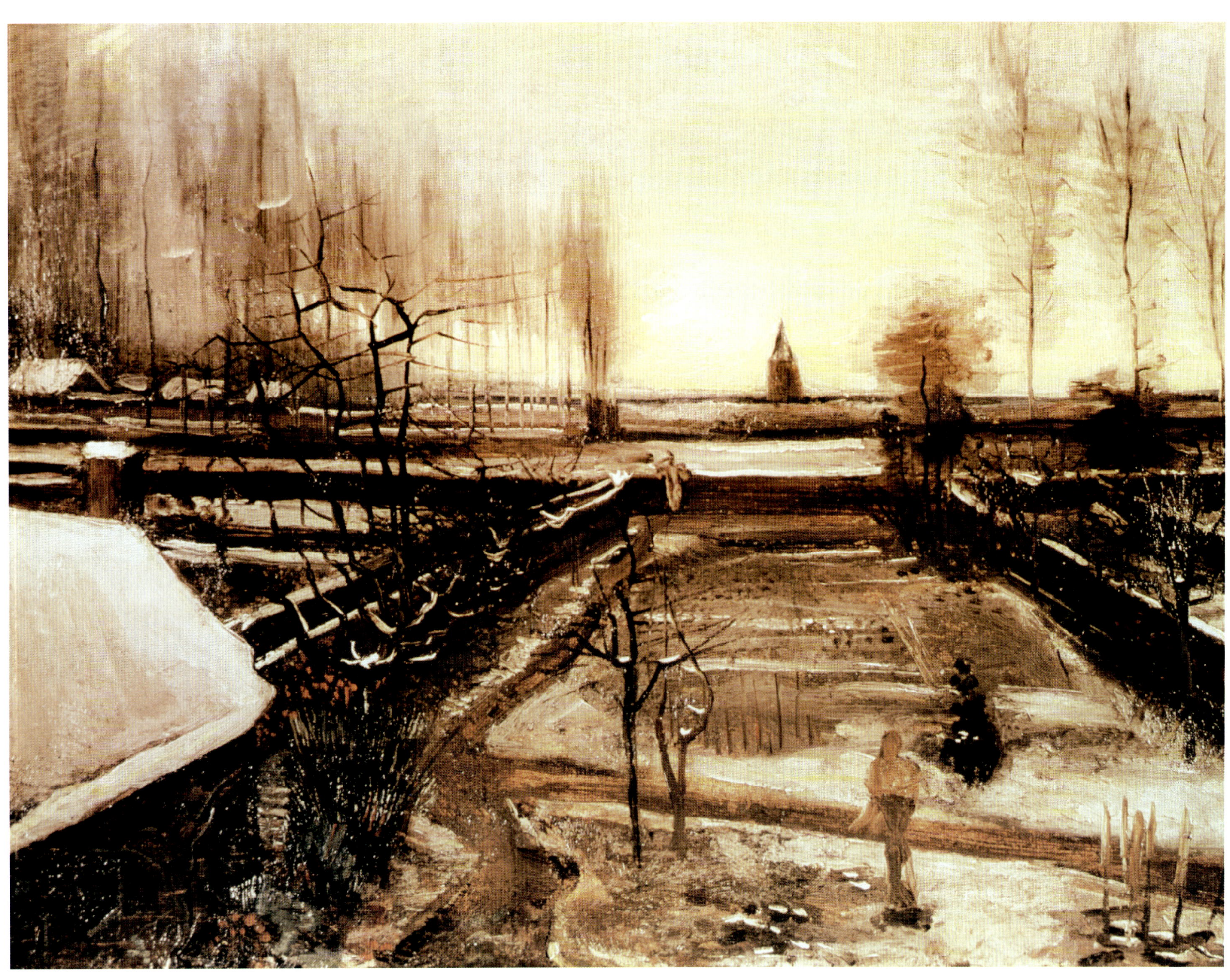

The Parsonage Garden in the Snow *(1885). The panoramic span of Vincent's view of the parsonage garden recalls the view he painted of the* Carpenter's Yard *out of his studio window at The Hague. There is a mournful aura in the starkness of the garden in winter, with bare trees and patches of snow on the hardened ground. But the sky in the distance has a golden glow, and the silhouette of the chapel rises high over the horizon.*

UCLA HAMMER MUSEUM, LOS ANGELES. OIL ON CANVAS ON PANEL (20¼×30¼ INCHES).

LAND OF PICTURES

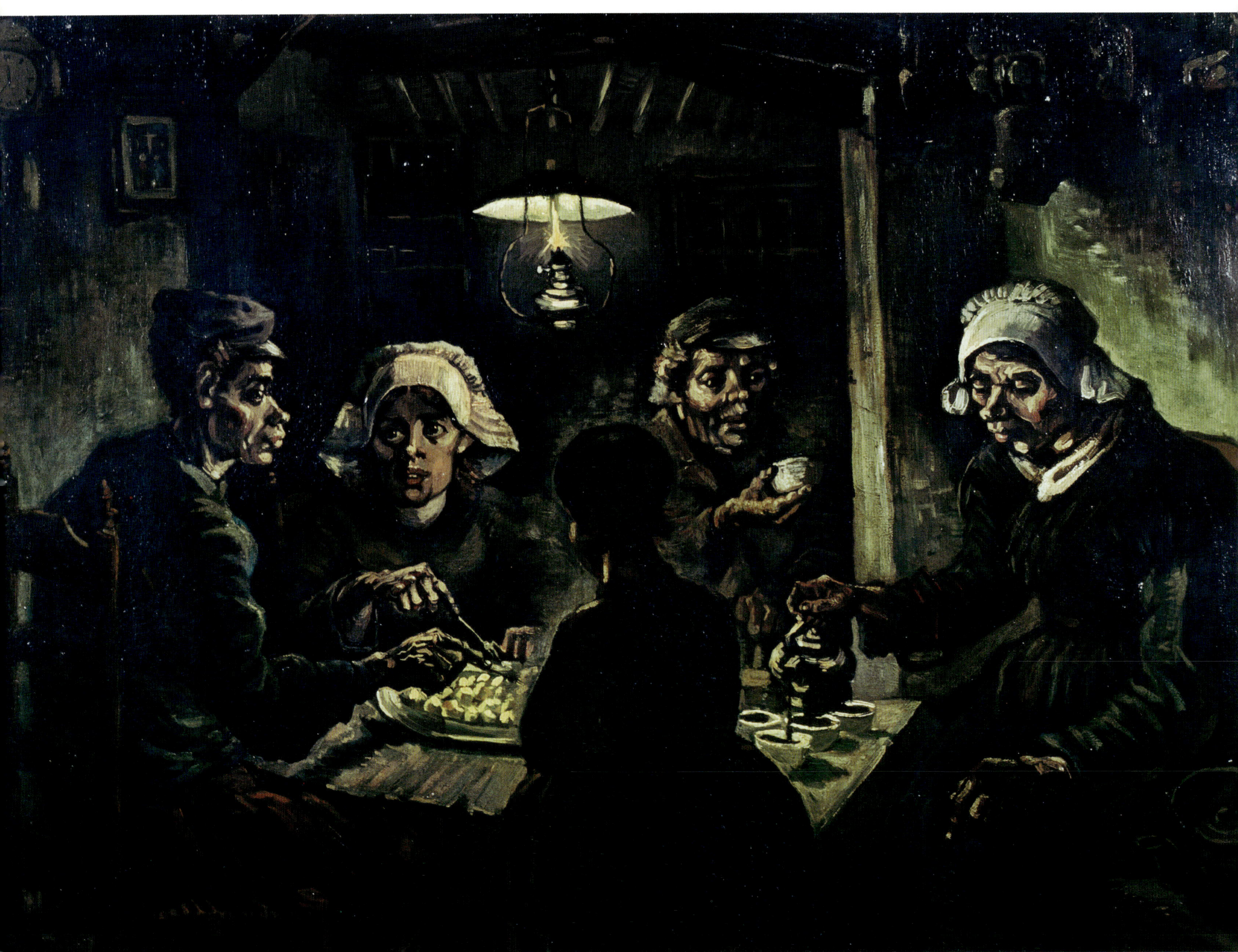

The Potato Eaters *(1885). After months of observing the local peasants' daily routines, Vincent depicted a family gathered around the table for a modest dinner of the potatoes grown in their own garden. He chose his colors purposefully to connect his sitters with the earth that sustained them. The stark interior, their rough hands, and weather-beaten faces were the legacy of their life of labor. Neither sentimental nor romantic,* The Potato Eaters *expressed the compassionate sincerity of Vincent's aims in art.*

Van Gogh Museum, Amsterdam. Oil on canvas (32¼×45 inches).

Woman Winding Yarn *(1885). After more than a year working in Nuenen, Vincent formulated a plan to create a large, important painting to launch his career. Late in 1884, he began a series of studies of figures absorbed in mundane work: sewing, spinning, and digging. He chose his models from the local farm community and limited his palette to dark, earthy tones. He wrote to Theo, "one must paint the peasants as being one of them."*

Van Gogh Museum, Amsterdam. Oil on canvas (16¼×12¾ inches).

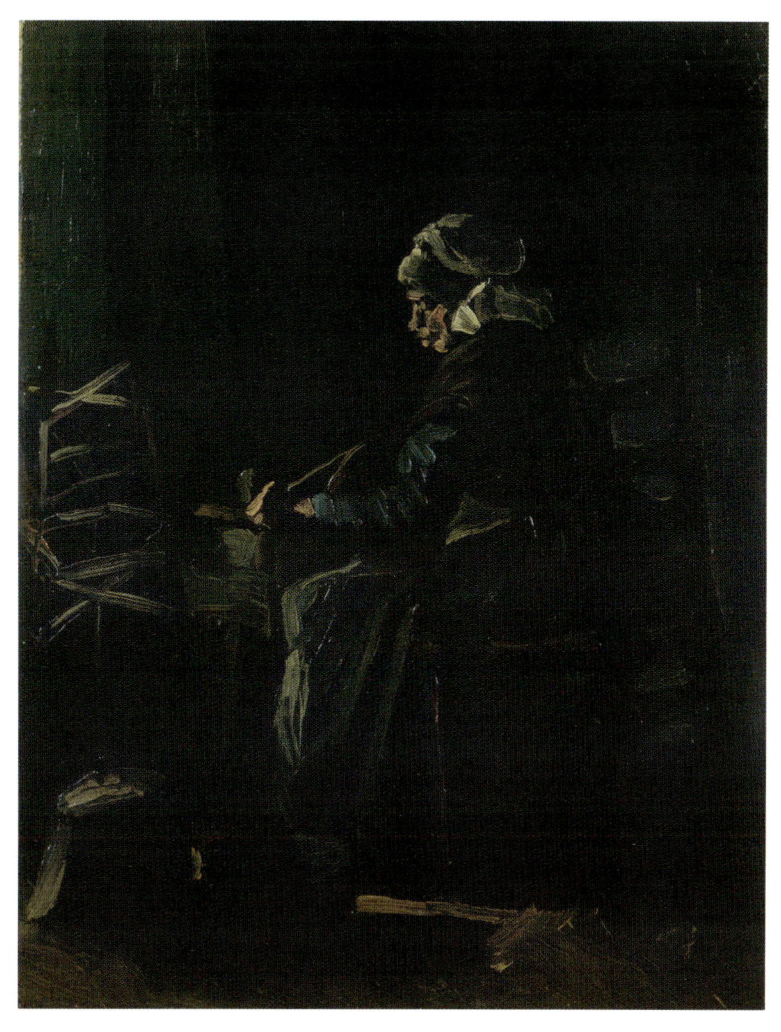

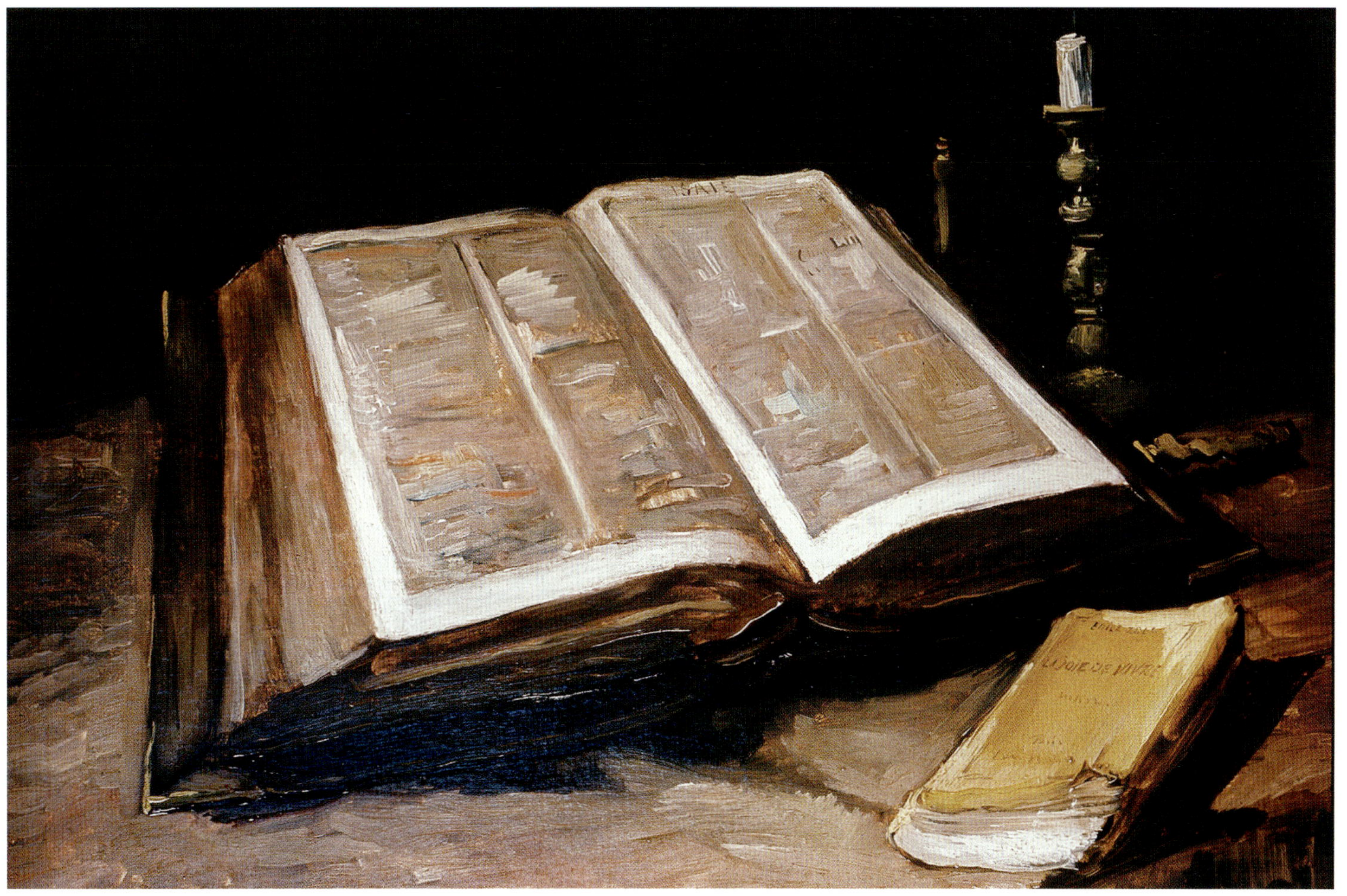

Still Life with Bible *(1885). In his quest to become a painter, Vincent arranged still lifes in the studio to train his eye and hand. He was following the tradition of his own heritage, admiring the compositions of the past masters of Holland that featured either the bounty of the merchant's import trade or the basic elements of a rustic repast. In this painting, Vincent featured deeply personal objects: the Bible of his father's religious traditions and a contemporary novel by Émile Zola. The harsh bright yellow of the novel's paper cover contrasts with the muted tones of the Bible pages yellowed with age, echoing a contrast of past and present ideas.*

Van Gogh Museum, Amsterdam. Oil on canvas (25½×30¾ inches).

LAND OF PICTURES

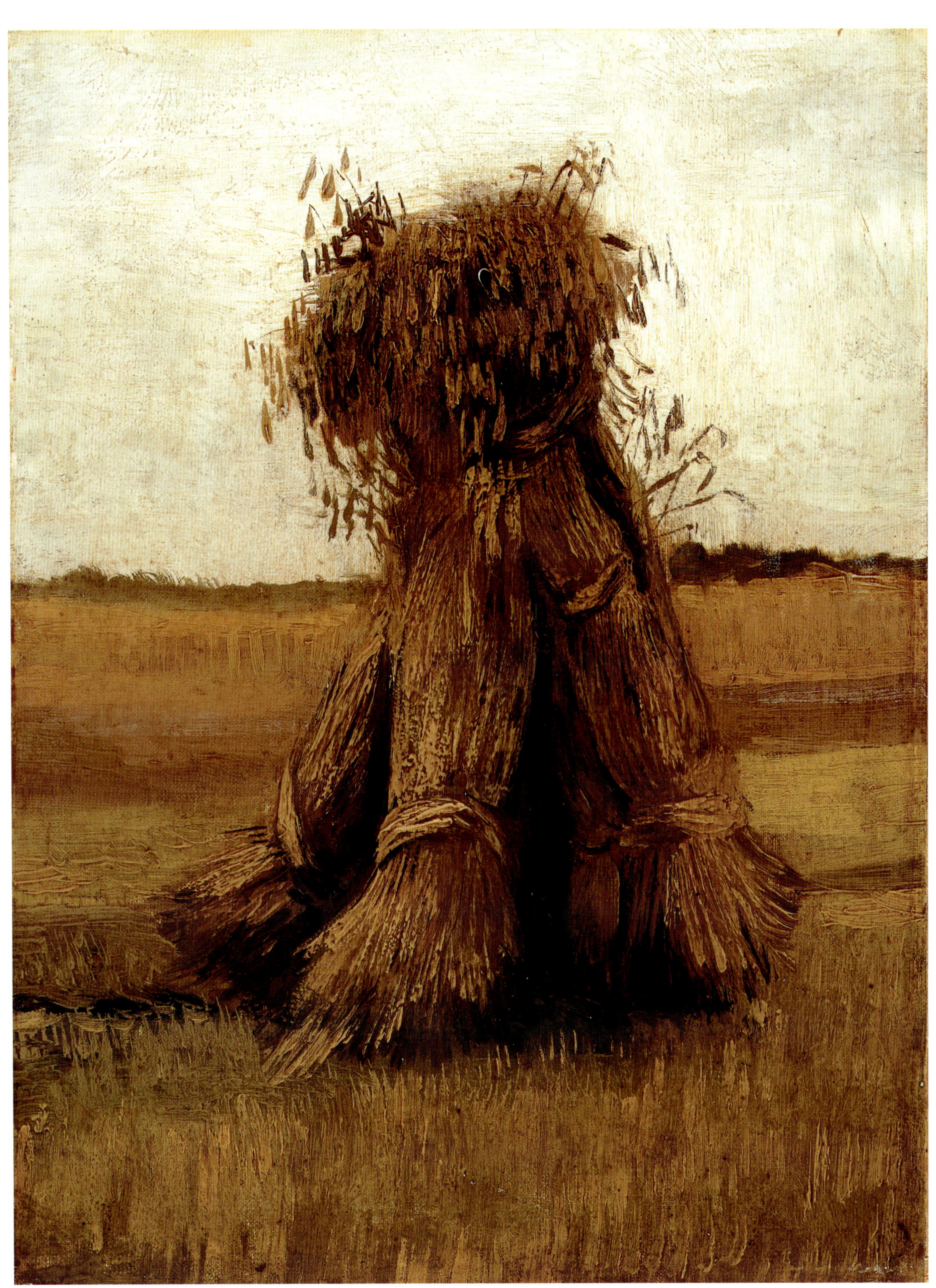

Sheaves of Wheat *(1885). Setting up his easel in the fields, Vincent painted the harvest during his last summer in Nuenen. He depicted the female workers digging and raking, but he also painted the sheaves of wheat, tied into bundles for storage. His dedication to painting outdoors endured because he believed that the natural light on the fields could not be duplicated in the studio.*

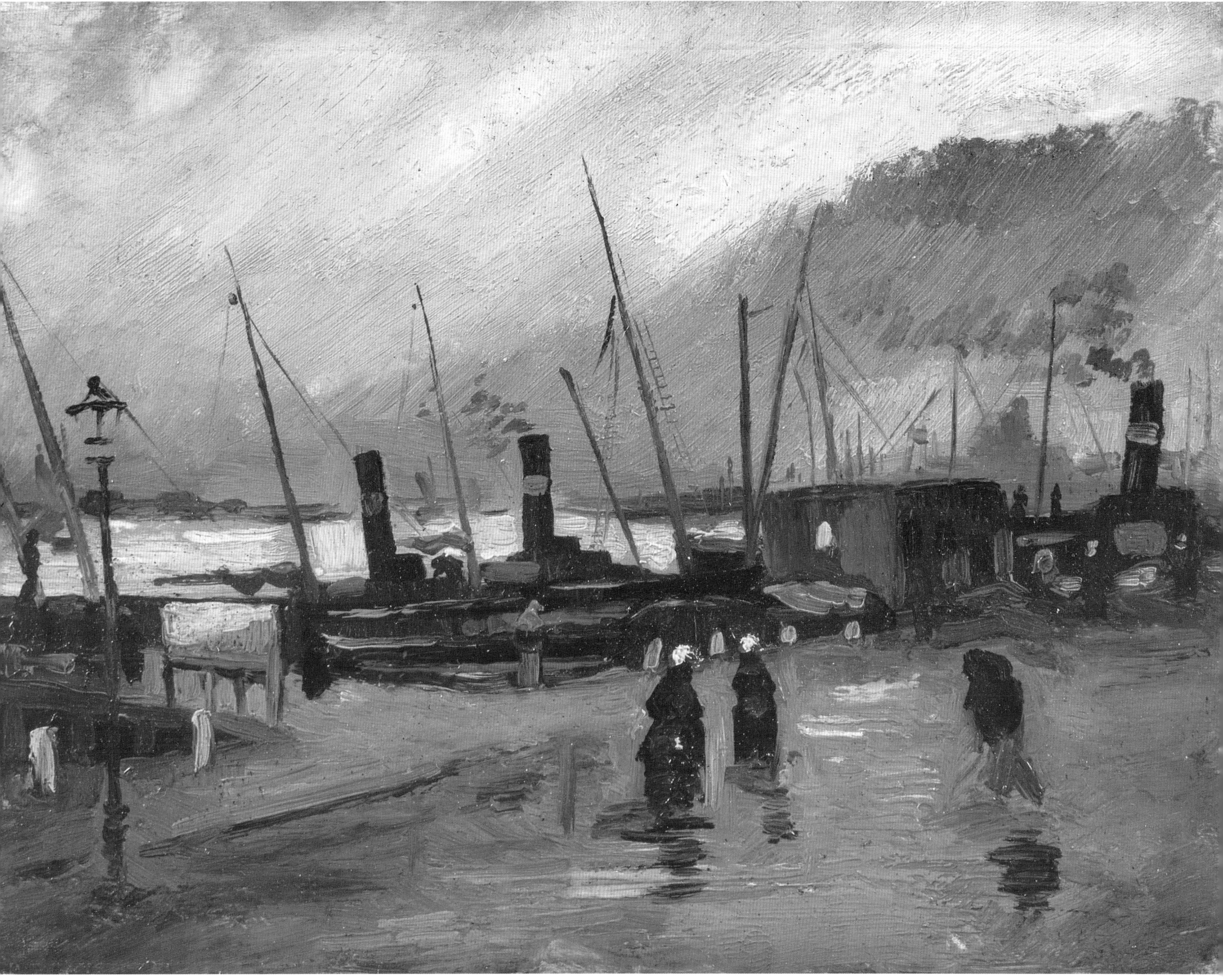

The De Ruijterkade in Amsterdam *(1885). Late in November, Vincent moved to Antwerp. With only a small allowance from Theo, he lived frugally, hoping to convince the local art dealers to sell his work from Nuenen. He made regular visits to the many art galleries and museums in Antwerp to study the works of Peter Paul Rubens and Franz Hals. But he found his subjects at the docks, where he set up his easel to paint the sea and the ships at various times of the day.*

Van Gogh Museum, Amsterdam. Oil on panel (8×10½ inches).

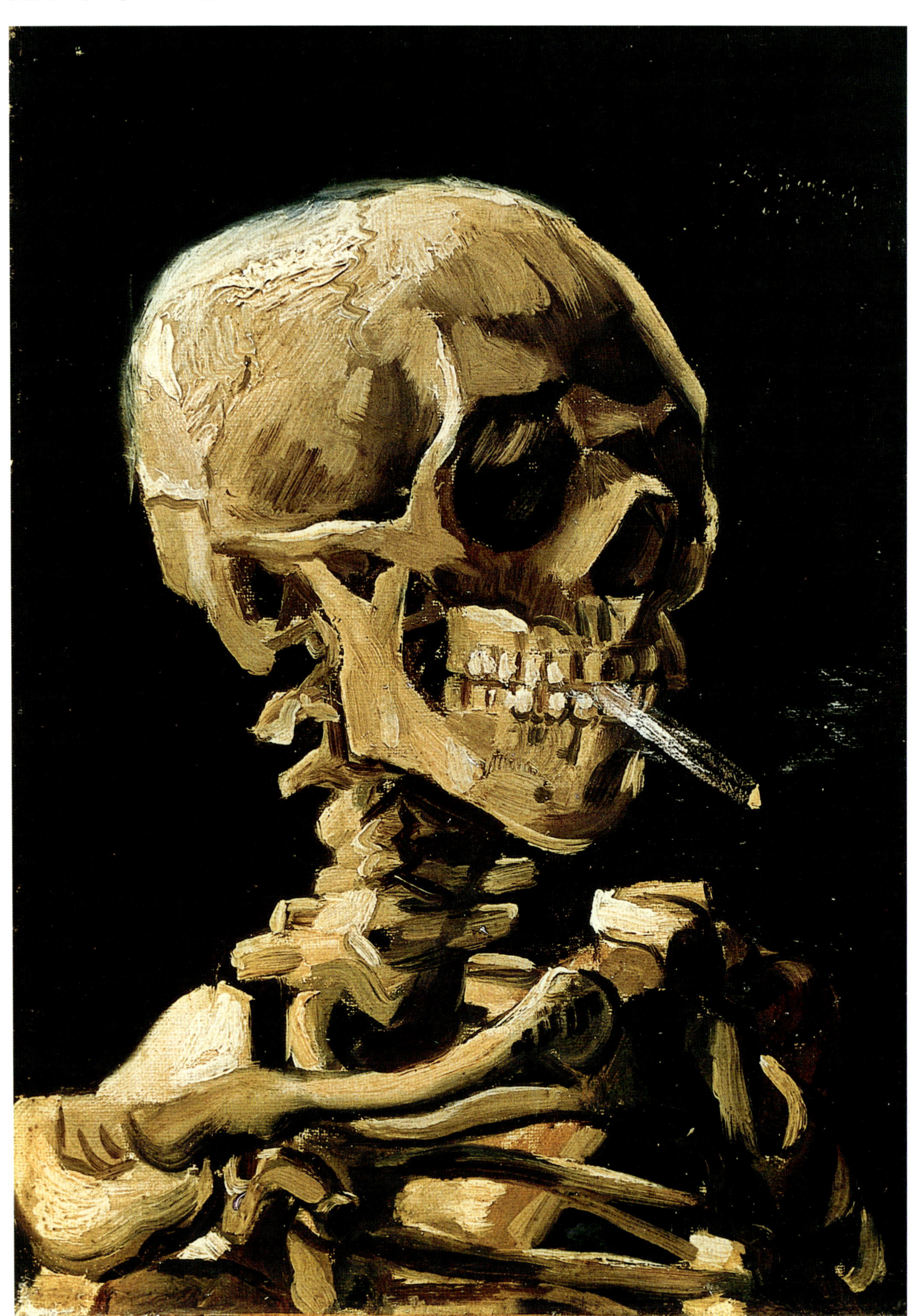

Skull of a Skeleton with Burning Cigarette *(1885–1886). To improve his command of the human figure, Vincent attended life classes at the Académie Royale des Beaux-Arts in Antwerp, where a skeleton was used to study anatomy. The burning cigarette placed between the teeth of this bare skull typifies the irreverent humor that often reigned among art students, but the striking feature of this painting is Vincent's vital and confident handling of a complex subject.*

Van Gogh Museum, Amsterdam. Oil on canvas (12½×9½ inches).

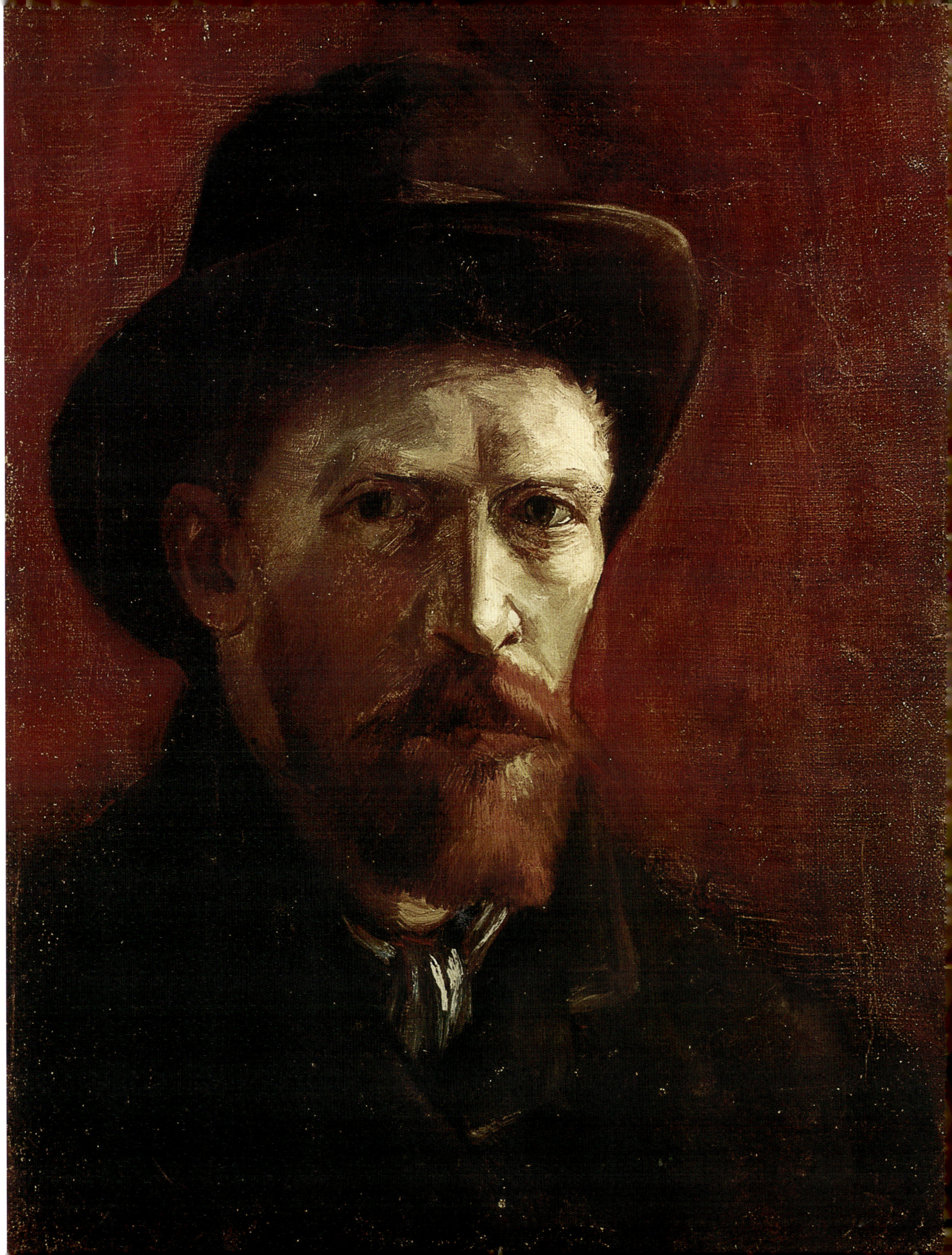

Self-Portrait with Dark Felt Hat *(1886). This is one of Vincent's early self-portraits. He is dressed in street clothes: a voluminous cloak and a dark brown felt hat pulled low on his forehead. His piercing blue eyes are deeply shadowed beneath his furrowed brow and his bright, ginger-red beard is muted in the low light of the painting. This portrait, painted shortly after his arrival in Paris, features the restrained and earthy range of hues that typified his peasant subjects. Vincent presents himself in a phase of transition, wary but ready to face a new life.*

COLOR SEEKING LIFE

"In color seeking life the true drawing is modeling with color."

VINCENT TO HORACE LEVENS, SUMMER 1886, FROM PARIS

IFE IN PARIS PLACED Vincent in the center of the most sophisticated art community in Europe. His brother Theo managed a contemporary art gallery where Vincent was able to see the latest works of artists whom he had previously known only by name and reputation. Theo introduced him to the innovators he had admired from a distance, including Claude Monet, Edgar Degas, and Camille Pissarro. In May, Vincent attended the eighth and final Impressionist exhibition, where he admired Georges Seurat's *A Sunday on La Grand Jatte* (1884–1886) for its daring concept of optical divisionism. For several months, Vincent attended the *Atelier Libre* (Free Studio) directed by Fernand Cormon. The curriculum was relatively unstructured, and in the studio Vincent met other aspiring painters such as Henri de Toulouse-Lautrec, Paul Signac, and Emile Bernard. These friendships endured well after Vincent left Cormon's *atelier,* and while in Paris he frequented the cafés with Toulouse-Lautrec and painted en plein air alongside Signac and Bernard in the fields just north of Montmartre and in the suburb of Asnières. Along with his brother, Vincent visited artists' studios, and in November 1887, they met Paul Gauguin, who showed them the vivid and colorful visions of the tropics he had painted during his recent stay in Martinique. Vincent absorbed all these new influences, intent on finding his own mode of expression. But more than anything, Vincent was determined to comprehend and master color.

Vincent had long been concerned with the expressive potential of color. In his letters, he often

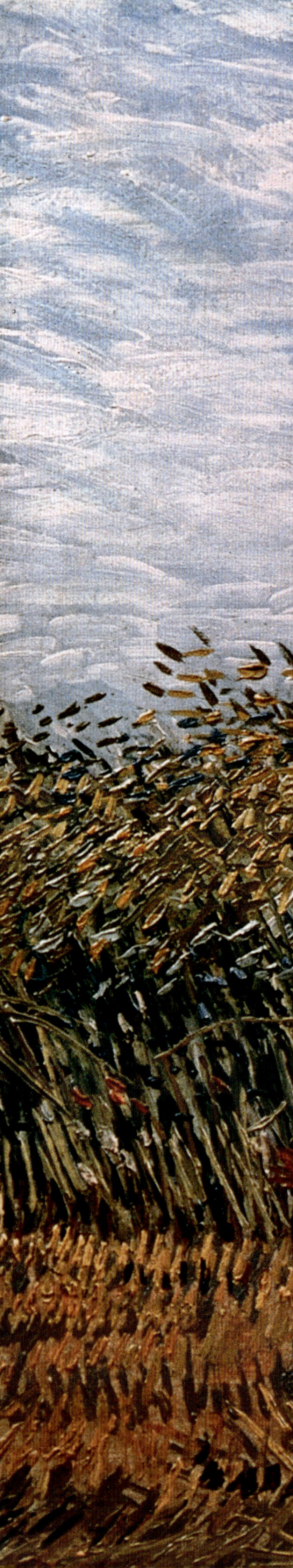

Wheatfield with a Lark (1887). Vincent painted Wheatfield with a Lark *in the fields outside Asnières. He portrayed the grain stalks at their fullest summer height, blowing in the wind of an approaching storm. A lark soars across the still-bright sky. Traditionally, the flight of a lark indicates happiness, but Vincent may have used the soaring bird to embody the sense of freedom he felt when working outdoors in the countryside.*

VAN GOGH MUSEUM, AMSTERDAM. OIL ON CANVAS (21¼×25¾ INCHES).

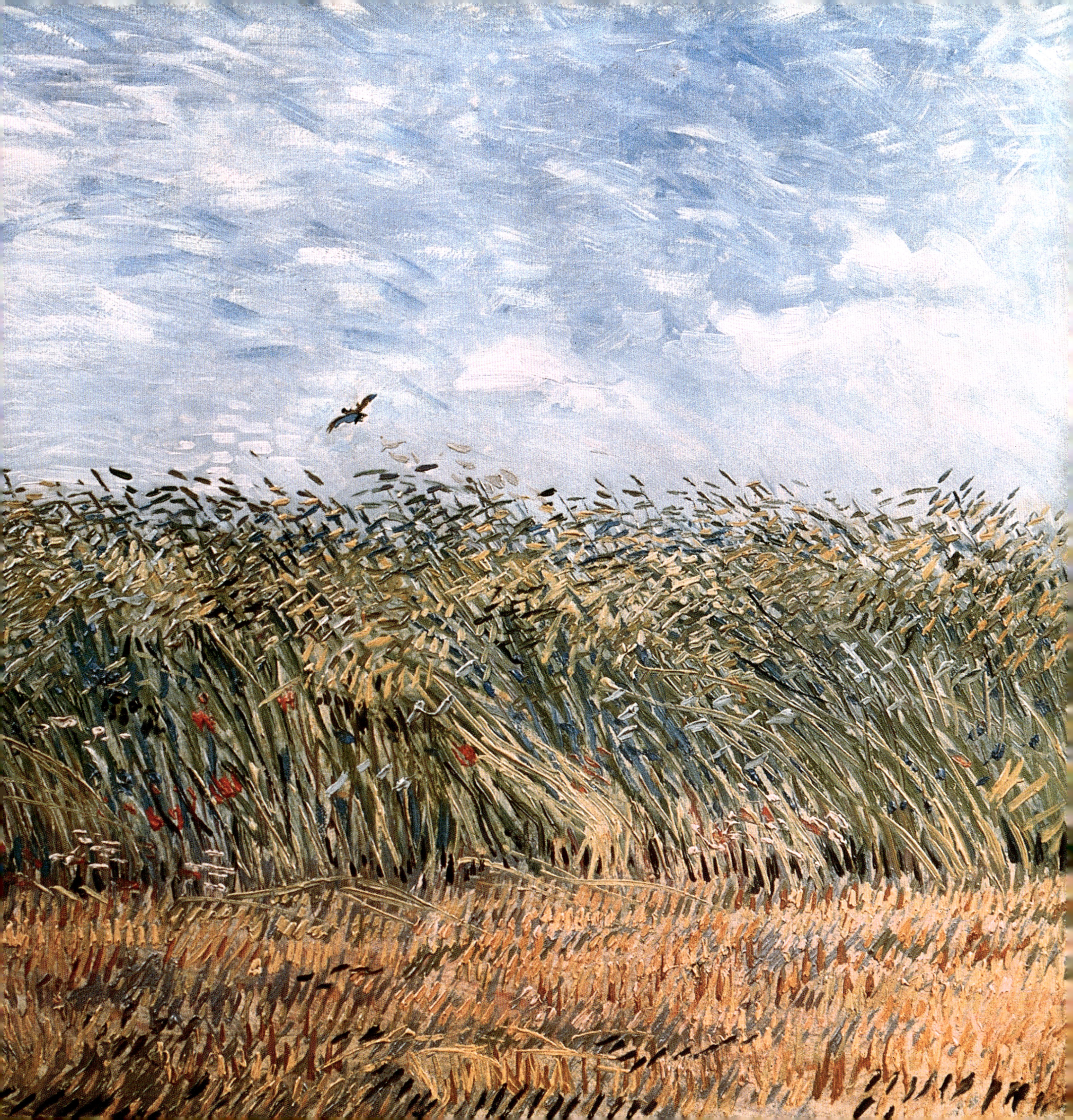

Color Seeking Life

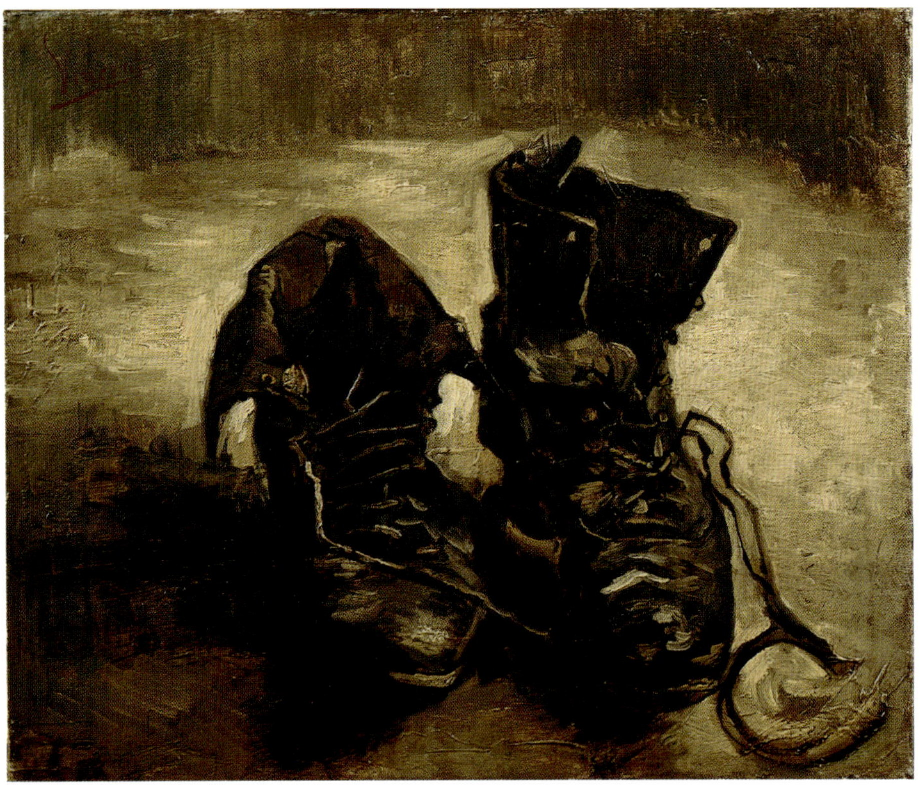

A Pair of Shoes *(1885).
A simple subject, such as
these worn work boots,
gave Vincent an opportu-
nity to concentrate on the
issues of color and brush
stroke in his painting. He
painted the boots in the
dull browns of his Nue-
nen palette, but he set
them against a fresh
background of gold. He
applied his paint thickly,
leaving distinct brush
strokes in the foreground
and working a crosshatch
pattern in the back,
giving as much impor-
tance to his surface as his
subject.*

reflected at length about the values and meanings of individual hues. He also described the tonal range of his current work in great detail. Writing to Theo from Nuenen in the summer of 1884, in part to justify a high bill to the color merchant, Vincent proposed that a painter could evoke a seasonal mood through colors in contrast: the delicate tints of "green young corn" and "pink apple blossoms" for spring, the "yellow leaves with violet tones" for autumn, and the black silhouettes on the snow for winter. He studied the color theories of Eugène Delacroix and, while in Antwerp, tried to incorporate some of the high warmth of Peter Paul Rubens's paintings in his own earthy palette. In Nuenen, he had used dark and somber tones to convey his serious regard for agricultural labor. But in Paris, he enlivened his palette by

painting bouquets of flowers in random combinations to study the range of natural hues. In the late summer of 1886, Vincent described his endeavors in a letter to Horace Levens, an English painter he had met in Antwerp. His color studies, he admitted, kept him from advancing his expertise at drawing figures, but flowers were more affordable than figure models. The vast variety he could purchase—poppies, daisies, roses, sunflowers, and carnations—taught him how "to render intense color" and rid his palette of restricted tones. He declared that these experiments confirmed his long-standing belief that "in color seeking life the true drawing is modeling with color."

Over the course of two years in Paris, Vincent painted more than 30 floral still lifes. He became bold in his experiments with contrasting color, as seen in the still life *A Pair of Shoes* (1885), where he introduced a deep, rich gold tonality into the somber browns of his palette. His intense devotion to plein air painting also brightened his tonal range, prompting him to use floral hues—pale violet and rose red—as well as jewel tones— turquoise, garnet, and burnished gold—to express atmospheric effects in works such as *The Hill of Montmartre with Stone Quarry* (1886) and *Boule- vard de Clichy* (1887). He advanced his color experiments by adopting—often briefly and eccen- trically—the innovative approaches he admired in contemporary art. To paint *Wheatfield with a Lark* (1887), he set his easel in a field near Asnières and

The Hill of Montmartre with Stone Quarry *(1886). Paris presented Vincent with an unprecedented opportunity to absorb everything that was new and innovative in art. He made regular visits to exhibitions and pursued introductions to artists, whom he liked to visit in their studios. This wealth of influence prompted him to experiment, as seen here with his daring introduction of violet and pink in the volatile sky and the square touch of the brush strokes, which conveys the solidity of the rock walls of the quarry.*

VAN GOGH MUSEUM, AMSTERDAM. OIL ON CANVAS (22×24½ INCHES).

instilled his subject with the sense of spontaneity associated with Impressionism by applying pure pigment with a deft, short stroke. He dabbed color on his canvas in his attempts to understand Seurat's optical theories, but his color combinations, such as the contrasting complements of red and green seen in his *Self-Portrait* (1887), and his natural inclination toward a gestural stroke, heightened the emotional content of his work beyond the reserve of the cerebral approach of Neo-Impressionism. While living in Paris, Vincent also expanded his collection of Japanese prints, and during the summer of 1887, he made detailed oil studies of two scenic views by Ando Hiroshige and one after a reproduction of a courtesan by Keisai Eisen. Vincent matched his colors to the subtle shades of the printed ink, but he applied his paint with an

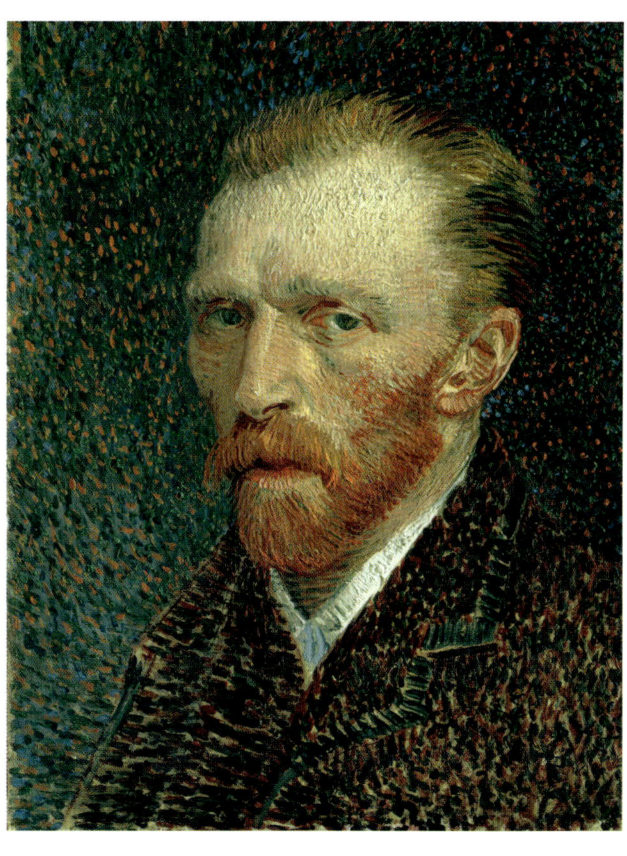

expressive hand that replaced the characteristic tranquility of the prints with a spirit of vibrant energy.

Late in the summer of 1887, Vincent painted several studies of cut sunflowers. He used contrasting colors: yellows that ranged from pale citron to deep ocher and fresh grassy greens shown against a background painted in shades of cerulean blue. He applied his bold color with confidence and a generous stroke. He used thick trails of pigment to describe the ragged petals and the twisted stems of the sunflowers, and this vigorous impasto conveyed the vitality and involvement of his approach. Every stroke he laid on his canvas echoed the intensity that he instilled in the act of painting. In writing to Theo in 1886, shortly before his sudden departure from Antwerp for Paris, Vincent had equated color with vitality. "What color is in a picture," he observed, "enthusiasm is in life." Vincent had come to Paris to rejuvenate his life and advance his art. His exploration of color transformed the way he painted and confirmed his conviction that his passion for art was the essential force in his life.

Self-Portrait *(1887). The stylistic innovations of Georges Seurat prompted Vincent to experiment with a pointillist brush stroke. His use of the color complements red and green illustrates his desire to understand Neo-Impressionism, but his stroke remained emphatically expressive in contrast to the neutral surface effect the optical approach was formulated to achieve. Rather than the cool, intellectual objectives of Seurat's pioneering theories, Vincent's work suggests emotional turbulence.*

JOSEPH WINTERBOTHAM COLLECTION, ART INSTITUTE OF CHICAGO. OIL ON ARTIST'S BOARD MOUNTED ON CRADLED PANEL (16¼×12¾ INCHES).

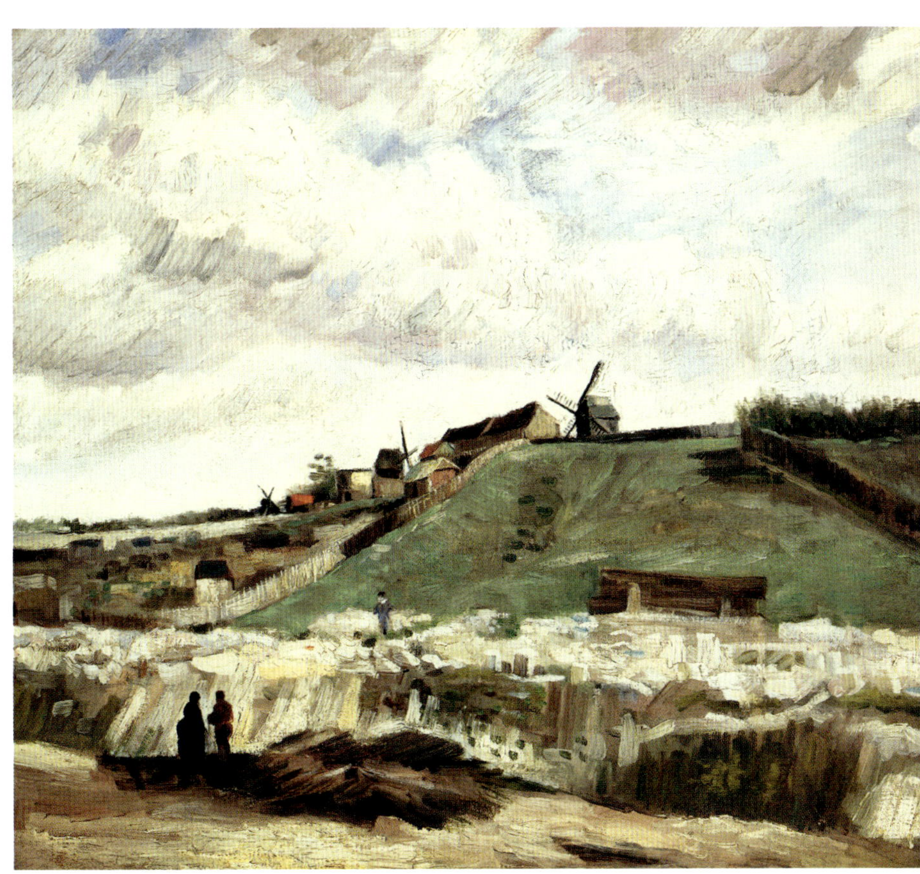

COLOR SEEKING LIFE

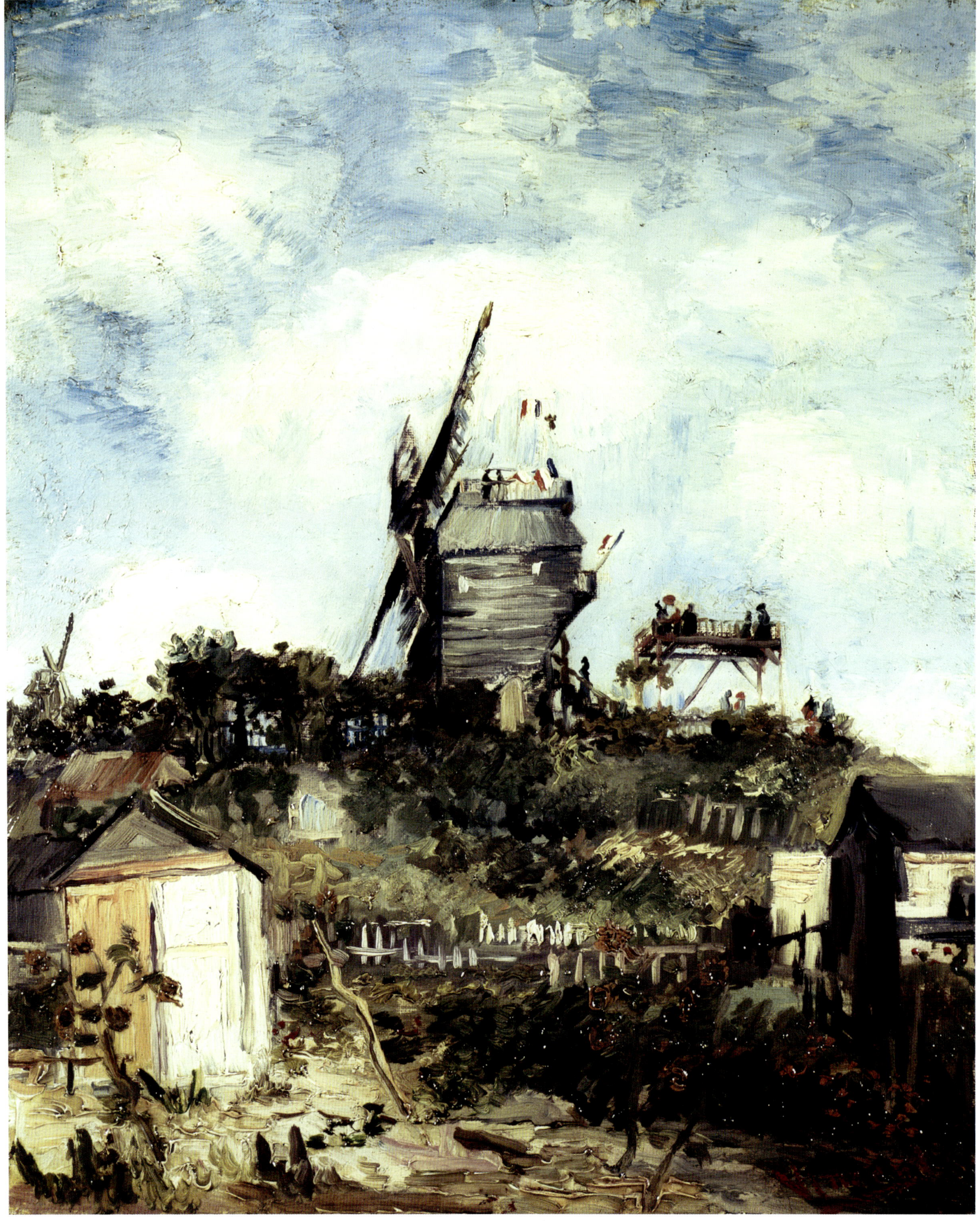

Le Moulin de la Galette
*(1886). Vincent enjoyed
living with his brother in
an apartment in Mont-
martre on the northern
edge of Paris. From there
it was an easy walk to the
outskirts of the city where
small cottage farms could
be found nestled among
the hills. Painting out-
doors helped him explore
the effects of natural light,
which gave his palette a
sun-drenched quality that
purged his rural subjects
of their characteristic
somber tonalities.*

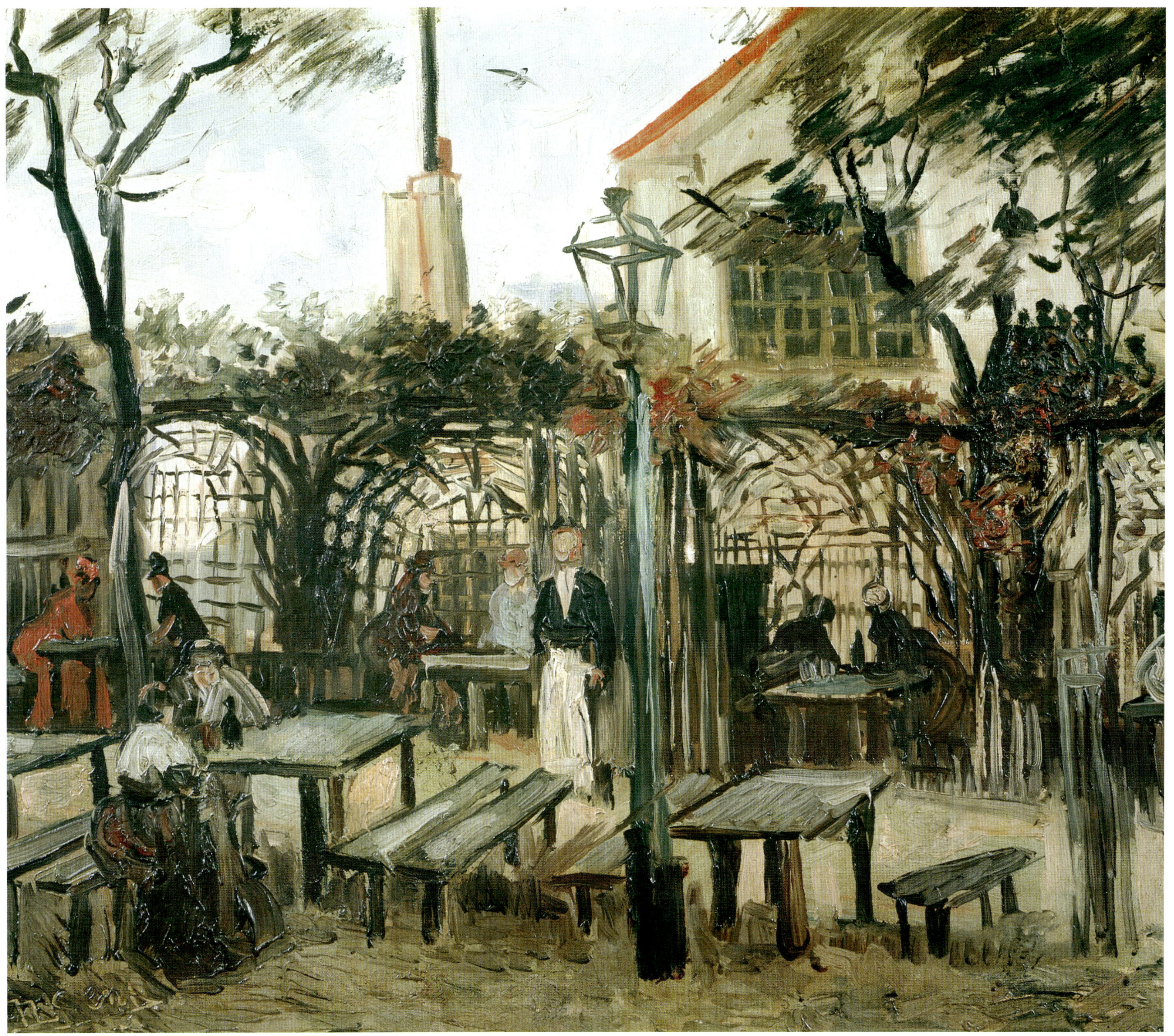

Terrace of a Café on Montmartre (La Guinguette) *(1886). Usually the setting for a lighthearted scene of leisure, notably in the work of Pierre-Auguste Renoir, the outdoor café takes on a sober note in the low autumn light. Vincent works in his figures as mere suggestions of form with weighted calligraphic strokes and a dark palette of brown and carmine red. The streak of aqua on the lamppost presents a startling contrast as does the free handling of the trees and volatile sky.*

MUSÉE D'ORSAY, PARIS. OIL ON CANVAS (19¼×25¼ INCHES).

COLOR SEEKING LIFE

Vegetable Gardens and the Moulin de Blute-Fin on Montmartre (1887). Vincent continued his experiments in color throughout the next year in Paris. He lightened his palette further as he worked outdoors, and he shifted his interest in the interaction of complements from red and green to yellow and blue. In this vista of a cottage farm and its windmill, Vincent also varied his application of pigment, using a pointillist touch for the fields and a broken brush stroke for the sky.

Van Gogh Museum, Amsterdam. Oil on canvas (17¾×32 inches).

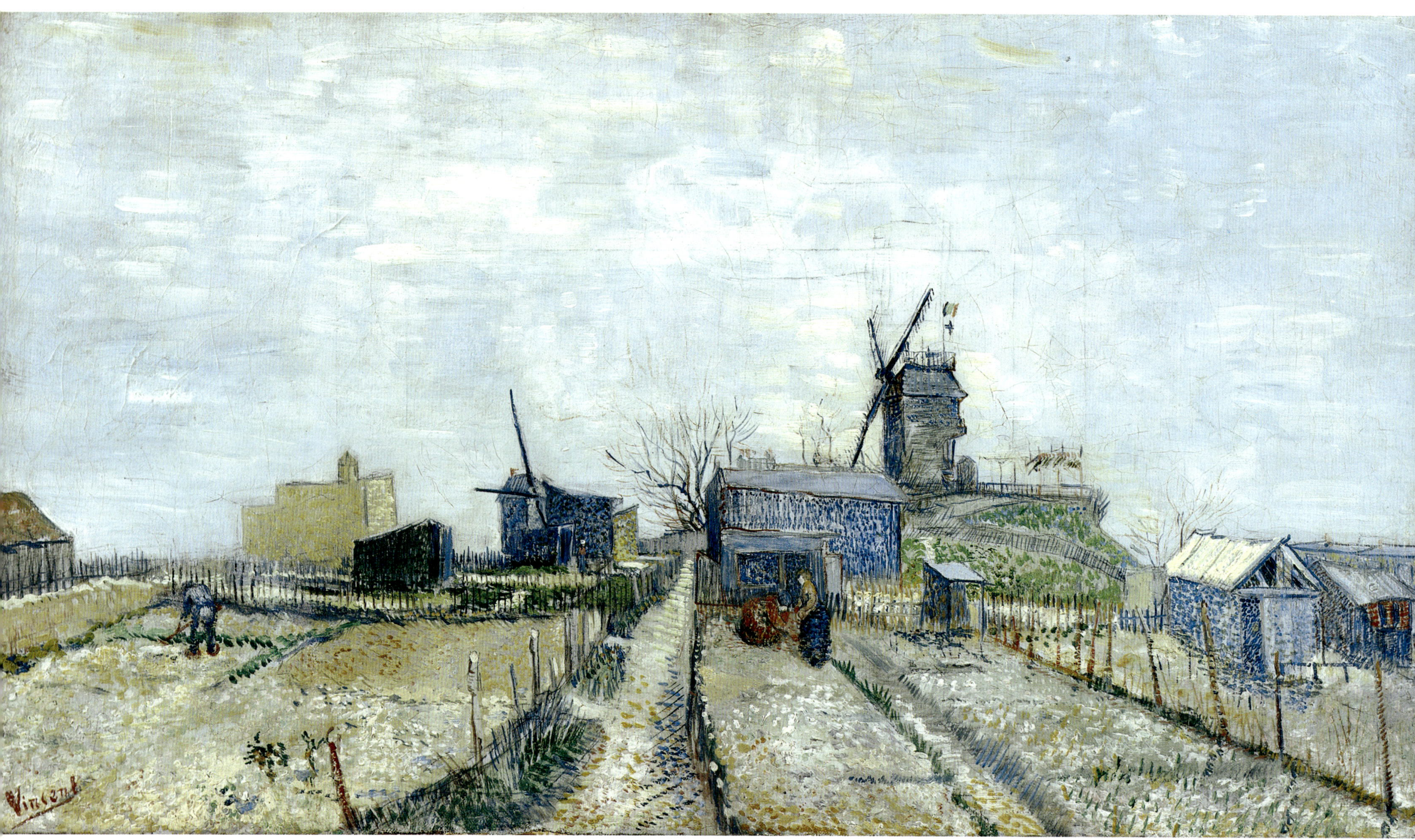

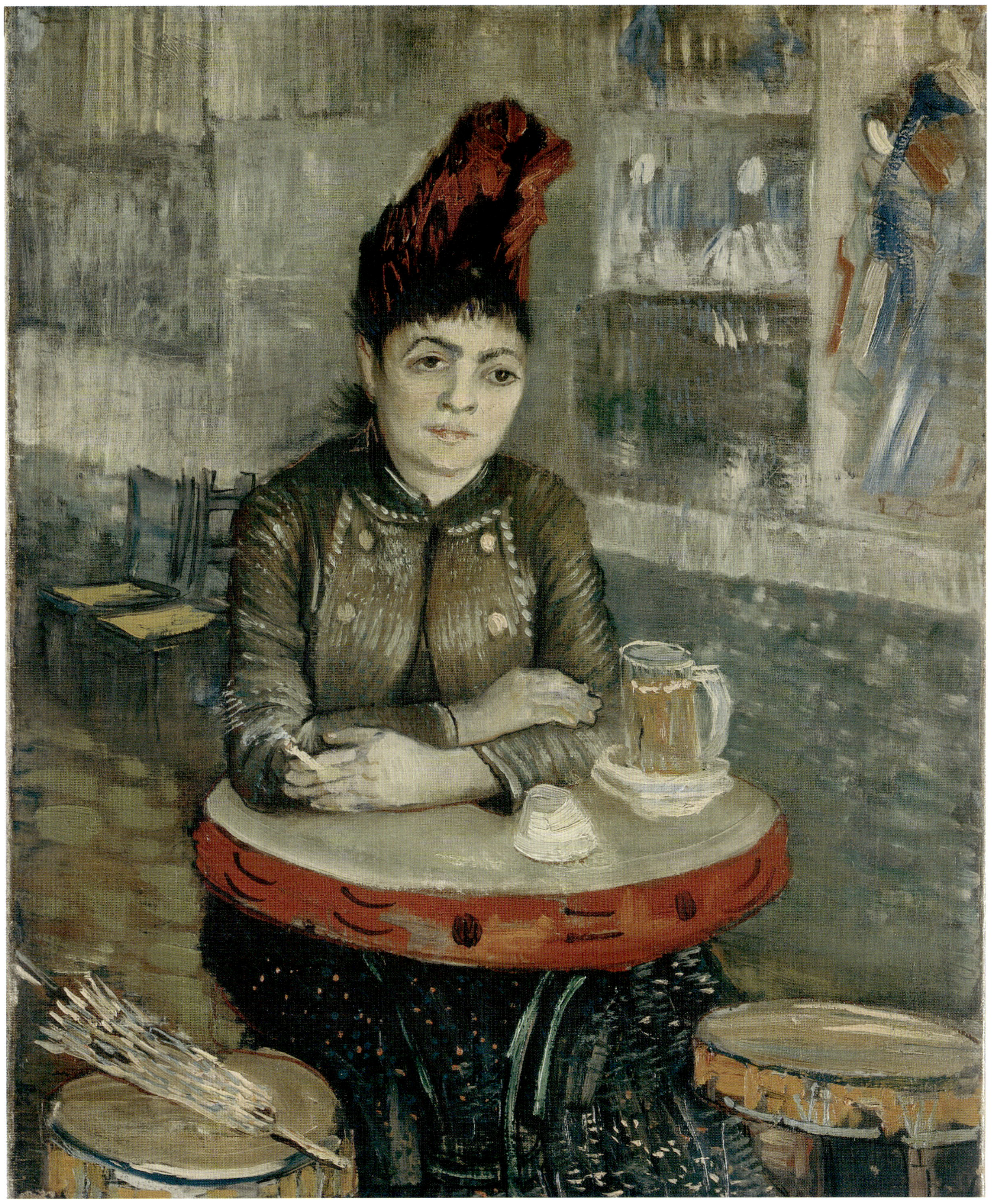

Agostina Segatori Sitting in the Café du Tambourin *(1887).*
Agostina Segatori was the proprietor of the Café Tambourin, a cabaret frequented by painters. She allowed Vincent to install an exhibition of his Japanese prints in her café, and she posed for him on several occasions. Here, he surrounds her with subtle variations in green with red and aqua highlights. The effect is both decorative and disturbing, due to the chromatic vibrations that result in the pairing of complementary colors. The table is in the form of a tambourine, the namesake of the café.

COLOR SEEKING LIFE

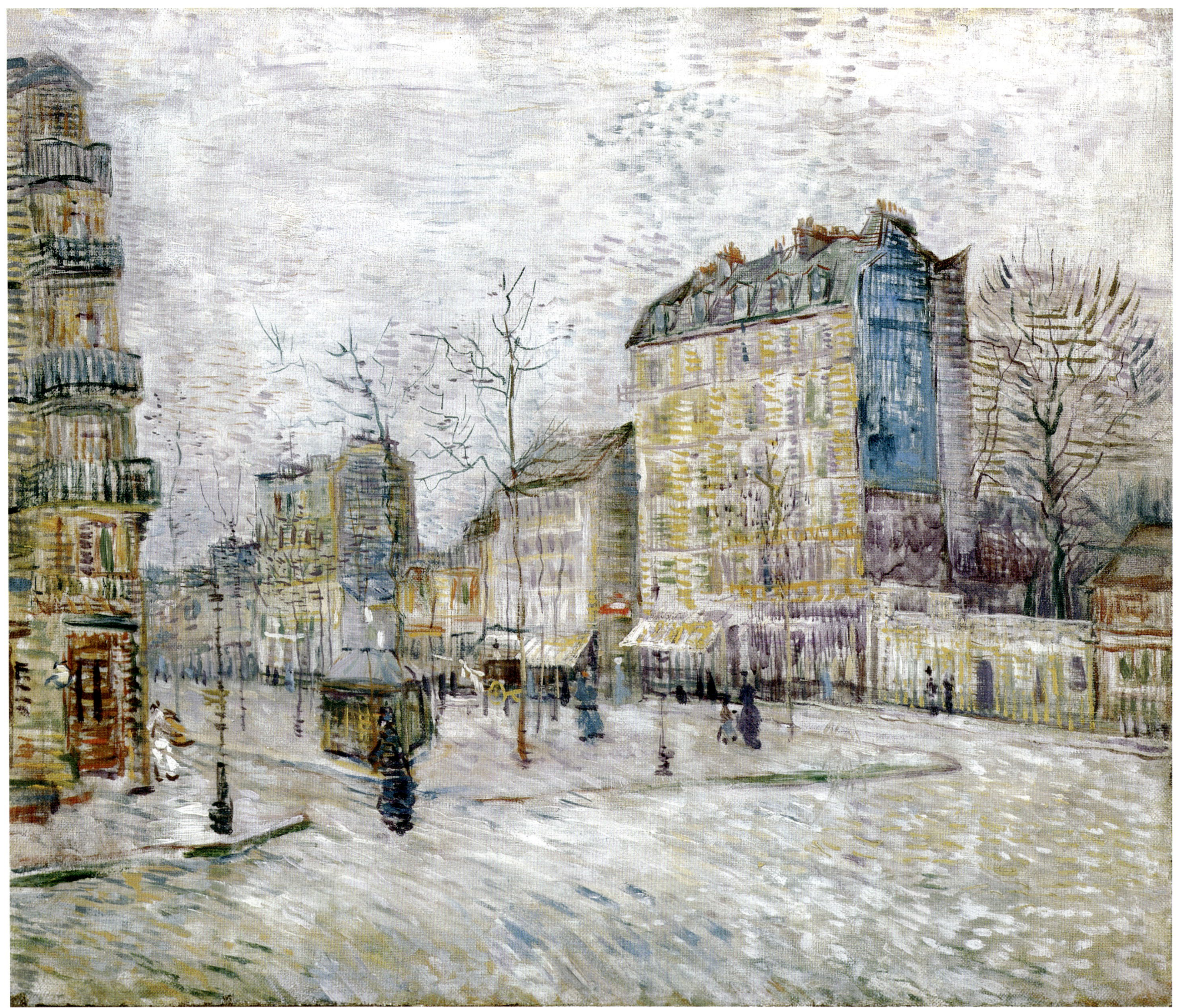

Boulevard de Clichy (1887). After a year of studying flowers, Vincent fulfilled his objective of adding brighter hues to his palette. With floral hues such as violet and rose, as well as jewel tones such as turquoise and burnished gold, Vincent painted the Boulevard de Clichy *with unprecedented lightness and freshness. His touch, expressive yet delicate, reveals that he had absorbed the Neo-Impressionist stroke and transformed it to his own advantage.*

Van Gogh Museum, Amsterdam. Oil on canvas (18×21¾ inches).

Fishing in the Spring, the Pont de Clichy (Asnières) *(1887). In the spring, Vincent made regular trips to the suburb of Asnières with fellow painters Paul Signac and Emile Bernard. He and his friends set up their easels in the park and along the riverbanks to catch the natural light. Vincent often built his composition up with color, as seen here.*

ART INSTITUTE OF CHICAGO. OIL ON CANVAS (19¼×22¾ INCHES).

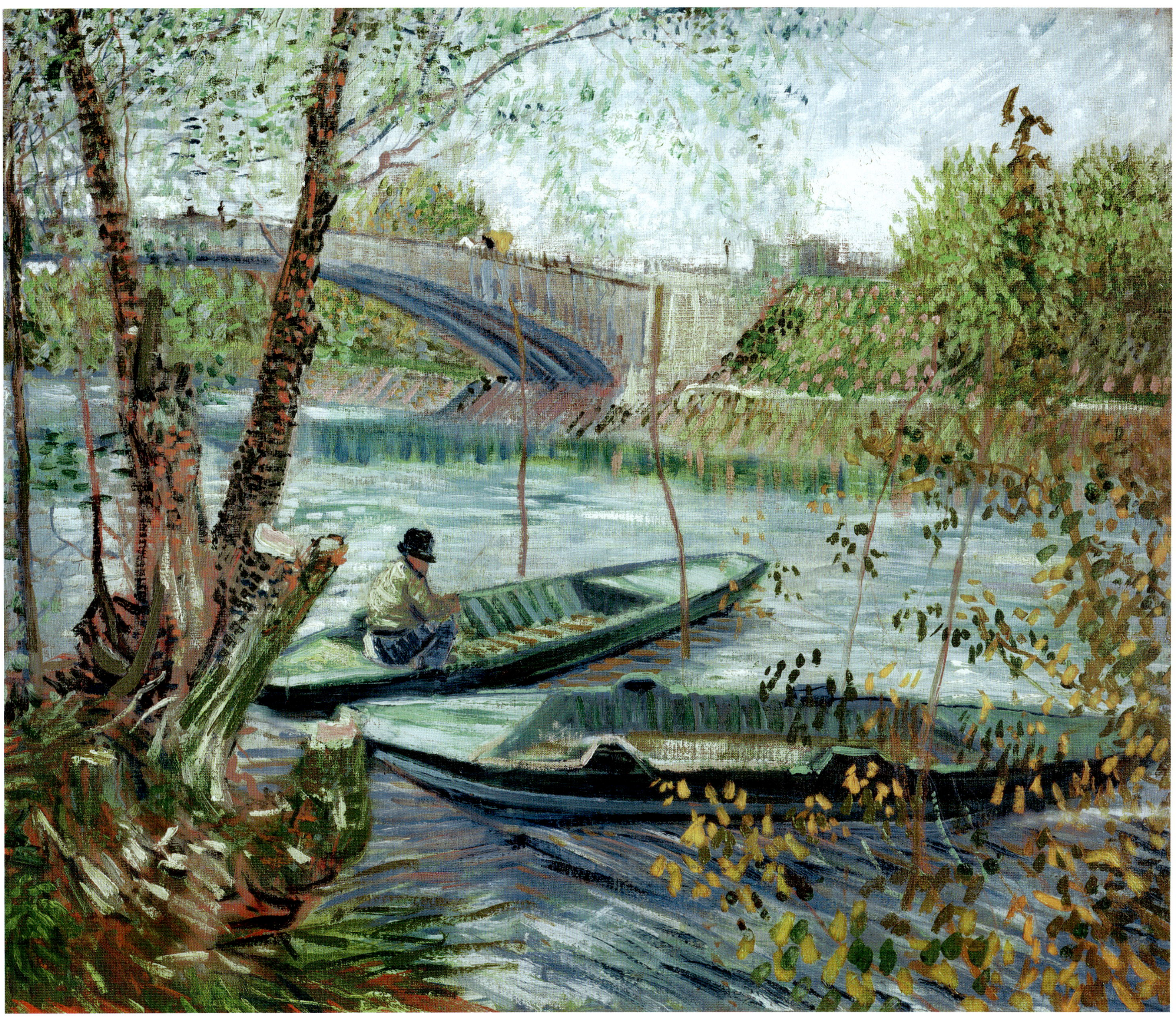

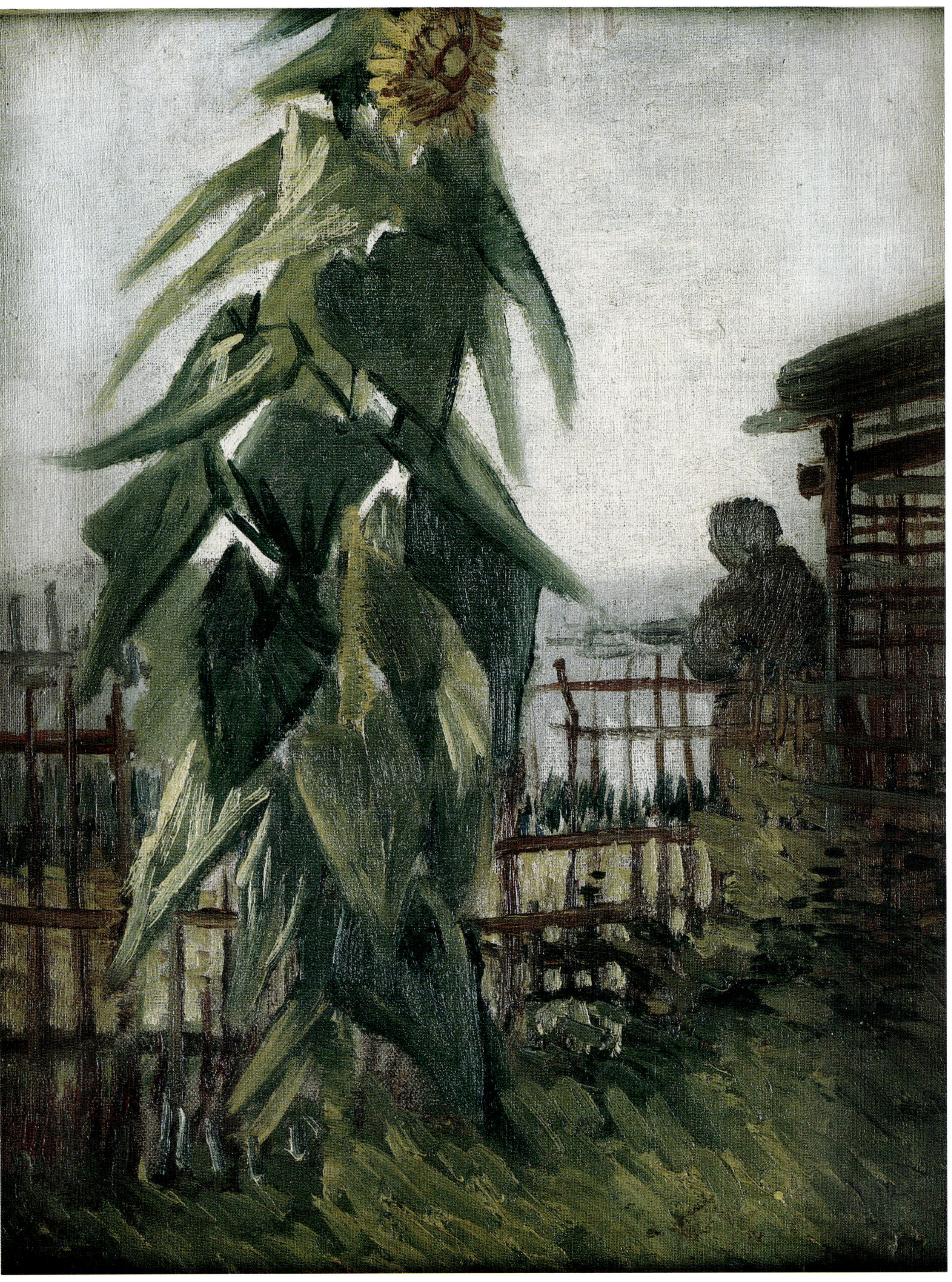

Garden with Sunflower *(1887). In the previous year, Vincent used a high point of view on Montmartre to paint a panoramic vista of the cultivated fields with their quaint windmills on the surrounding rolling hills to the north or the cityscape to the south. In the summer of 1887, he made several studies of cottage gardens with giant golden sunflowers nodding atop their sturdy stalks and towering above the cottage fences.*

Van Gogh Museum, Amsterdam. Oil on canvas (16¾×14 inches).

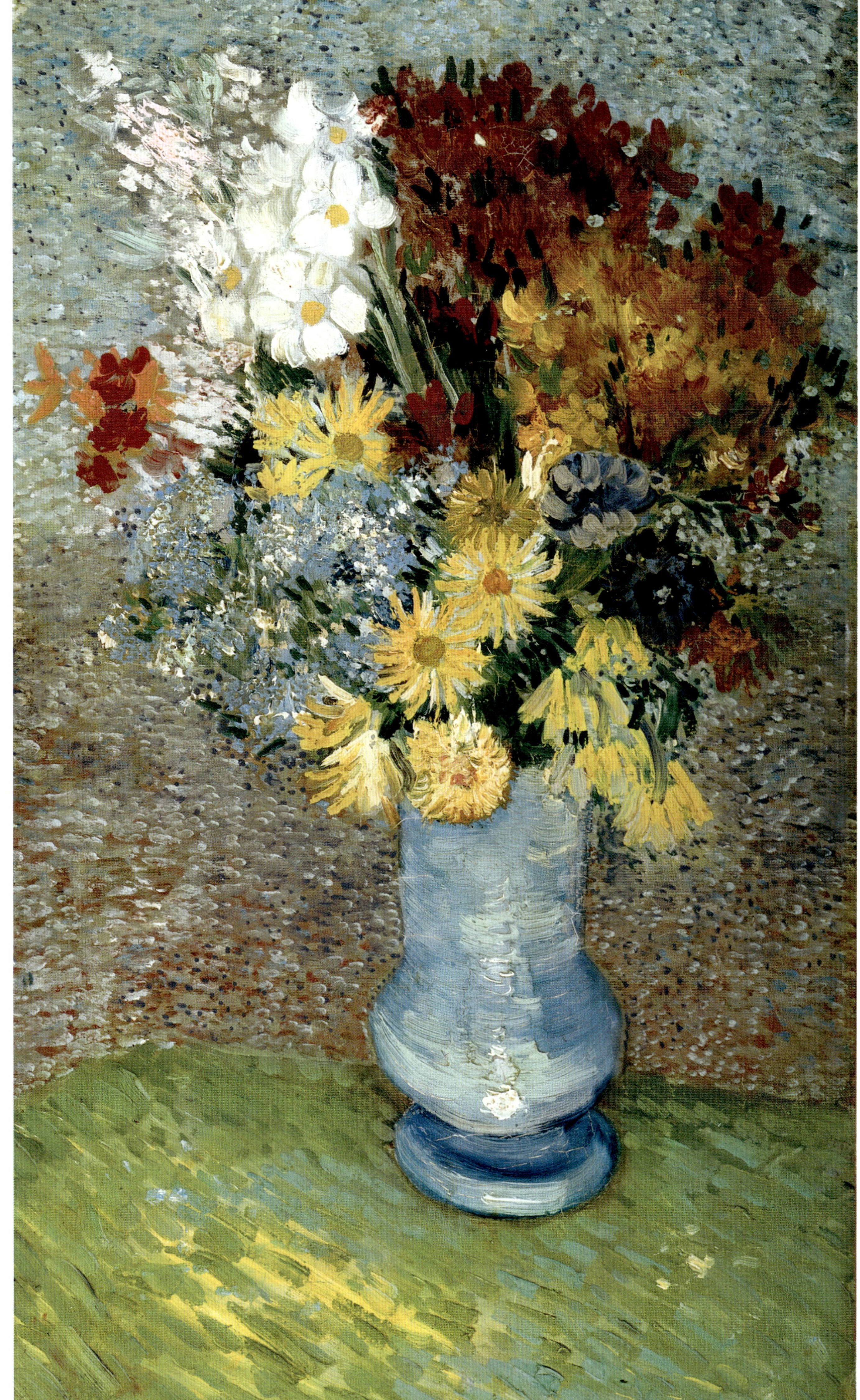

Flowers in a Blue Vase *(1887). Fresh and luminous, Vincent's study of a mixed bouquet reveals the successful results of his experiments in color. Bold, yet natural, his palette displays a full tonal range from deep brown and violet shadows to pearly whites and opalescent pinks. In his letters to his sister Wil, he listed the colors he had added to his palette: "pink, soft or bright green, light blue, violet, yellow, glorious red."*

KRÖLLER-MÜLLER MUSEUM, OTTERLO, NETHERLANDS. OIL ON CANVAS (24×15 INCHES).

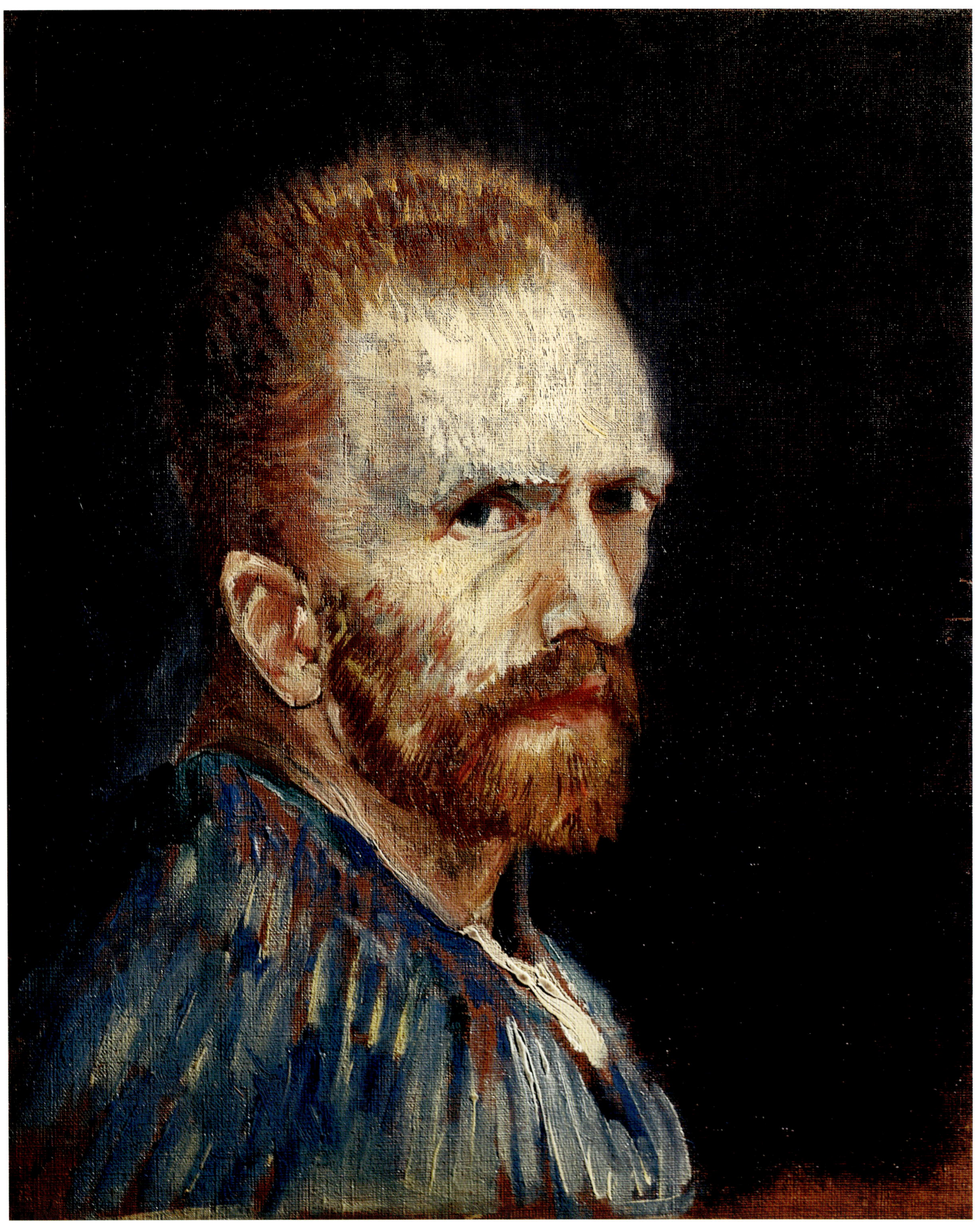

Self-Portrait (1887). Over the summer of 1887, Vincent painted a series of self-portraits. Although many of these employ a warm, yellow-based palette, here Vincent modulated his tonalities from the ginger red of his beard and hair, the muddied greens of his jacket, to the stark pale of his complexion. Set against a deeply shadowed background, this portrait recalls the influence of Rembrandt, who also painted his own portrait repeatedly and with great variation.

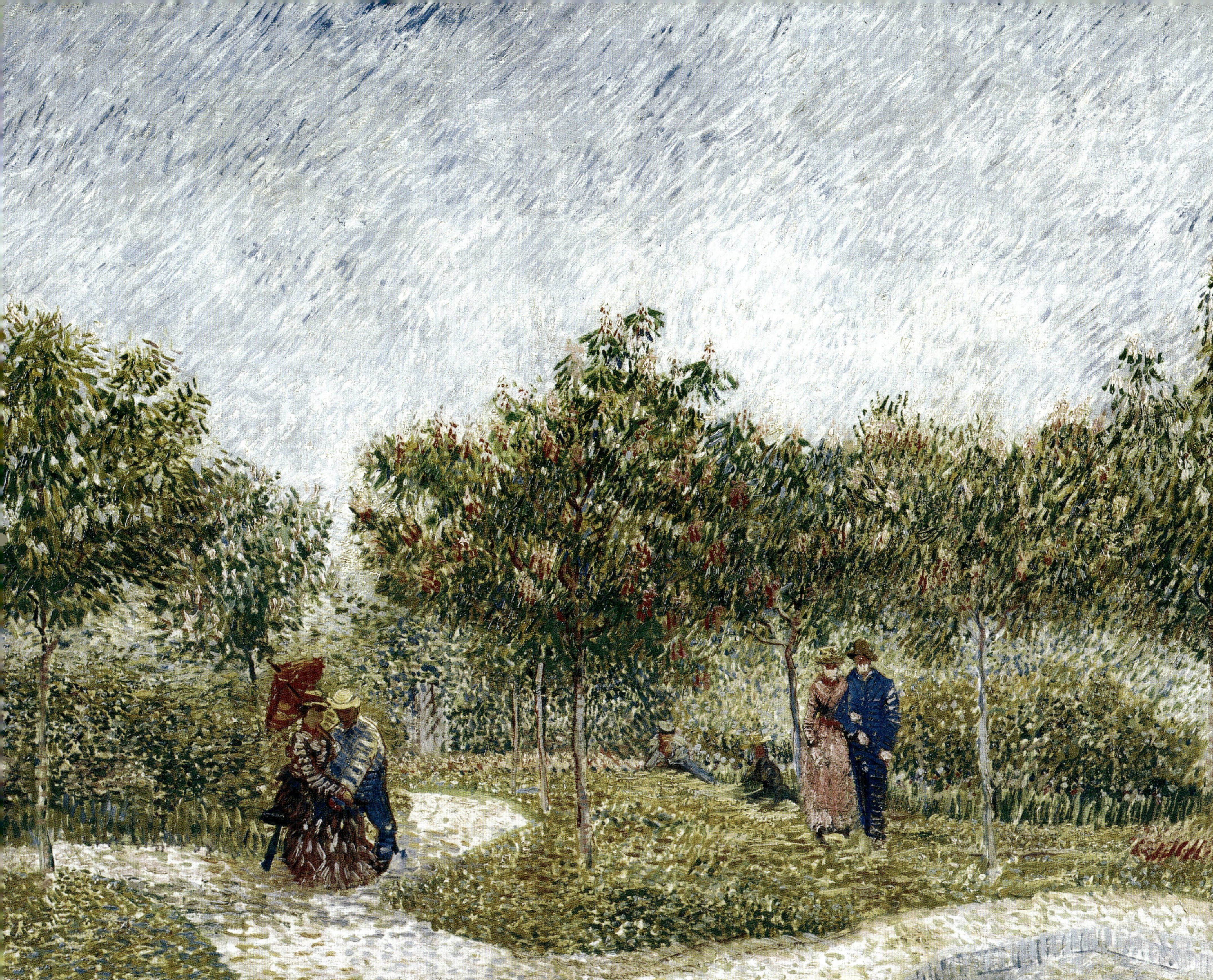

Courting Couples in the Voyer d'Argenson Park at Asnières *(1887). Vincent painted strolling couples in the park with a bright palette and an exuberant touch. The foliage of the trees reflect his study of complementary tones; the sky is feathered with tiny strokes of the palest shades of blue, violet, and green. In a letter to his sister Wil, he compared the fundamental harmony of chromatic pairs that together "shine brilliantly" to a human couple declaring, the colors "complete each other like a man and woman."*

COLOR SEEKING LIFE

Two Cut Sunflowers *(1887). In the summer of 1887, Vincent painted several studies of cut sunflowers. To contrast with the wide range of the color yellow—from pale citron to deep ocher—he set the flower heads against a complementary background of bright blue. The thick impasto he used to describe the radiant petals and twisted stem evoke the robust vigor of the flower in full growth.*

METROPOLITAN MUSEUM OF ART, NEW YORK. OIL ON CANVAS (17×24 INCHES).

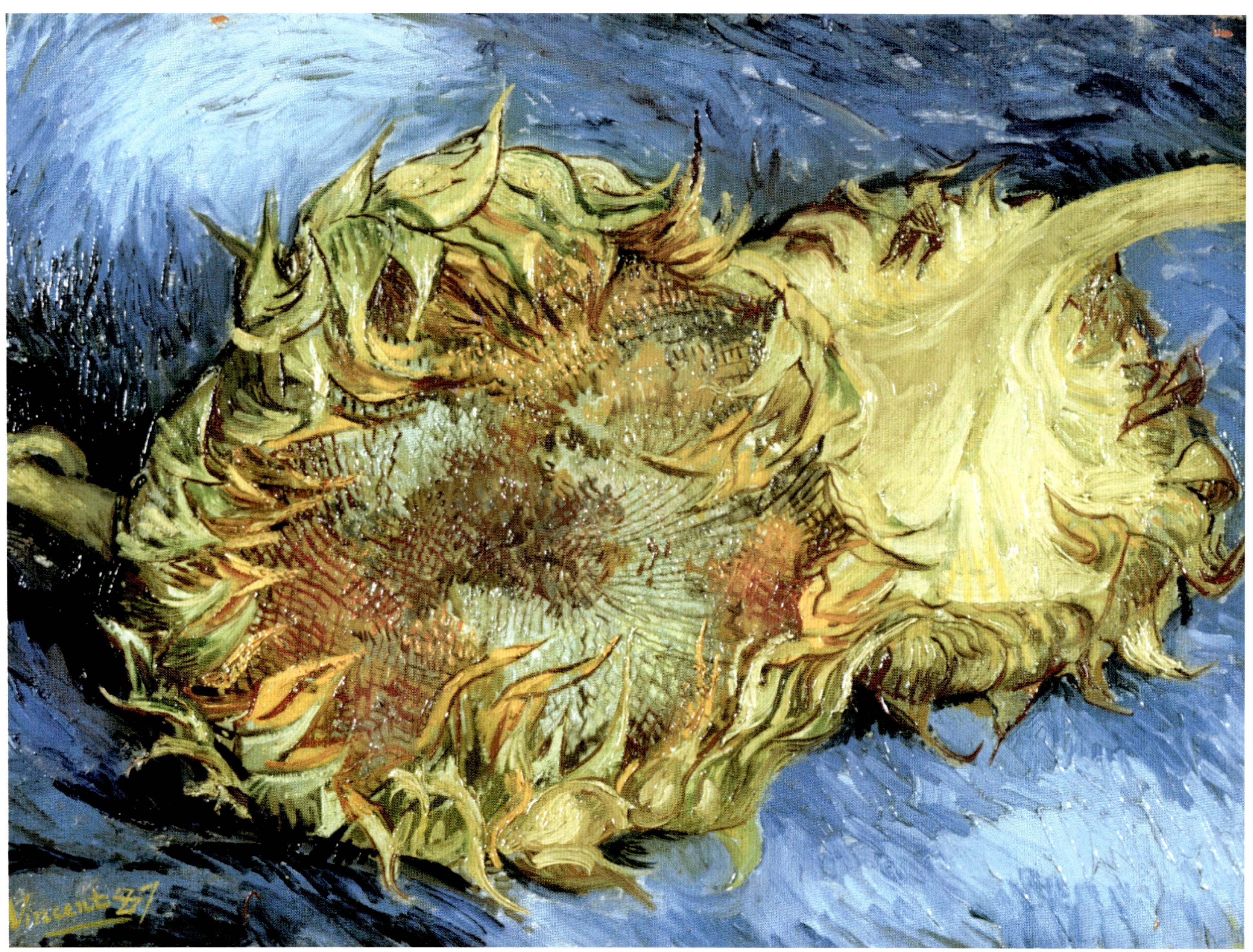

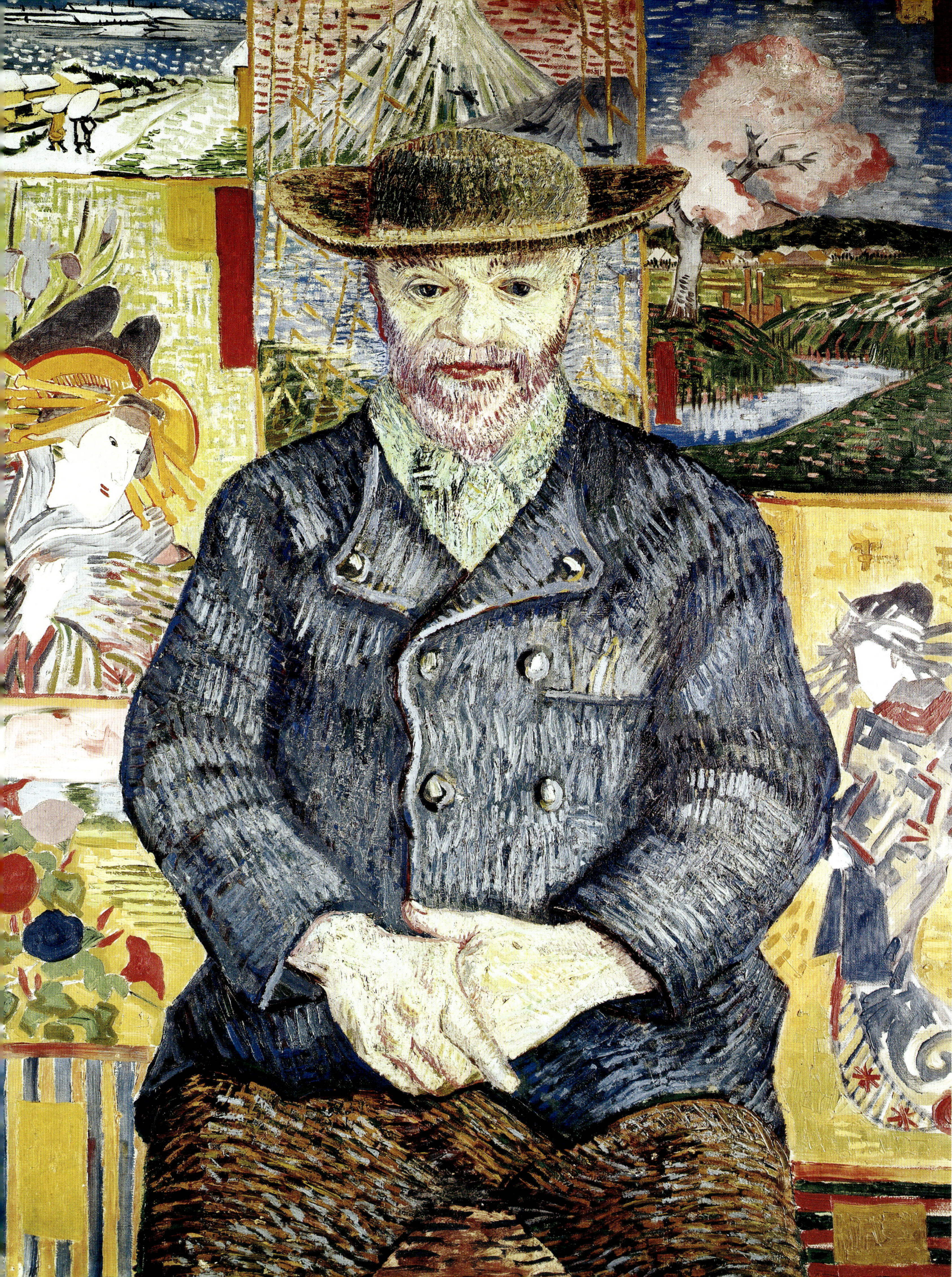

Le Père Tanguy *(1887).
Julien Tanguy, known as
"Père" or "Papa," sold
artists' materials, and
Vincent frequented the
shop to purchase paint
and to visit the informal
gallery housed in the back
rooms. Tanguy displayed
the work of innovators
such as Georges Seurat
and Paul Cézanne. He
also sold Japanese prints.
Vincent began collecting
works of the* ukiyo-e
*masters in Antwerp, and
in honor of their shared
interest, he painted
Tanguy's portrait in front
of a selection of famous
prints.*

Nature Under a Brighter Sky

"My dear brother, you know that I came to the South and threw myself into my work for a thousand reasons. Wishing to see a different light, thinking that looking at nature under a brighter sky might give us a better idea of the Japanese way of feeling and drawing."

VINCENT TO THEO, SEPTEMBER 10, 1889, FROM SAINT-RÉMY

THE EARLY ONSET of a harsh, gray winter in 1887 made Vincent yearn for sunshine and a warmer climate. The years in Paris had been invigorating, but Vincent was now feeling physically drained and emotionally overstimulated. He had gained little recognition for his work and was estranged from professional art circles, which he came to regard as fiercely competitive and unsupportive. Vincent longed for a community of like-minded painters who would live and work together in harmony with nature and one another, as he imagined artists lived in Japan. To pursue these ideals, Vincent decided to move to Arles where he hoped to live like a simple crafter, working in the countryside under the southern sun. Never having traveled to Arles, Vincent pictured it as a French counterpart to the charming and tranquil world depicted in Japanese prints, where people led peaceful and purposeful lives. He reflected back on his decision in a letter to Theo written in September 1889: "My dear brother, you know that I came to the South and threw myself into my work for a thousand reasons." But above all he wished "to see a different light" and look "at nature under a brighter sky."

Vincent arrived in Arles during the middle of a heavy snowstorm late in February 1888. Although spring seemed distant, he noticed an appealing and subtle difference in the color of the landscape from that of the north. There were yellow rocks and red soil, as well as mountains beyond the village that appeared lilac in the chilly air. He compared the vista "with the sum-

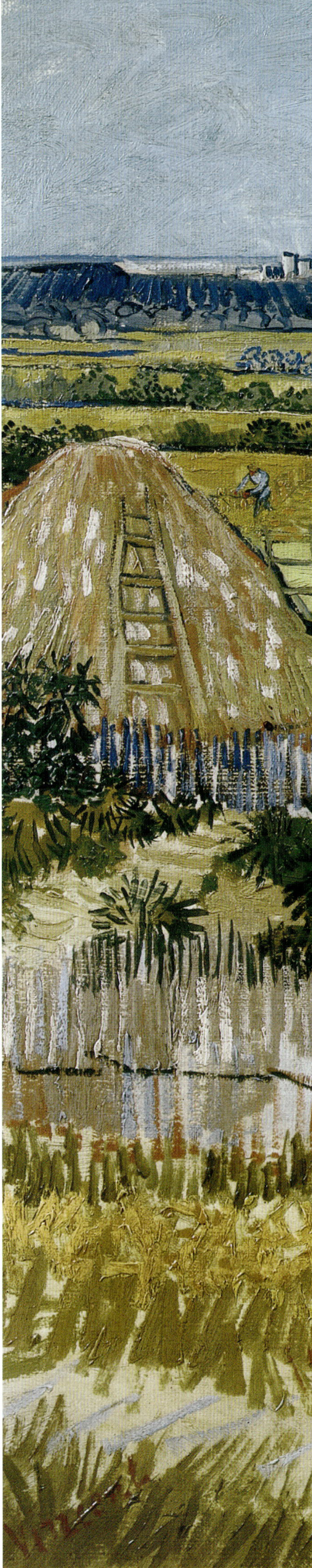

The Harvest *(1888). Vincent returned to his earlier panoramic approach to depict the first harvest of the year. His deliberate approach to spatial organization— the crops in the foreground, the fields above, and the mountains on the high horizon—reveals his desire to attain some of the epic grandeur Paul Cézanne achieved with similar subjects. He worked with intense focus, writing to Emile Bernard that he had seven studies in progress and felt like one of the harvesters working under the blazing sun.*

VAN GOGH MUSEUM, AMSTERDAM. OIL ON CANVAS (28¾×36¼ INCHES).

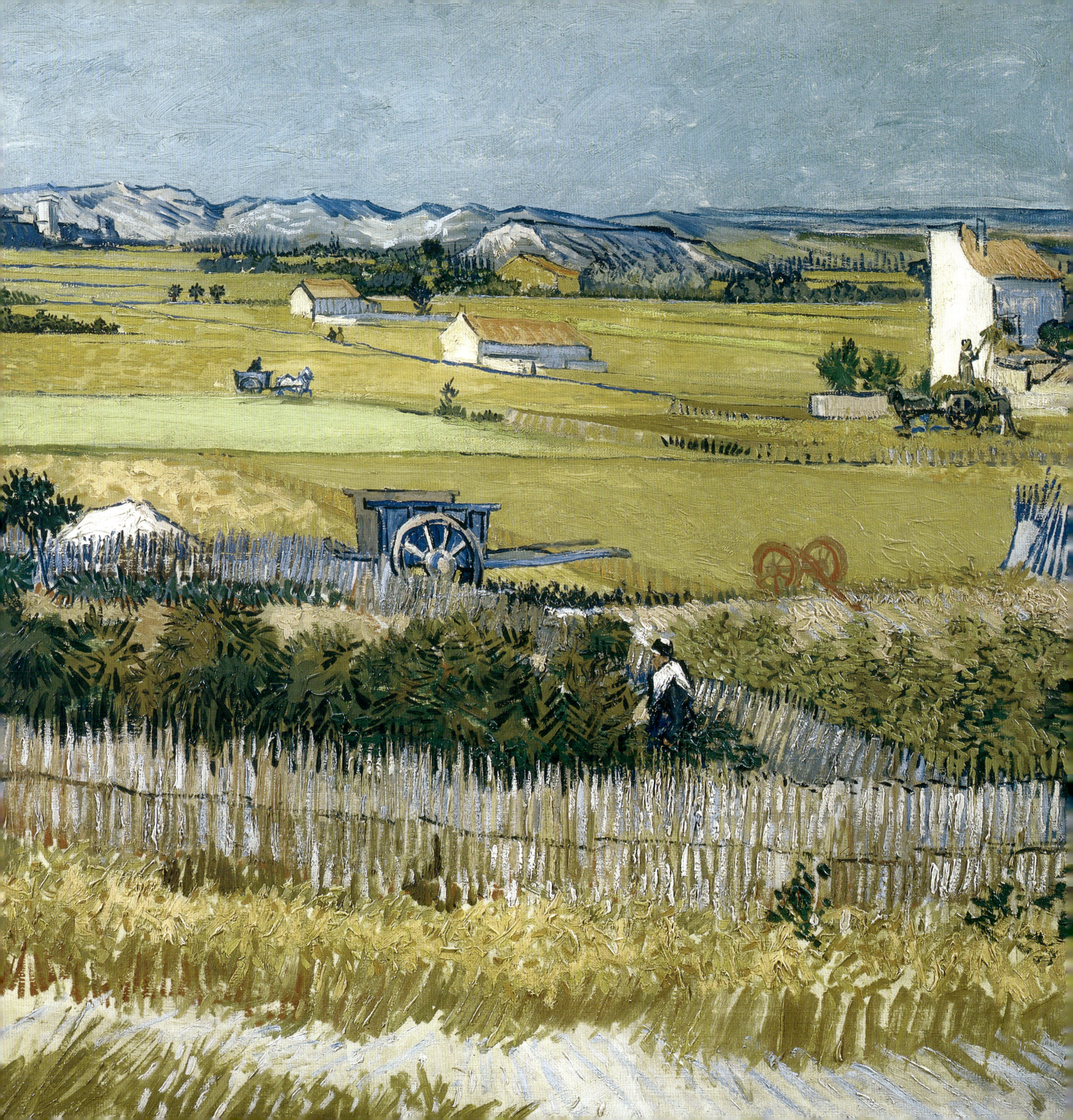

BRIGHTER SKY

mits white against a sky as luminous as the snow" to the winter landscapes he had seen in Japanese prints. He immediately tried to paint outdoors but found it too arduous in the cold and wind. But as Vincent explored the countryside, he saw that there already were tiny green buds on the otherwise bare branches of the almond trees. He snapped off a twig and placed it in a glass of water in his room. It soon bloomed, and Vincent painted two small oil studies of the sprig of flowering almond, using tints of pink and yellow to shade the white petals on their rose-brown stems, against a background of pale violet and blue that evoked the mountains in the mist.

Vincent soon wrote to Theo of his new project: "I'm up to my ears in work, for the trees are in

blossom and I want to paint a Provençal orchard of astonishing gaiety." After years of painting bouquets in Paris, Vincent was now inspired by the spectacle of the flowering fruit trees in the early spring. He set up his easel in the orchards, working swiftly to capture the ephemeral beauty before the burgeoning fruit replaced the flowers. To make the most of his time, Vincent worked on several canvases at once. He used pure pigment to get the freshest tones and applied it to his canvas with a light touch to echo the pale, translucent petals flickering on the branches. Vincent abandoned the self-conscious approach to painting he had practiced in Paris and followed his own instincts. In a letter to his friend Emile Bernard, he proclaimed, "My brush stroke has no system at all." He worked freely over the surface of his paintings, applying thick paint on some areas while allowing bare patches of raw canvas to remain exposed. Of all his flowering trees, Vincent took the greatest delight in painting a pink peach tree, which he dedicated to Anton Mauve, the first painter to encourage him to work in color.

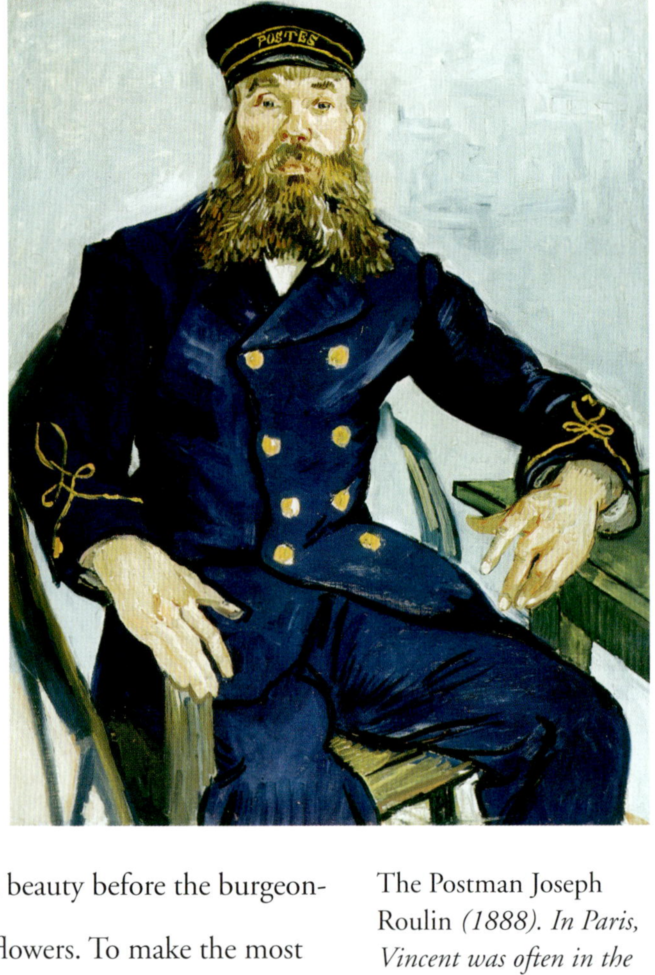

Sprig of Flowering Almond Blossom in a Glass (1888). Vincent hoped that Arles would provide a tranquil and quiet setting for his life and work. Once settled, he painted a sprig of an almond branch, which he forced into early flowering in a glass of water. The irregular pattern of the little branch, covered with pale, translucent blooms, gave him a subject that recalled the depiction of flowers in Japanese prints. The simple division of the silvery, violet background with a scarlet band pays tribute to the Japanese aesthetic.

Van Gogh Museum, Amsterdam. Oil on canvas (9½×7½ inches).

The Postman Joseph Roulin *(1888). In Paris, Vincent was often in the company of like-minded friends, whom he met in the cafés and galleries that were frequented by artists. In Arles he generally was alone, but he struck up a strong friendship with Joseph Roulin and his family. Vincent painted several portraits of the postal worker in his official uniform, conveying his admiration for the man in the solidity of his form and the quiet dignity of his expression.*

Museum of Fine Arts, Boston. Oil on canvas (32×25¾ inches).

Late in April, Vincent wrote to Theo to request more paint and canvas. He was working at a furious pace with the awareness that the flowers would not last. But he also recognized that he possessed a restless nature, and he reminded Theo: "You know I am changeable in my work; and this craze for painting orchards will not last forever." By the time the season ended in mid-May, Vincent had completed at least 20 canvases. He turned his attention to the green fields now ablaze with wildflowers. In a letter to Bernard, he characterized Arles as a painter's paradise. "The town," he wrote, "is surrounded by immense meadows all abloom with countless buttercups—a sea of yellow—in the foreground these meadows are divided by a ditch full of violet irises." Vincent was particularly drawn to the wild iris, and to capture the bolder tonality of the upcoming summer, he turned to more vivid hues in resonant combinations such as chrome yellow and ultramarine blue. The contrast of these primary colors created a vibrant effect that Vincent used for many of his subjects, ranging from a portrait of his friend the postman Joseph Roulin (1888) to a scene of nightlife in *Café Terrace on the Place du Forum, Arles, at Night* (1888) to a vision of an evening sky sparkling with stars in *Starry Night over the Rhone* (1888). He wrote to Theo that he now approached his color with little regard to theory or analysis: "I use color more arbitrarily, in order to express myself more forcibly."

In June, Vincent painted the first grain harvest of the season. *The Harvest* (1888) presents a panoramic vista of rural grandeur. He used the natural elements of the landscape to structure his composition. Horizontal bands of golden wheat stir in the foreground. They are anchored by the delineated plots of the plowed fields at mid-distance with the mountains defining the broad horizon against a vivid cerulean sky. He wrote to Bernard, "There is no blue without yellow," and in *The Harvest,* Vincent used his hard, bright colors in a vibrant combination to evoke the vitality of the fields beyond Arles under the summer sun.

Café Terrace on the Place du Forum, Arles, at Night *(1888). After a summer of painting in the sunny fields, Vincent began to explore the potential of plein air painting at night. The café offered a study in contrasts: the glow of the gas-lit square and the dark sky illuminated with stars. Vincent described the painting as "a night picture without any black in it" and admitted, "it amuses me enormously to paint the night right on the spot."*

KRÖLLER-MÜLLER MUSEUM, OTTERLO, NETHERLANDS. OIL ON CANVAS (32×25¾ INCHES).

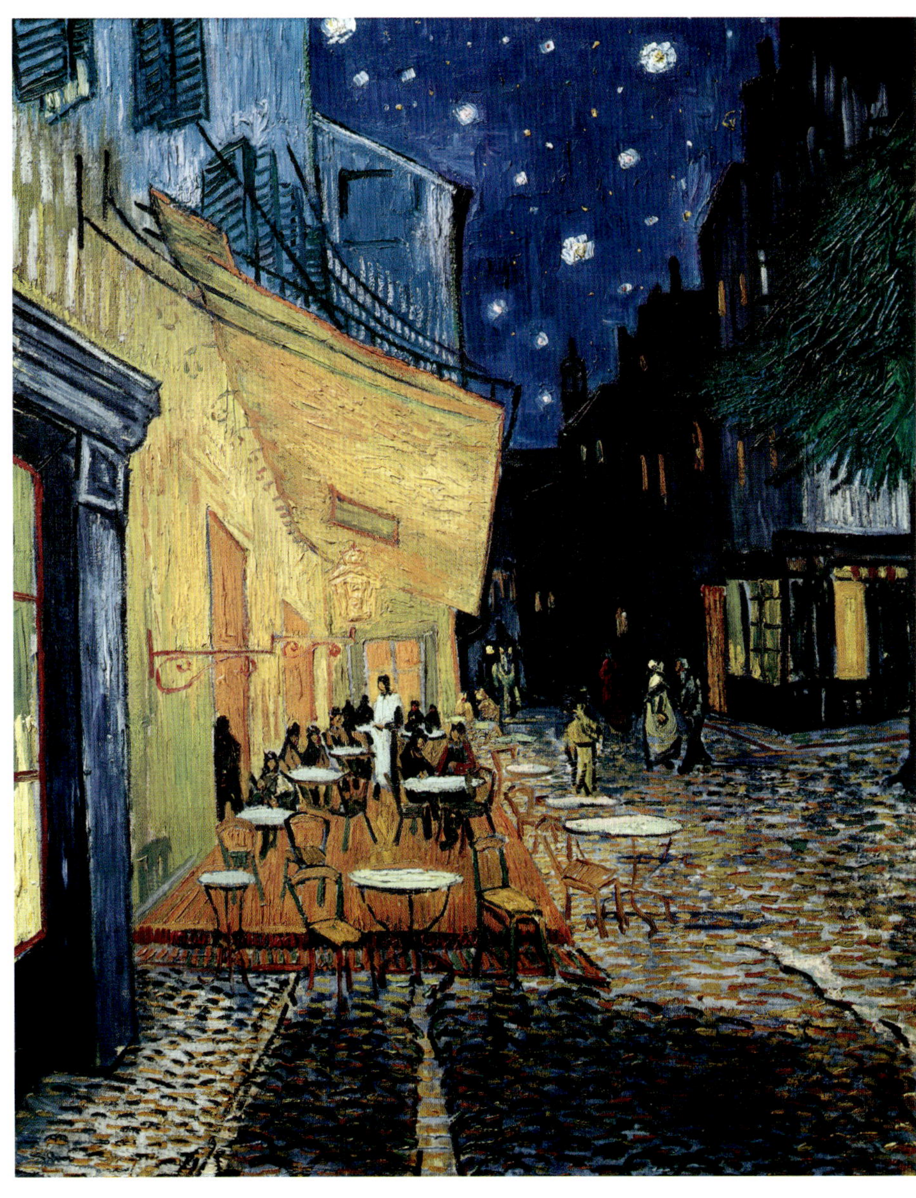

Brighter Sky

Landscape with Snow *(1888). The desire to work in a warmer climate motivated Vincent's move from Paris to Arles. Upon his arrival in February, he was surprised to find the region blanketed in snow. Despite the damp cold, he set up his easel outdoors to paint the exquisite landscape, notable for the pale lilac hue of the mountains.*

Solomon R. Guggenheim Museum, New York. Thannhouser Collection, Gift, Hilde Thannhouser, 1984.
Oil on canvas ($15\frac{1}{16} \times 18\frac{3}{16}$ inches).

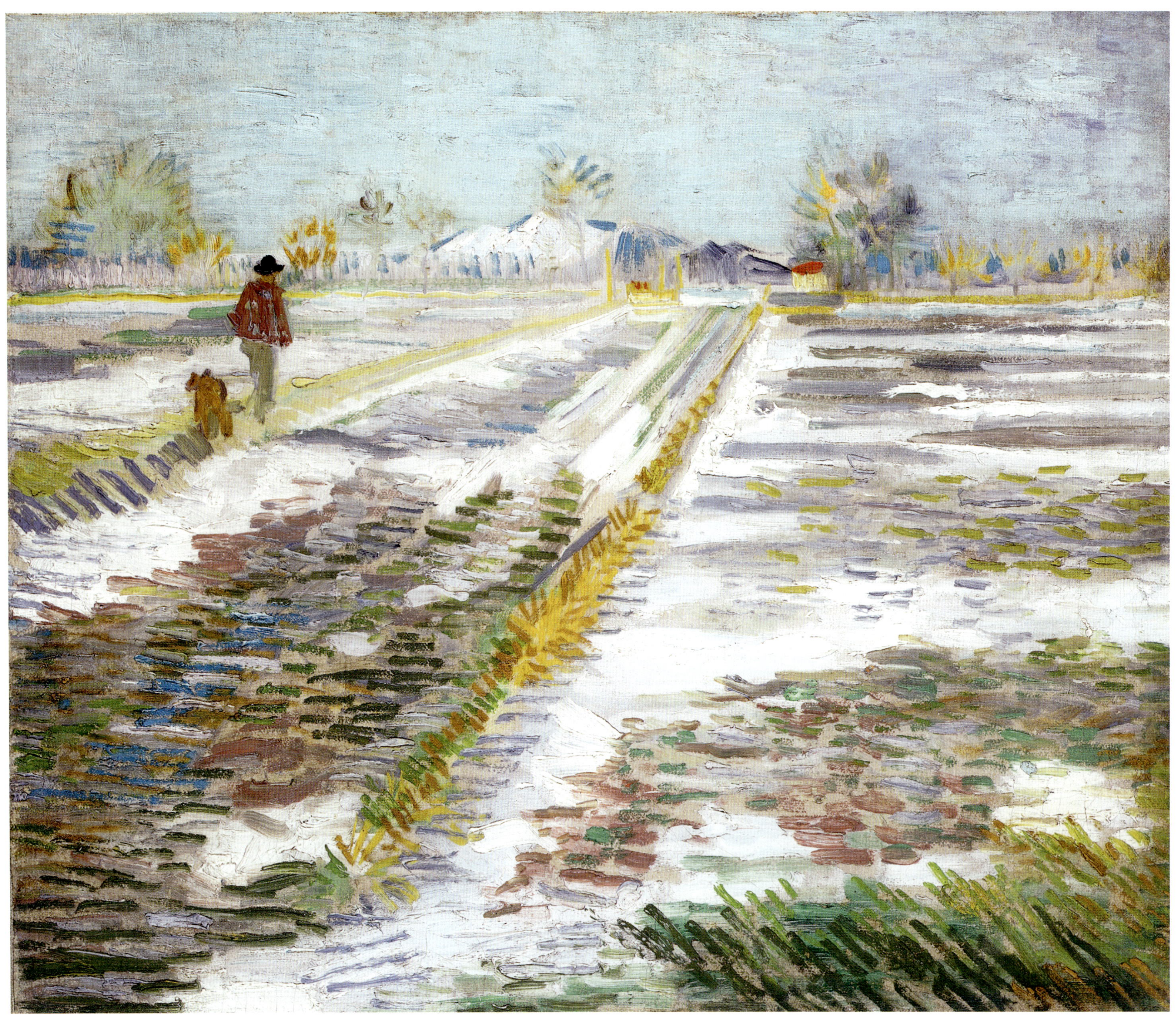

Peach Trees in Blossom
(Souvenir de Mauve)
*(1888). The weather
turned mild in March,
and Vincent went out to
paint every day. By the
end of the month all the
fruit trees—plum, apri-
cot, pear, apple, and
cherry—were either
budded or in full bloom.
He worked rapidly, with
flickering strokes to
capture the beautiful but
fleeting effect. While
painting pink peach trees
he received news of the
death of Anton Mauve.
The older painter had
urged Vincent to use color
freely, and Vincent
dedicated this painting to
his memory.*

Kröller-Müller Museum,
Otterlo, Netherlands. Oil on
canvas (28¾×23½ inches).

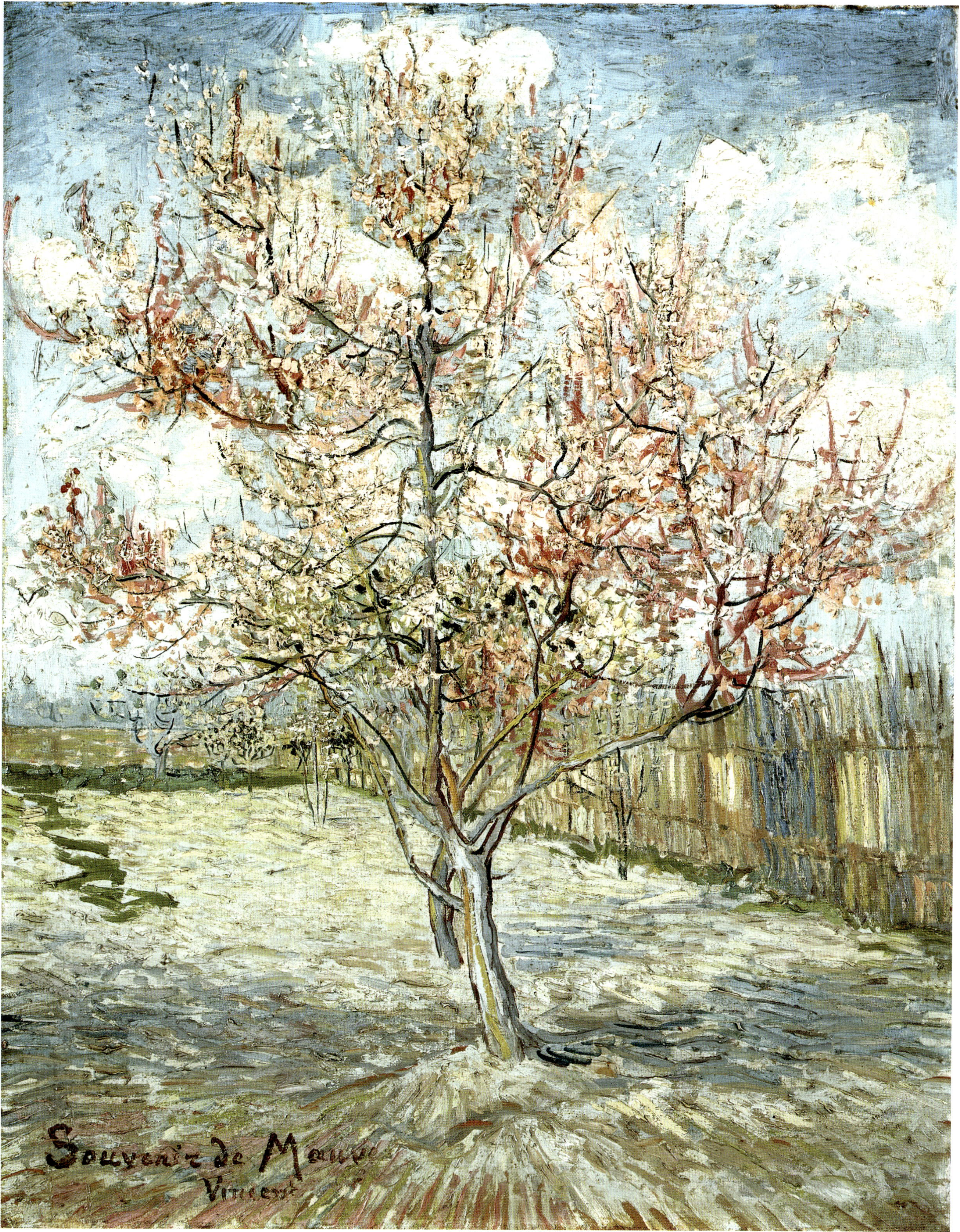

BRIGHTER SKY

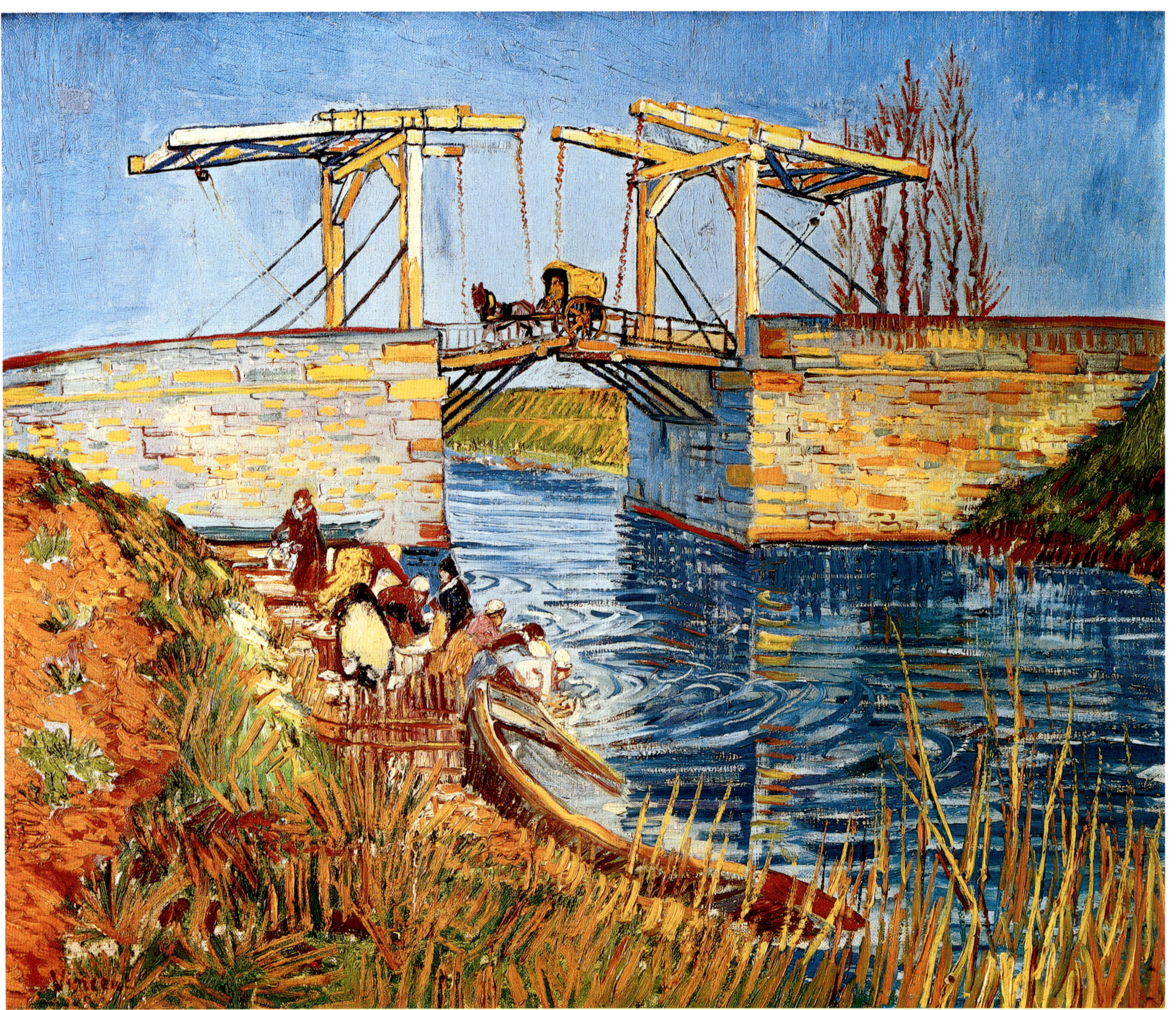

Langlois Bridge at Arles with Women Washing *(1888). Vincent thought of Arles as a French counterpart to the world he saw in the Japanese prints: clear air, blossoming trees, and the local people purposefully working in harmony with nature. He longed to see "nature under a brighter sky" to better understand what inspired the artists in Japan. He approached the subject of the Langlois Bridge mindful of the Japanese example, employing clear color and emphasizing the linear patterns of the bridge structure against the sky.*

KRÖLLER-MÜLLER MUSEUM, OTTERLO, NETHERLANDS. OIL ON CANVAS (21¼×25½ INCHES).

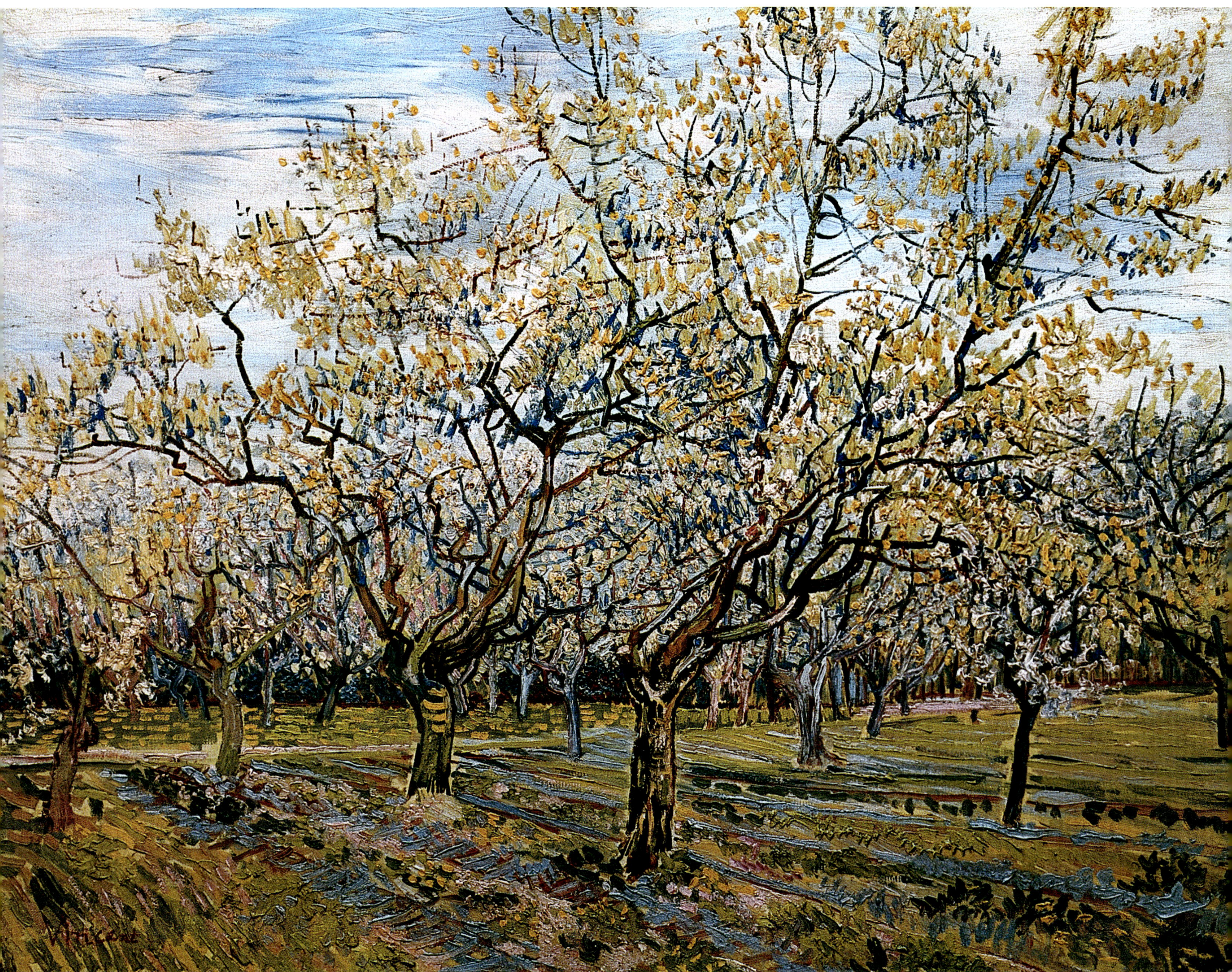

The White Orchard *(1888). Well aware that time was short to paint the trees in flower, Vincent worked with a sense of urgency. He wanted to capture the natural spectacle of the petals sparkling in the clear spring sun. The tones Vincent chose were luminous and light, shades of pink, aqua, and green that marked a change from the rich, jewel-toned palette he developed in Paris. His immersion in plein air painting restored his sense of vitality, as well as his sense of purpose.*

Van Gogh Museum, Amsterdam. Oil on canvas (23½×32 inches).

BRIGHTER SKY

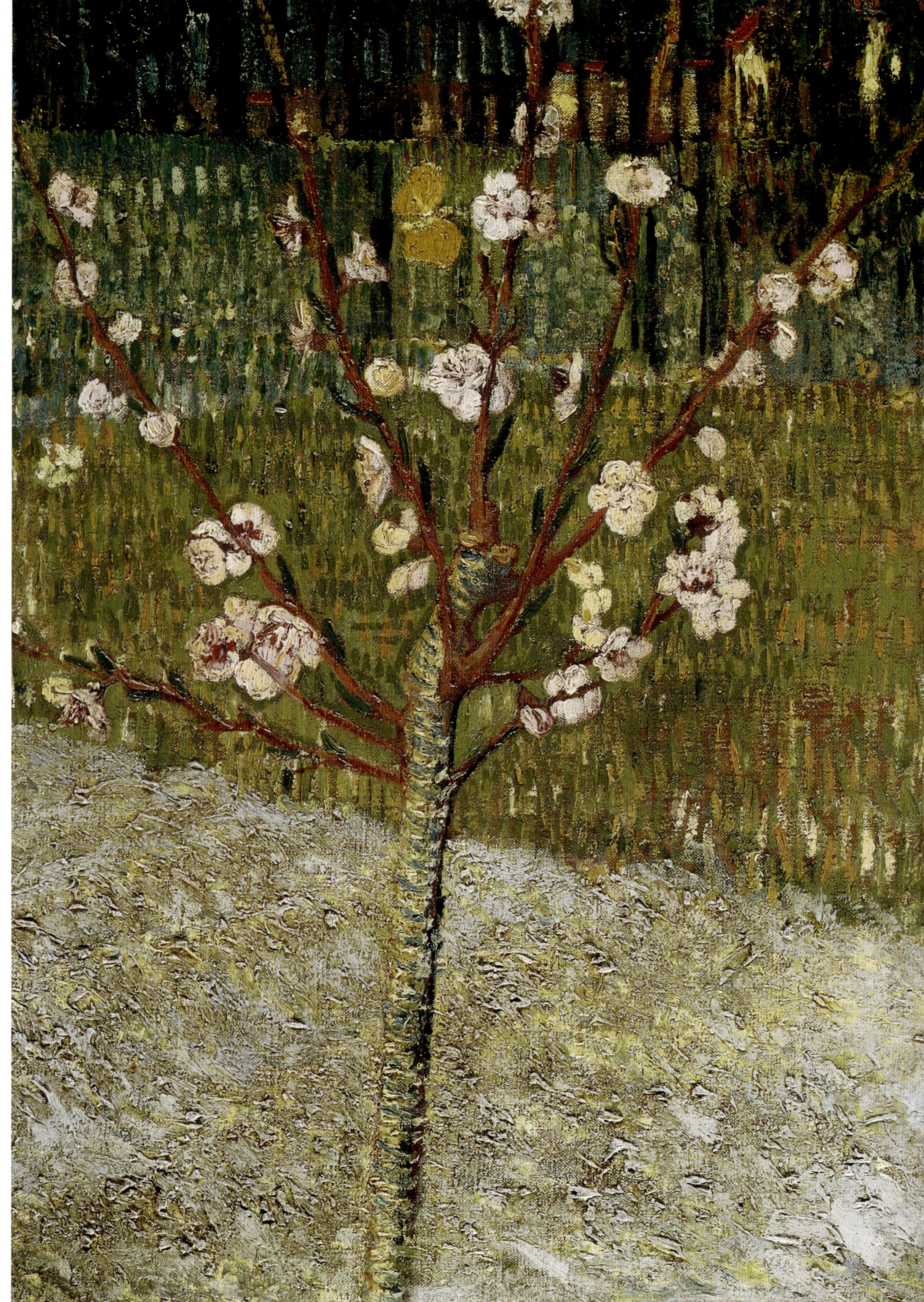

Almond Tree in Blossom *(1888).*
Painting in the orchards freed
Vincent's approach from the analyti-
cal path he had established as a
mode of self-education in Paris. He
now worked with unprecedented
spontaneity, dabbing color, building
impasto, and painting with broken
and calligraphic strokes uninhibited
by his previous concern for prevail-
ing theory or technique. He readily
adapted every effect to serve the
purpose of painting the spectacle of
nature coming into full flower.

Van Gogh Museum, Amsterdam. Oil on canvas (19×14 inches).

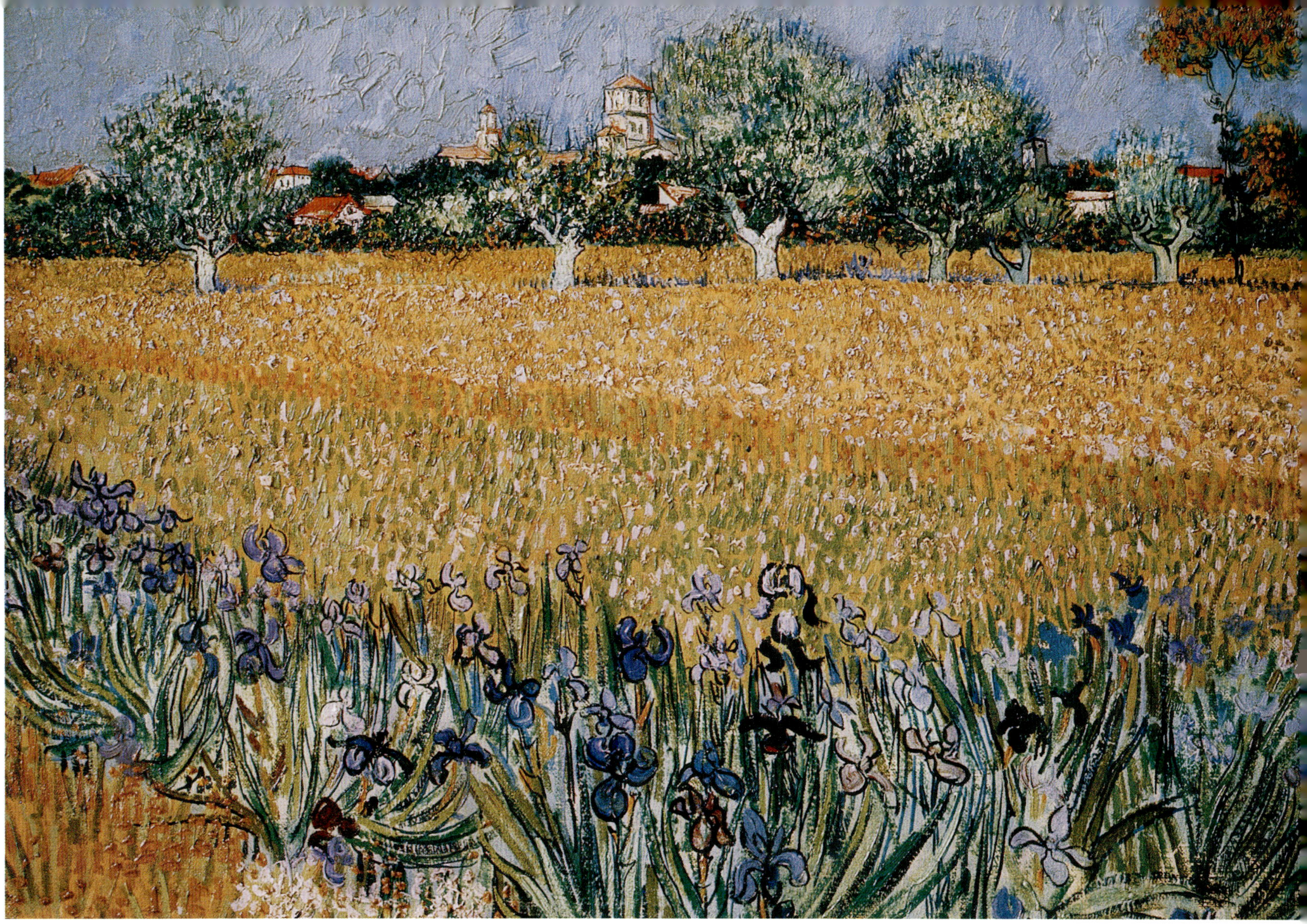

Field of Flowers near Arles *(1888). Summer arrived early in Arles, and the wild irises bloomed in the meadows. Vincent described the delightful scene in a letter to his brother: "A little town surrounded by fields all covered with yellow and purple flowers… just like a Japanese dream." The seasonal change prompted Vincent to brighten his pale palette, reintroducing the strong clear blues and golden yellows that had fascinated him the previous summer.*

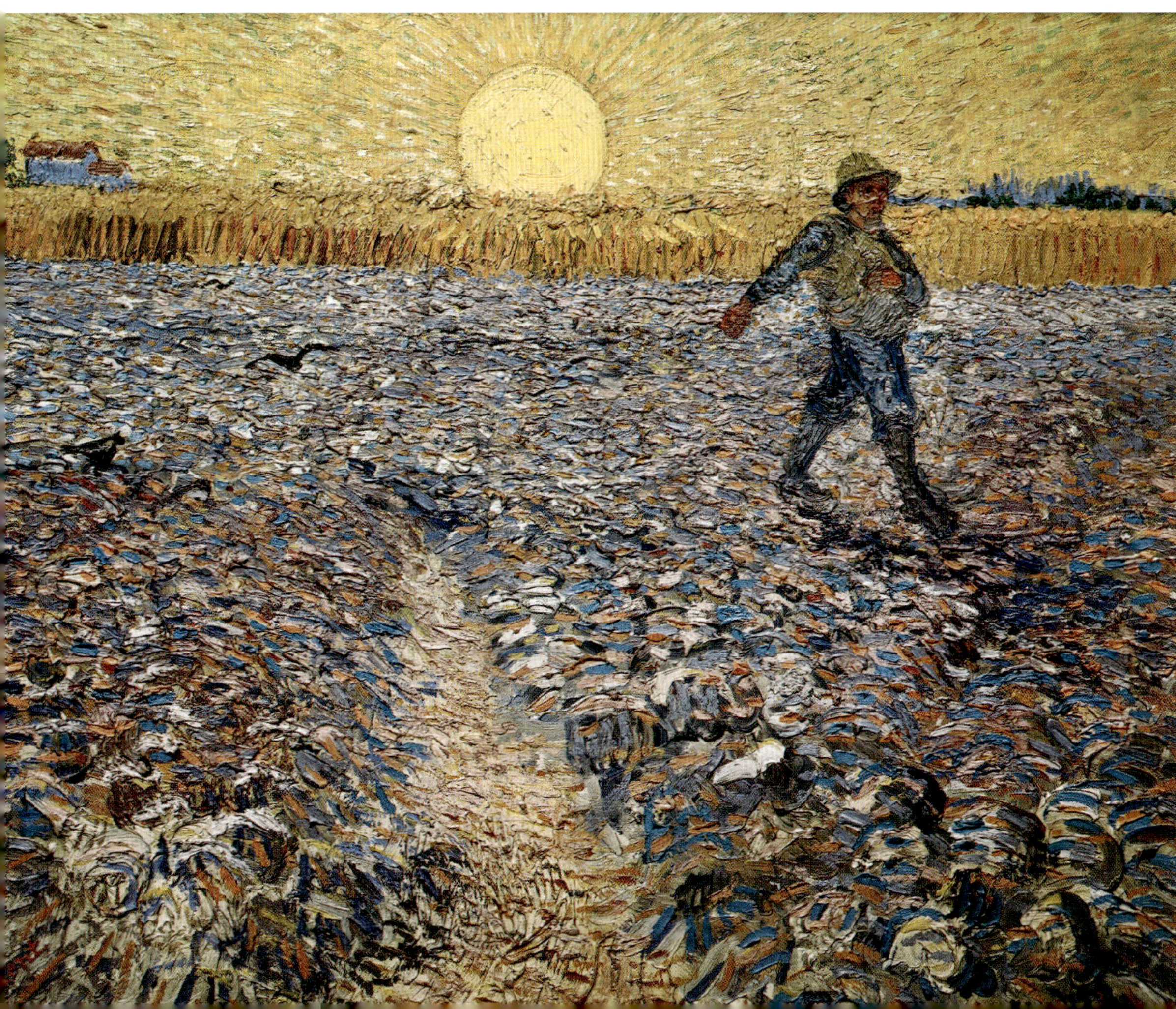

The Sower *(1888). The field in which the sower casts the new seeds vibrates with dabs of blue and yellow. With flickers of black, Vincent depicted birds descending to feast on the seeds, and he used vertical impasto strokes to paint the stalks of grain. A burning sun hovers in the yellow sky, and its thickly painted rays streak through the background. The modest, calm figure of the sower is subsumed into the chromatic vitality of the world that surrounds him.*

Kröller-Müller Museum, Otterlo, Netherlands. Oil on canvas (25¼×31¾ inches).

BRIGHTER SKY

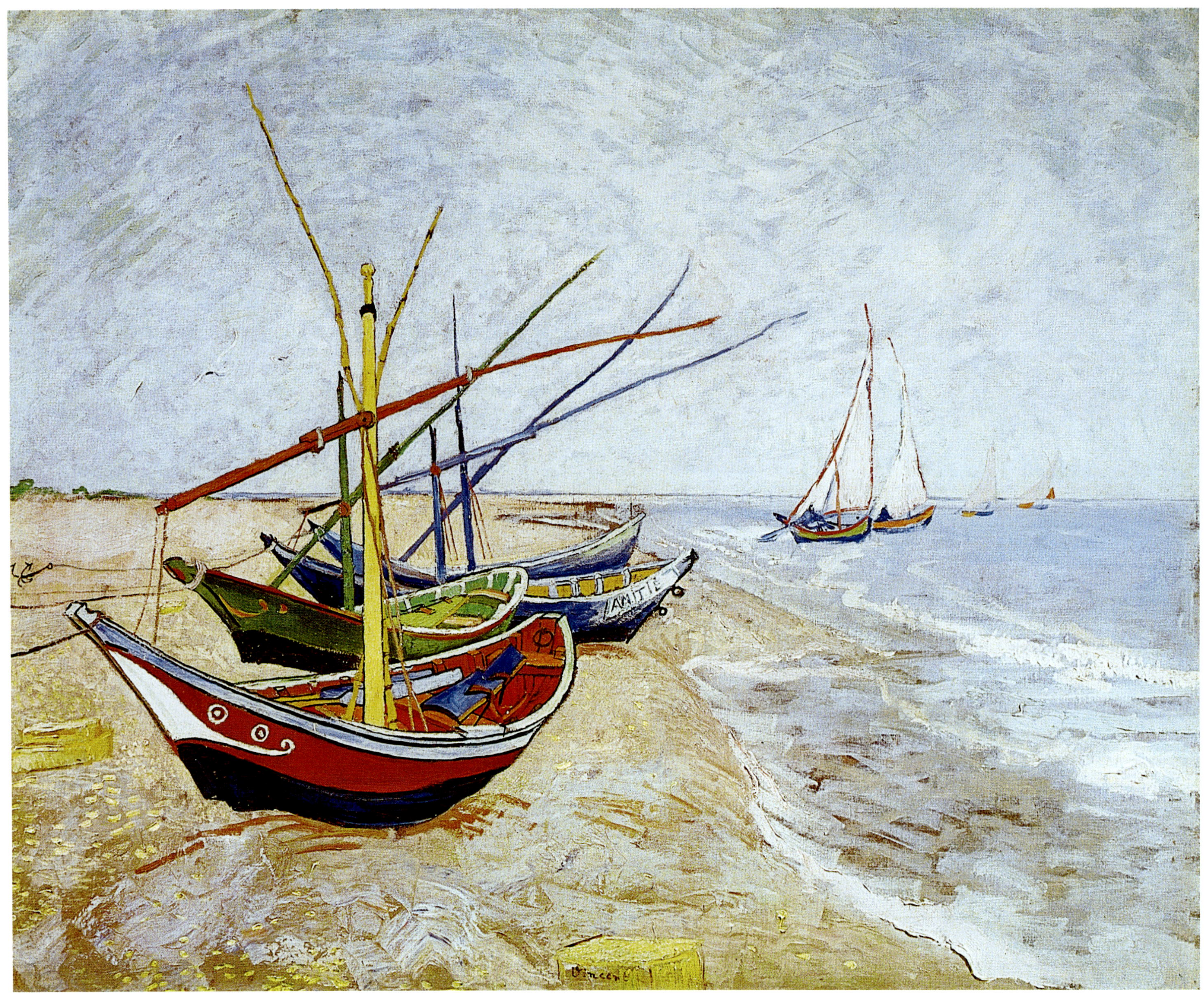

Fishing Boats on the Beach at Saintes-Maries-de-la-Mer *(1888). Vincent traveled to Saintes-Maries-de-la-Mer, a fishing village on the Mediterranean coast. He sketched on the shore, planning to work his ideas into paintings when he returned to his studio. There is a high level of control in his composition, with its nearly even division of land and sky and the boats positioned to break through the division and unite the separate zones. Even the color is controlled, and individual objects are bound within black contour lines.*

VAN GOGH MUSEUM, AMSTERDAM. OIL ON CANVAS (25½×32 INCHES).

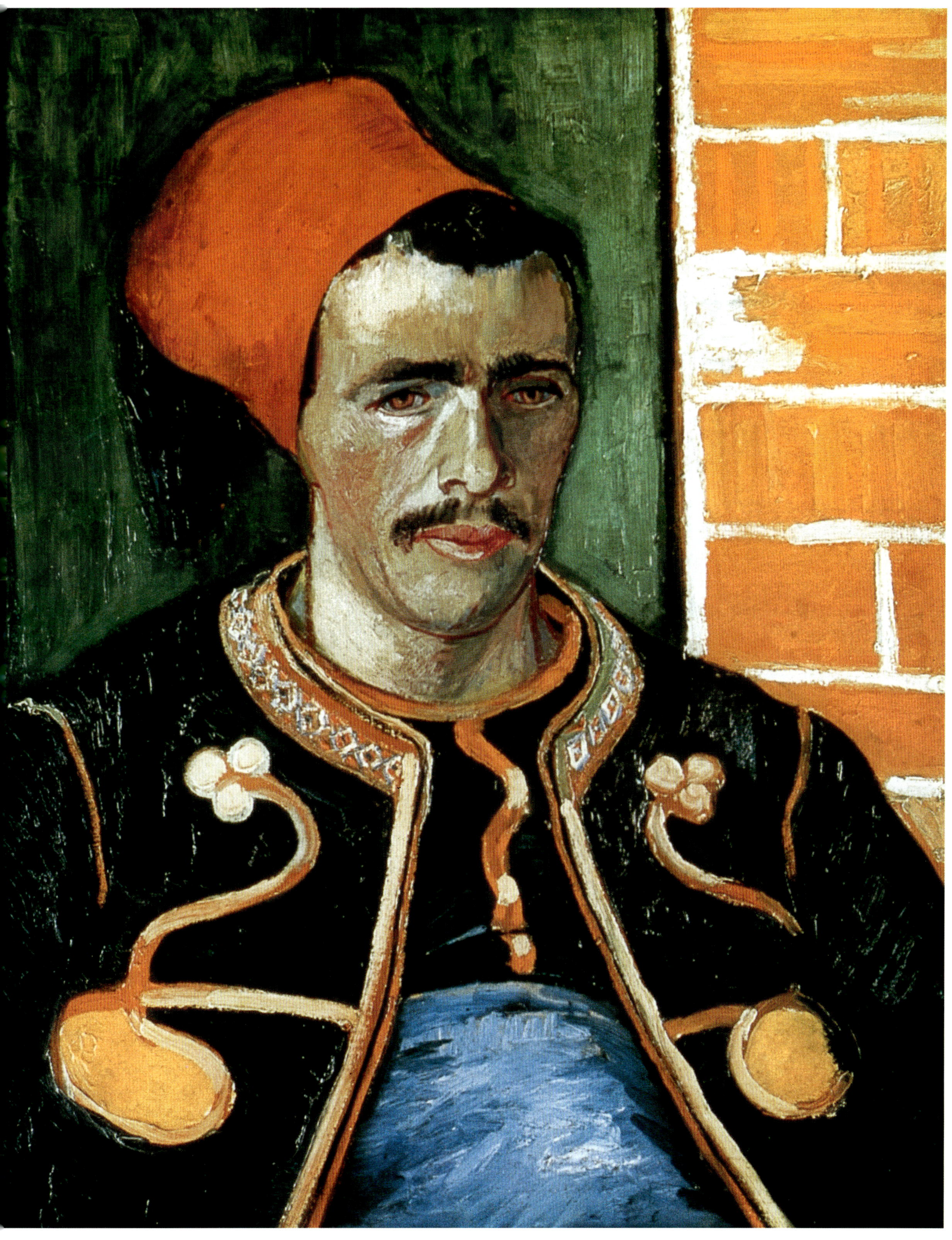

The Zouave *(1888). Vincent's portrait of a soldier in his uniform signals a change in his approach to color. The paint is applied thickly, in broad areas, in heavily saturated tones of green, red, and blue that appear more sober than bright. A division of French-Algerian soldiers billeted in Arles, the Zouaves were notorious for their recklessness on and off the battlefield. Vincent asserted that the subject inspired the palette, which he described as "a savage combination of incongruous tones."*

VAN GOGH MUSEUM, AMSTERDAM. OIL ON CANVAS (25½×21½ INCHES).

Brighter Sky

Corn Fields and Poppies *(1888). By June, Vincent had attained the full assimilation of his sources. As seen in this lyrical composition of wheat waving above a flowering field, he had mastered the Impressionist approach of painting quickly to achieve the sensation of immediacy. His variable touch, from dabs to descriptive strokes, transcended the Neo-Impressionist example in its expressive power. His bold compositions and vivid palette were the rewards of his study of Japanese art.*

The Israel Museum, Jerusalem. Gift of Yad Hanadiv. Oil on canvas (21¼×25½ inches).

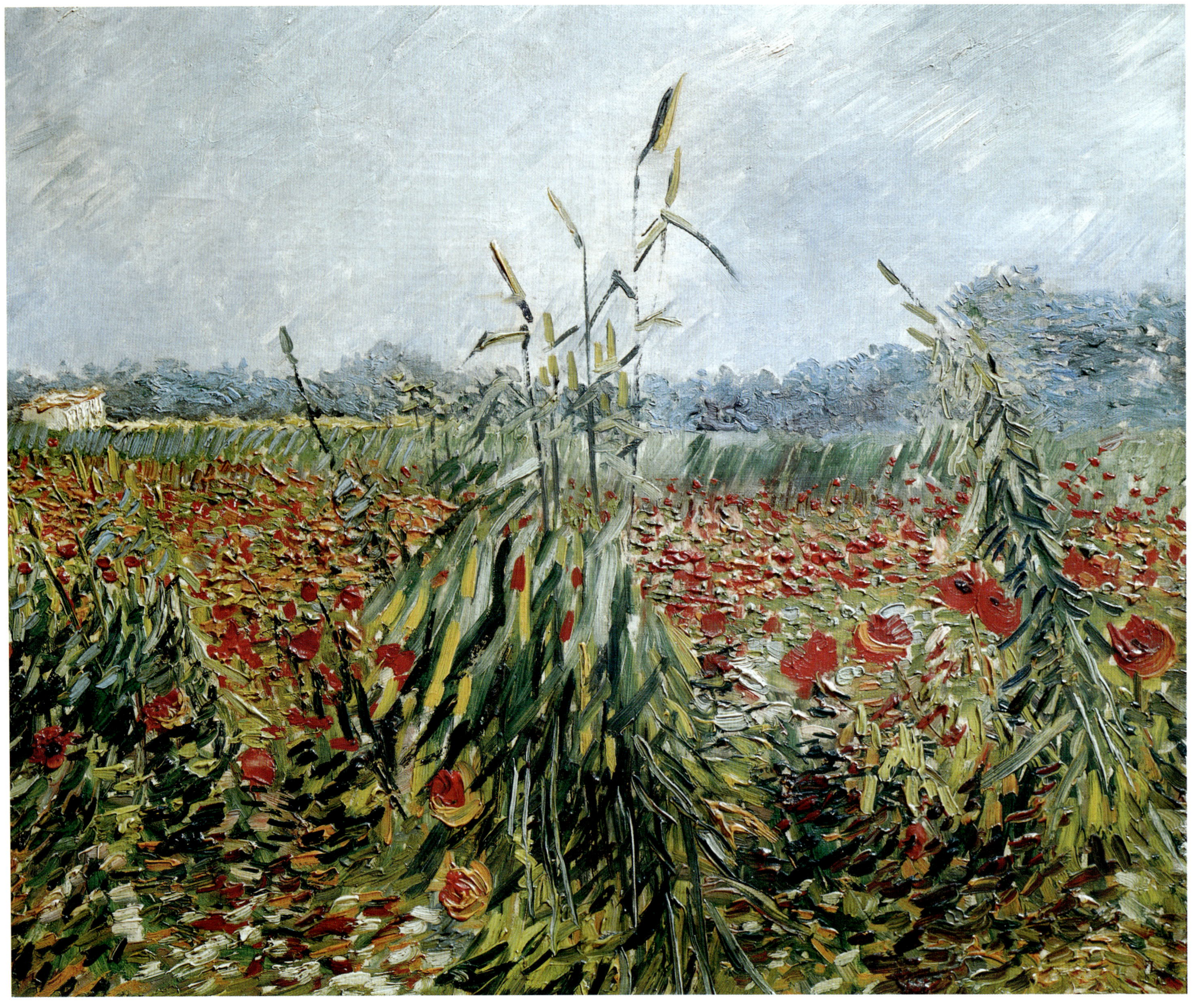

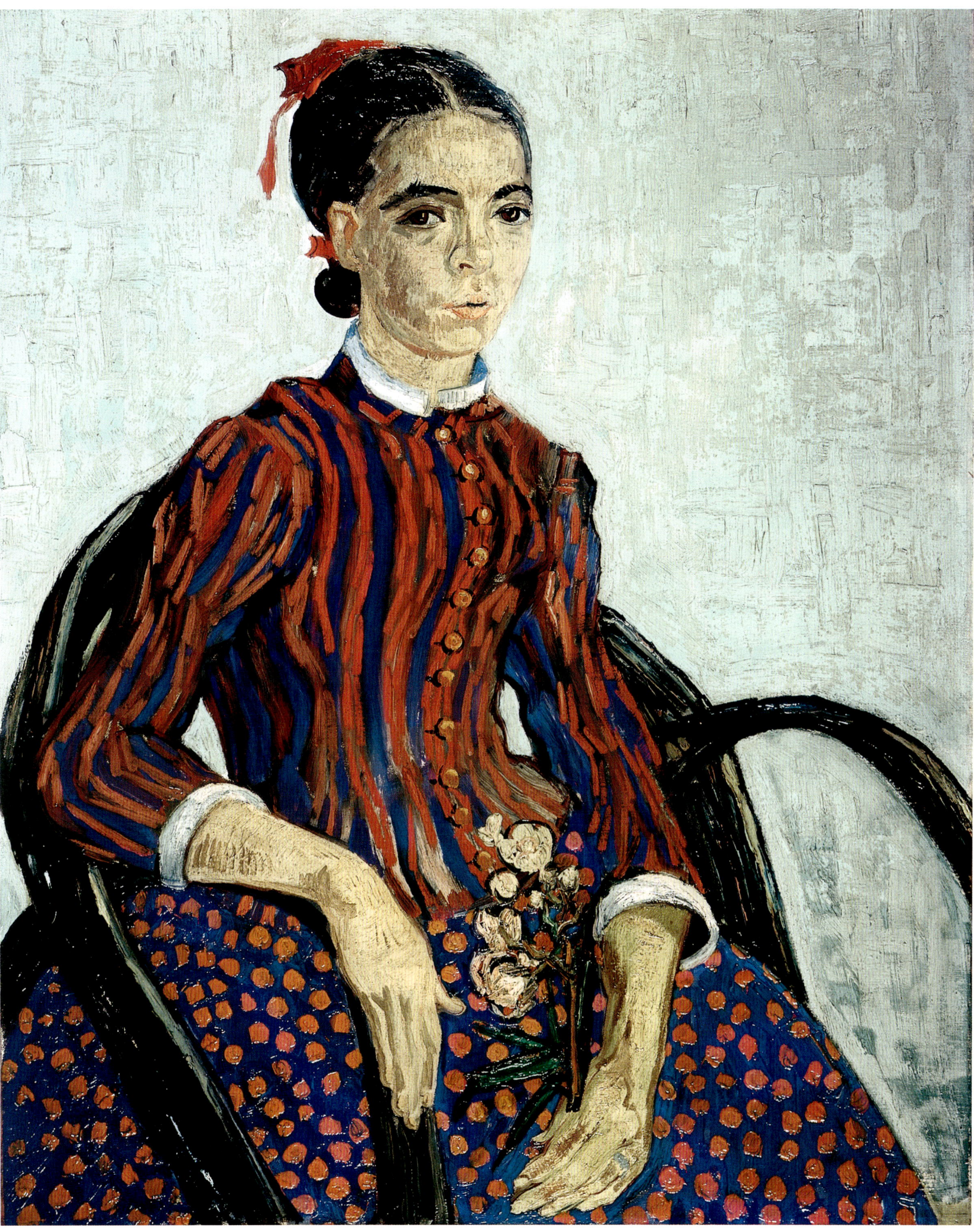

La Mousmé, Sitting
*(1888). Always an avid
reader, Vincent was
inspired by Pierre Loti's
novel* Madame Chrysan-
theme *to paint a portrait
of a* mousmé. *He
explained in a letter to
Theo that a* mousmé *was
a young Japanese girl.
Loti's novel describes the
temporary marriage of a
French sailor to a young
Japanese woman. In his
painting, Vincent sought
a sitter—young, comely,
and modest—who
embodied the characteris-
tics Loti portrayed in his
title character.*

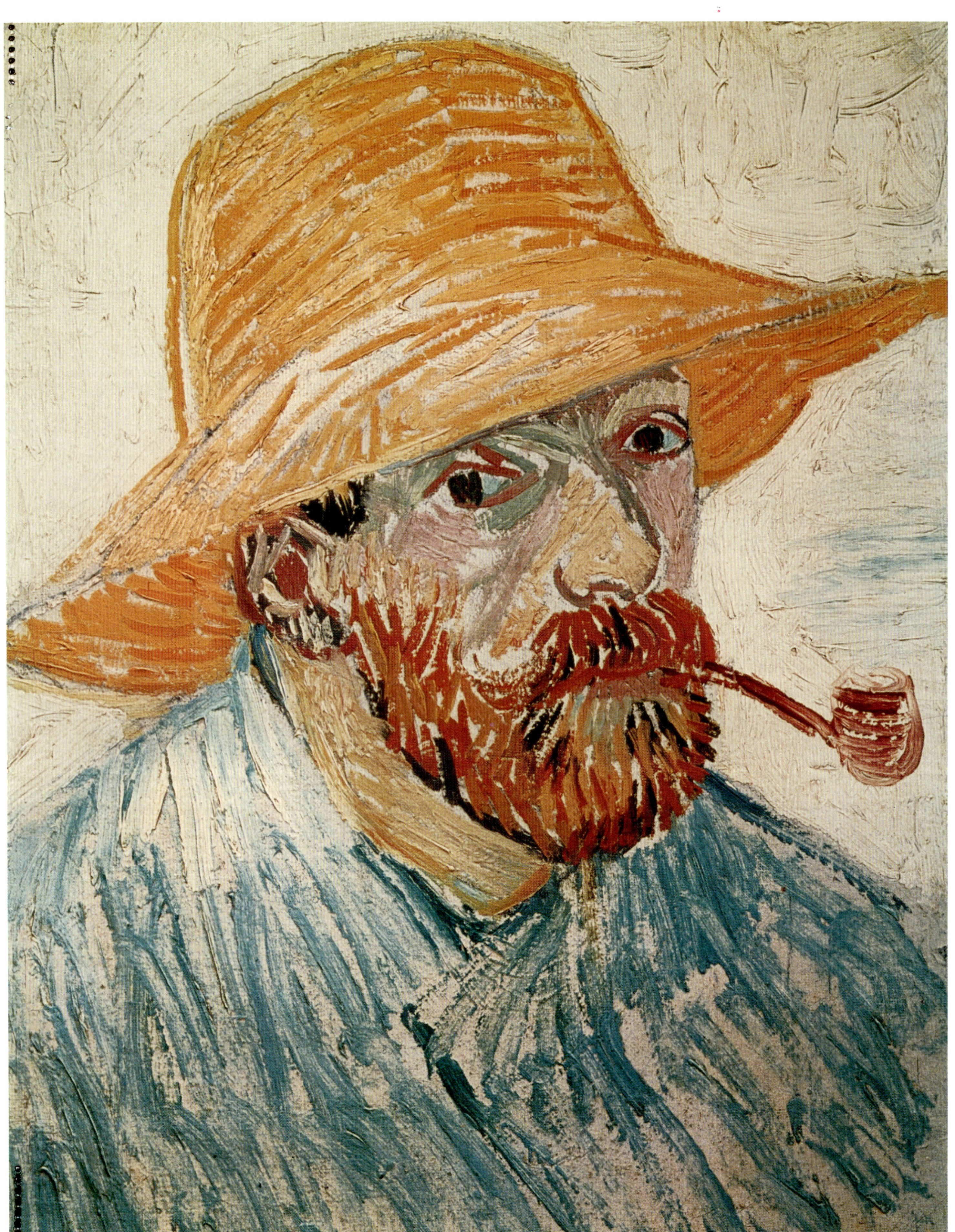

Self-Portrait with Pipe and Straw Hat *(1888). Vincent's many self-portraits record his sense of identity. Here, near the end of his summer in Arles, he wears a coarse peasant shirt and a common straw hat and smokes a long pipe, expressing his feelings of kinship with the local farmers. But these portraits also allowed him to continue his chromatic experiments, laying tone next to tone—such as the pink and gray strokes on his cheeks—for color effects rather than naturalistic depiction.*

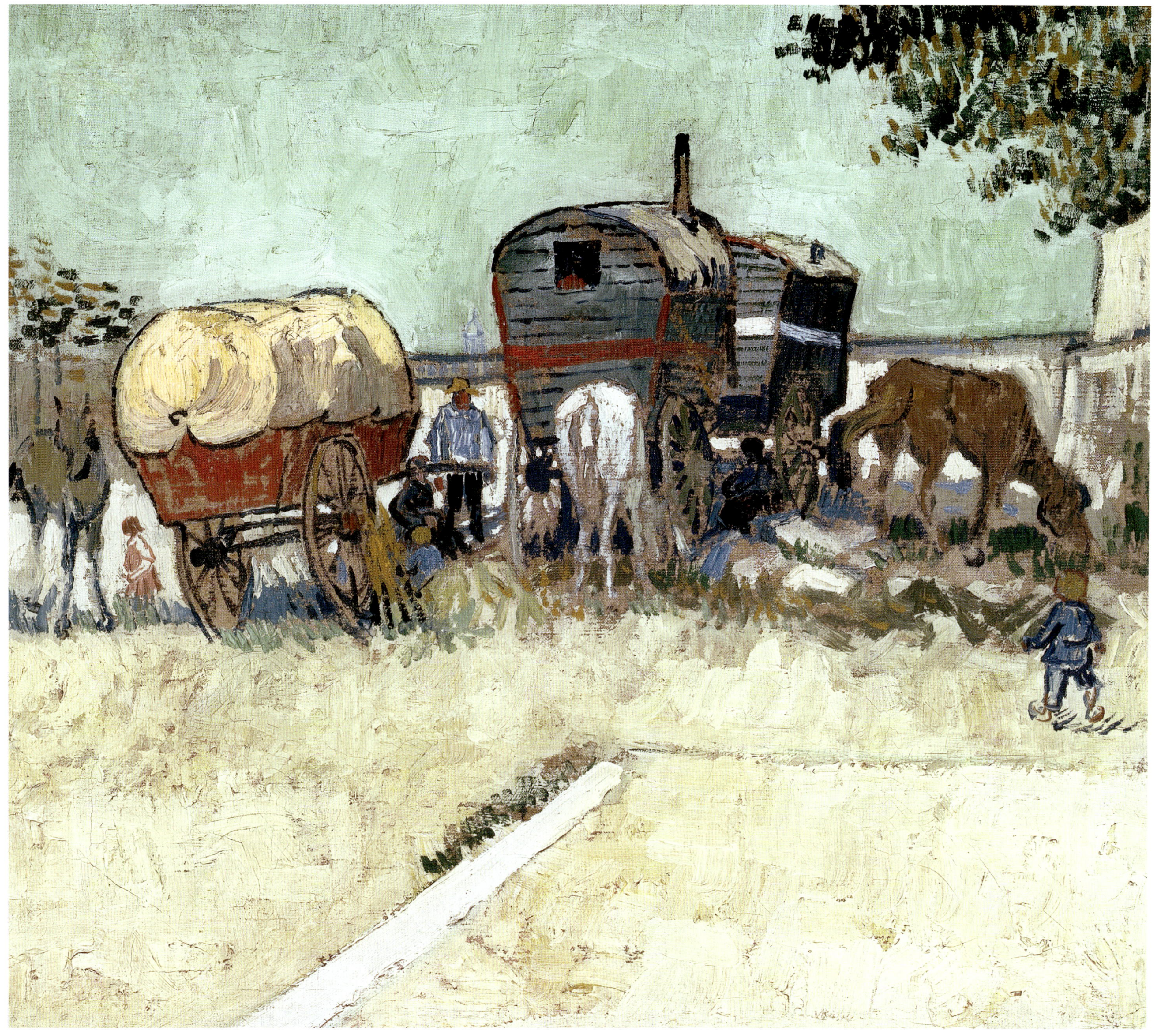

Encampment of Gypsies with Caravans *(1888). Vincent downplayed the narrative aspect of his painting of a gypsy encampment, focusing instead on the application of his pigment to the canvas. The thick layers of impasto recorded the action of his brush, rising off the canvas to mark the end of every stroke. This approach had become central to his work, giving the process of painting an expressive significance in the result. His technique required so much paint that he regularly asked Theo for extra money to buy new supplies.*

Musée d'Orsay, Paris. Oil on canvas (17¾×20 inches).

BRIGHTER SKY

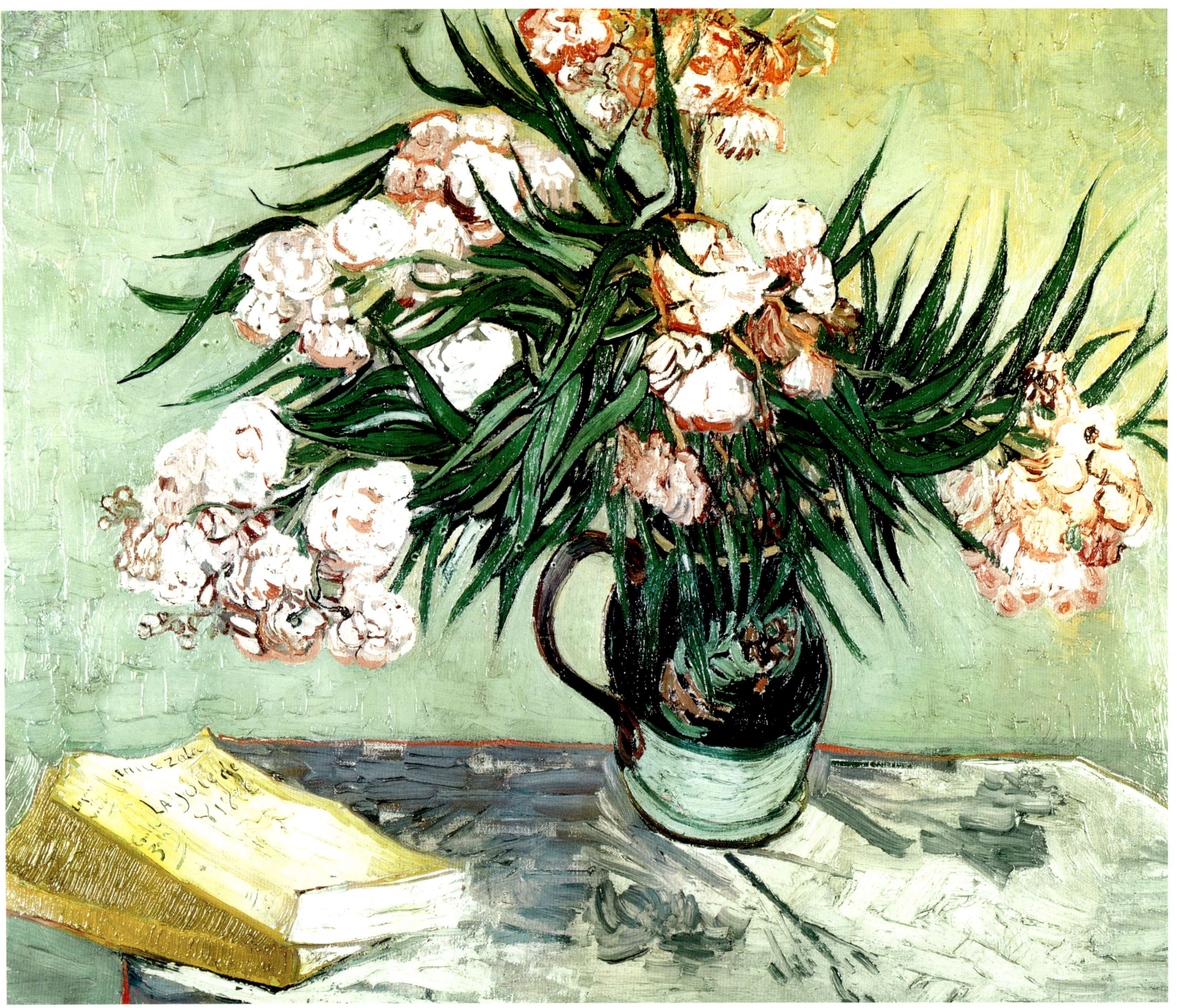

Oleanders *(1888). For Vincent, flowers and books were always objects of significance.
These books have the characteristic yellow jackets of contemporary Naturalist novels—
one is Émile Zola's* La joie de vivre. *But color is Vincent's supreme concern in this still
life, as seen in the strong contrasts of the thickly painted pink petals, which cast lilac
shadows on the table, and the heavily worked background in pure bright green.*

Metropolitan Museum of Art, New York. Oil on canvas (23¾×29 inches).

Ploughed Field *(1888). With thick strokes of yellow ocher, Vincent worked the patterns of the ploughed field onto his canvas. Individual brush strokes are evident, creating a descriptive texture through color. In the sky, it is possible to observe every time he lifted his brush as he applied the heavy pigment. He wrote to Theo demanding more tubes of paint: "I need another dozen of white zinc as soon as possible."*

Van Gogh Museum, Amsterdam. Oil on canvas (28½×36½ inches).

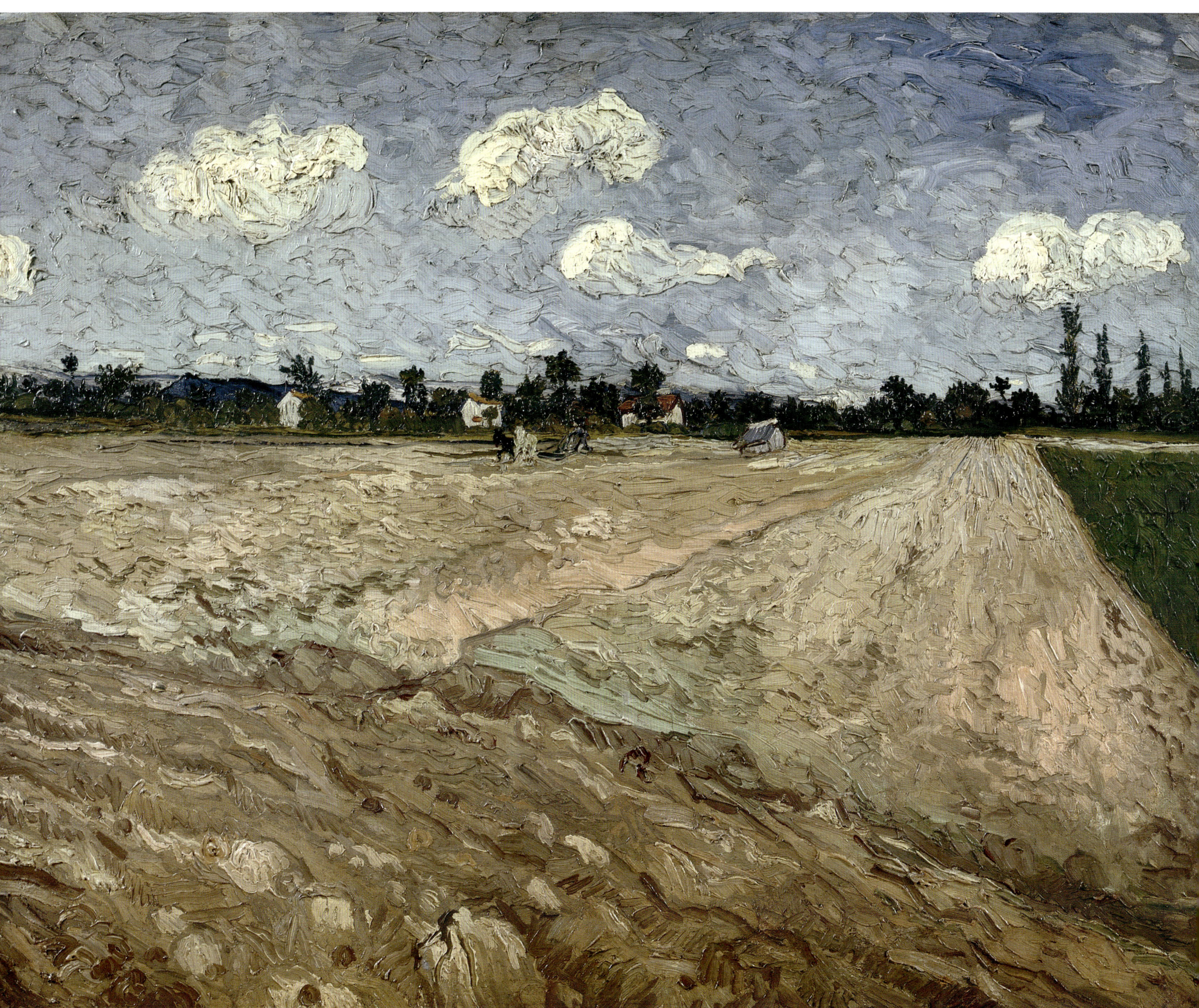

BRIGHTER SKY

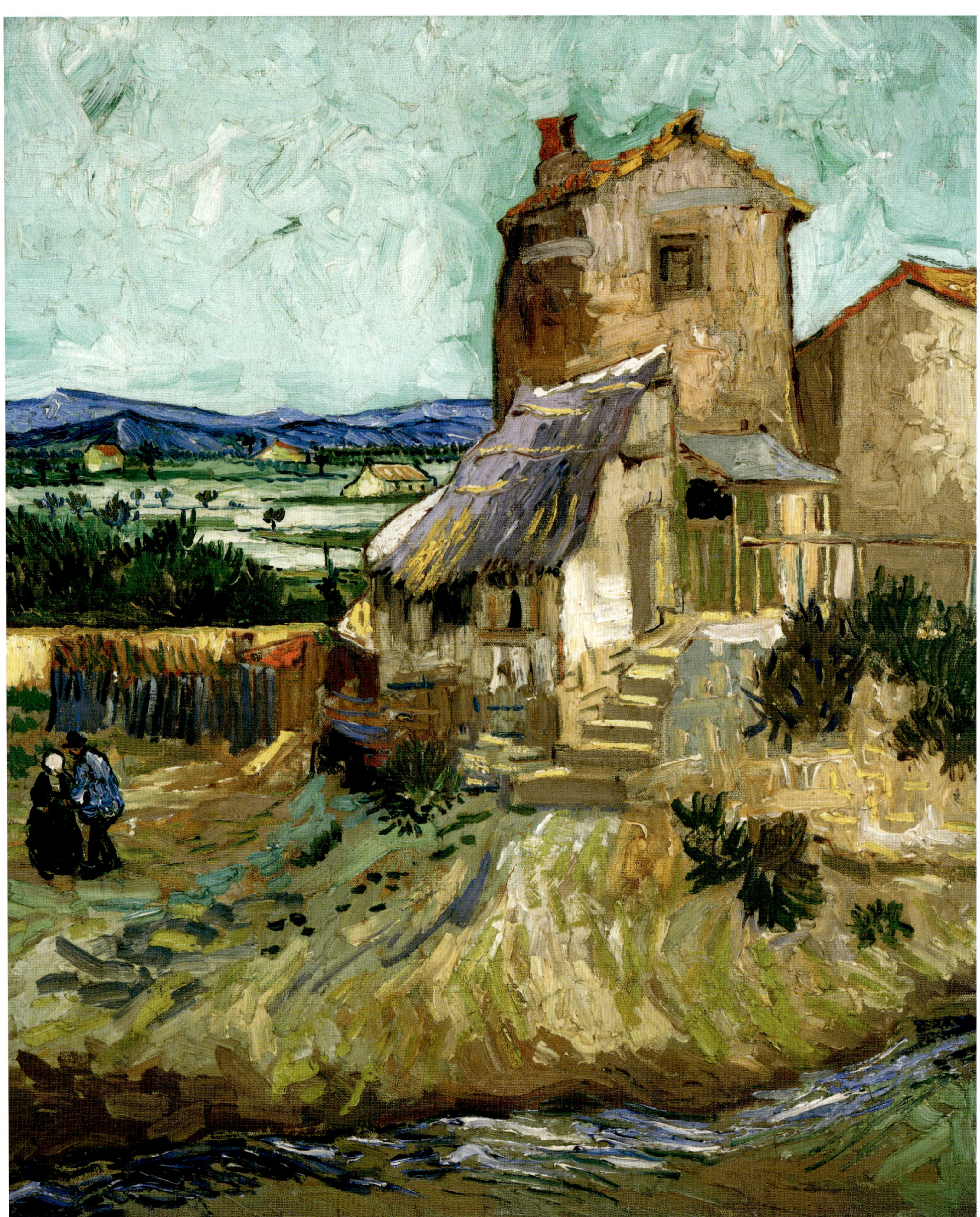

The Old Mill *(1888).*
Working at top speed,
Vincent poured all his
energy into his painting.
He became so immersed
in the physical process of
brushing pigment on
canvas that his brush
strokes took on an expres-
sive quality quite apart
from the subject of the
painting. The apparently
serene subject of an old
mill with a strolling
couple in the foreground
and cultivated fields in
the distance has a dis-
turbing emotional effect
as a result of the thick
articulation of the strokes.

Albright-Knox Art Gallery,
Buffalo. Oil on canvas
(25½×21¼ inches).

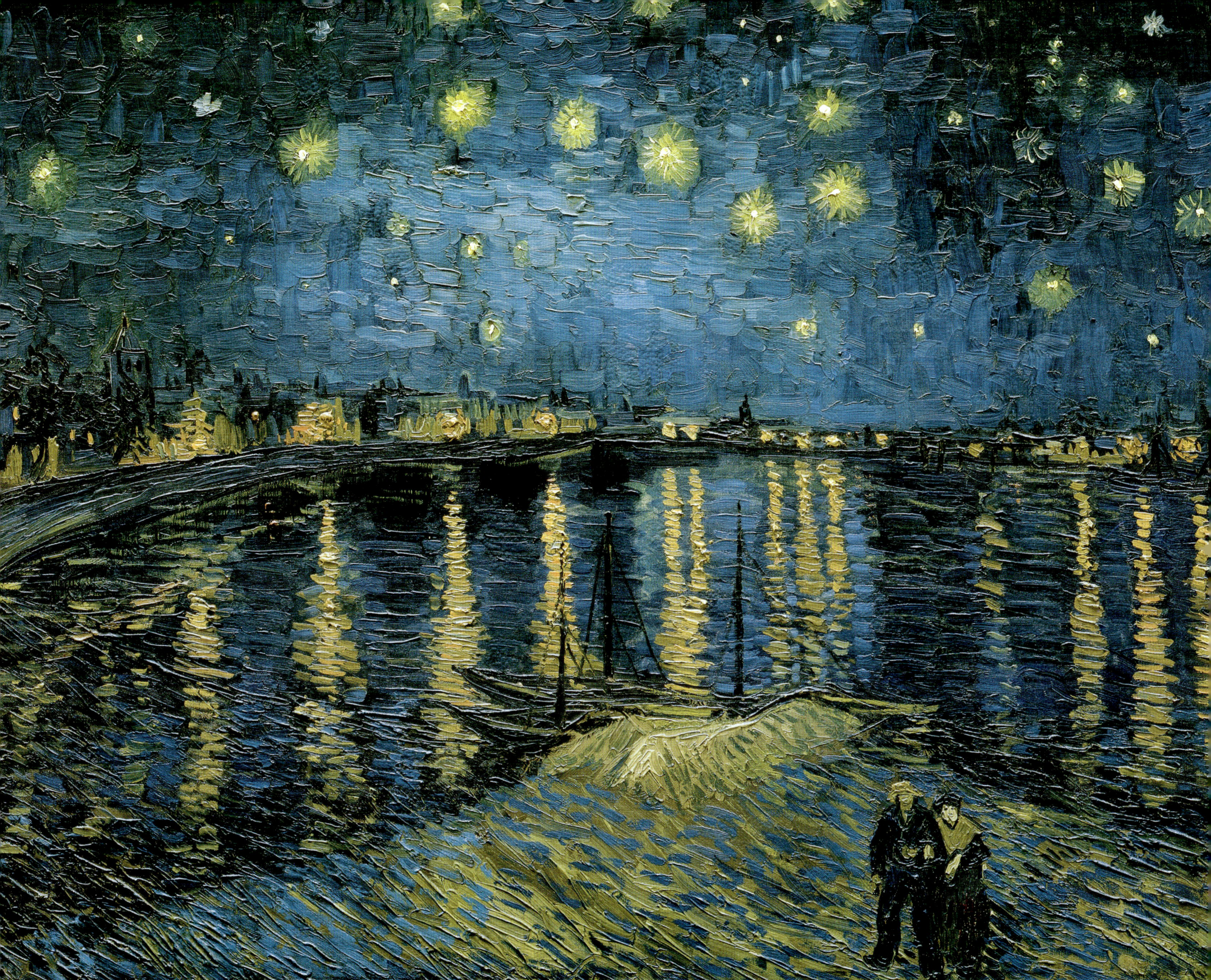

Starry Night over the Rhône *(1888). Vincent wrote to Theo that despite his rejection of conventional religion, he felt the need for an affirmation of faith, which prompted him to "go out at night into the open and paint the stars." In his first "starry night," he evoked evening's darkness with deep shades of blue, violet, and green, broken by the illumination of the stars with their citron-yellow auras and the lamps on the dock in the distance casting pale yellow reflections across the water.*

Musée d'Orsay, Paris. Oil on canvas (28½×36¼ inches).

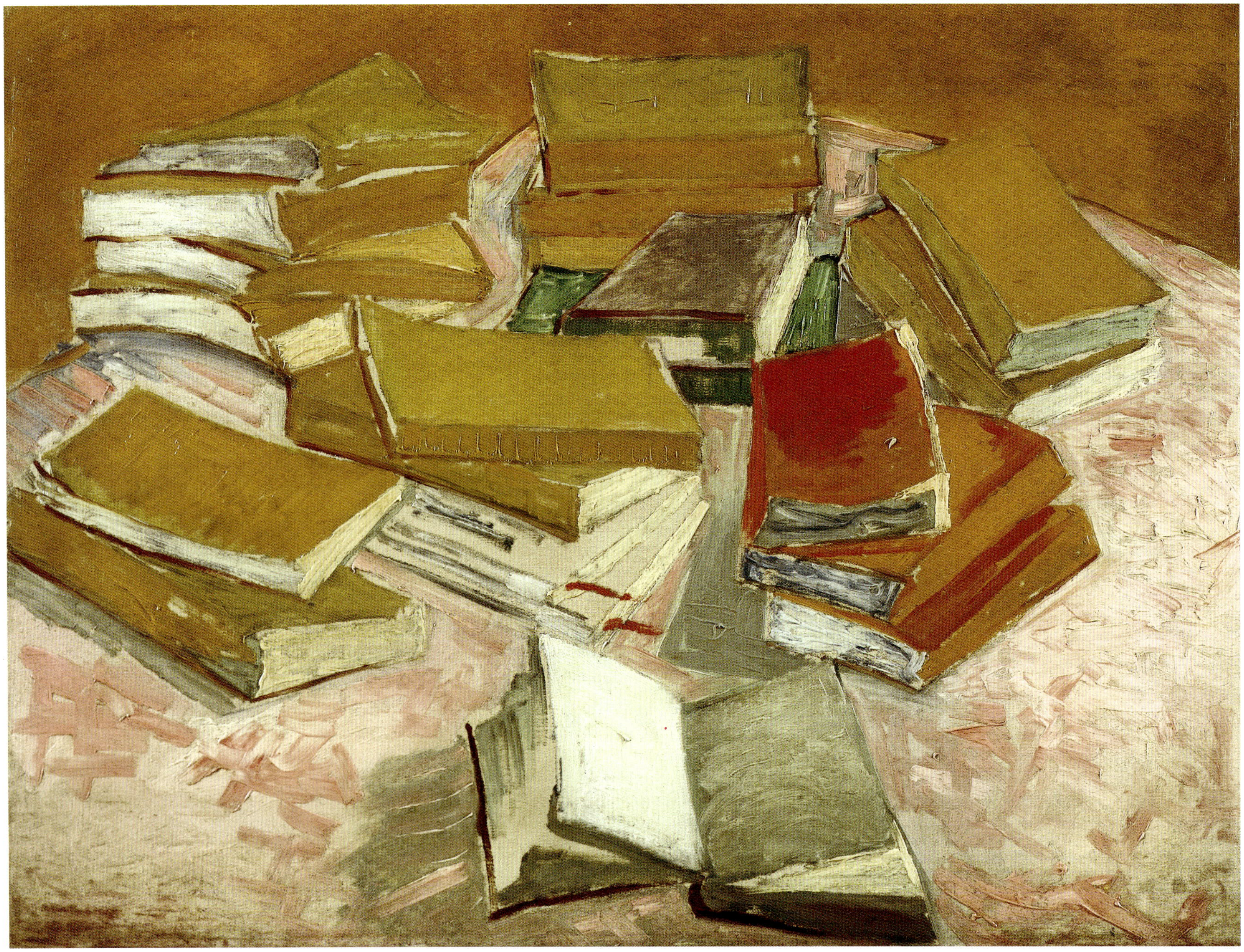

Study for 'Romans Parisiens' *(1888). As the weather turned colder, Vincent renewed his interest in still life. He piled a stack of novels on the table and painted their bright yellow jackets on a modulated surface of yellow and against a thickly painted background of gold. With bent pages and broken spines, the books appear well read, and Vincent continued to find comfort in their narratives. He was trying to instill his paintings with a kindred sympathy to the conditions of modern life.*

VAN GOGH MUSEUM, AMSTERDAM. OIL ON CANVAS (20¾×28¾ INCHES).

Willows at Sunset *(1888). The vivid tones of Vincent's palette announce the change of season from summer to autumn. After months of passionate and unrelenting work in solitary circumstances, he was physically drained and deeply lonely. He felt a parallel in the ebbing vitality of the cycle of the seasons. The bare branches of the willows appear animated, as if they twist to reach out into the last rays of vigorous heat cast by the setting sun.*

KRÖLLER-MÜLLER MUSEUM, OTTERLO, NETHERLANDS. OIL ON CARDBOARD (12½×13½ INCHES).

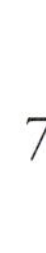

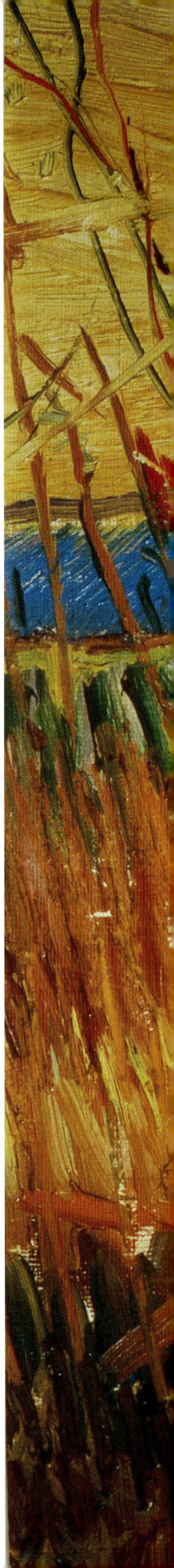

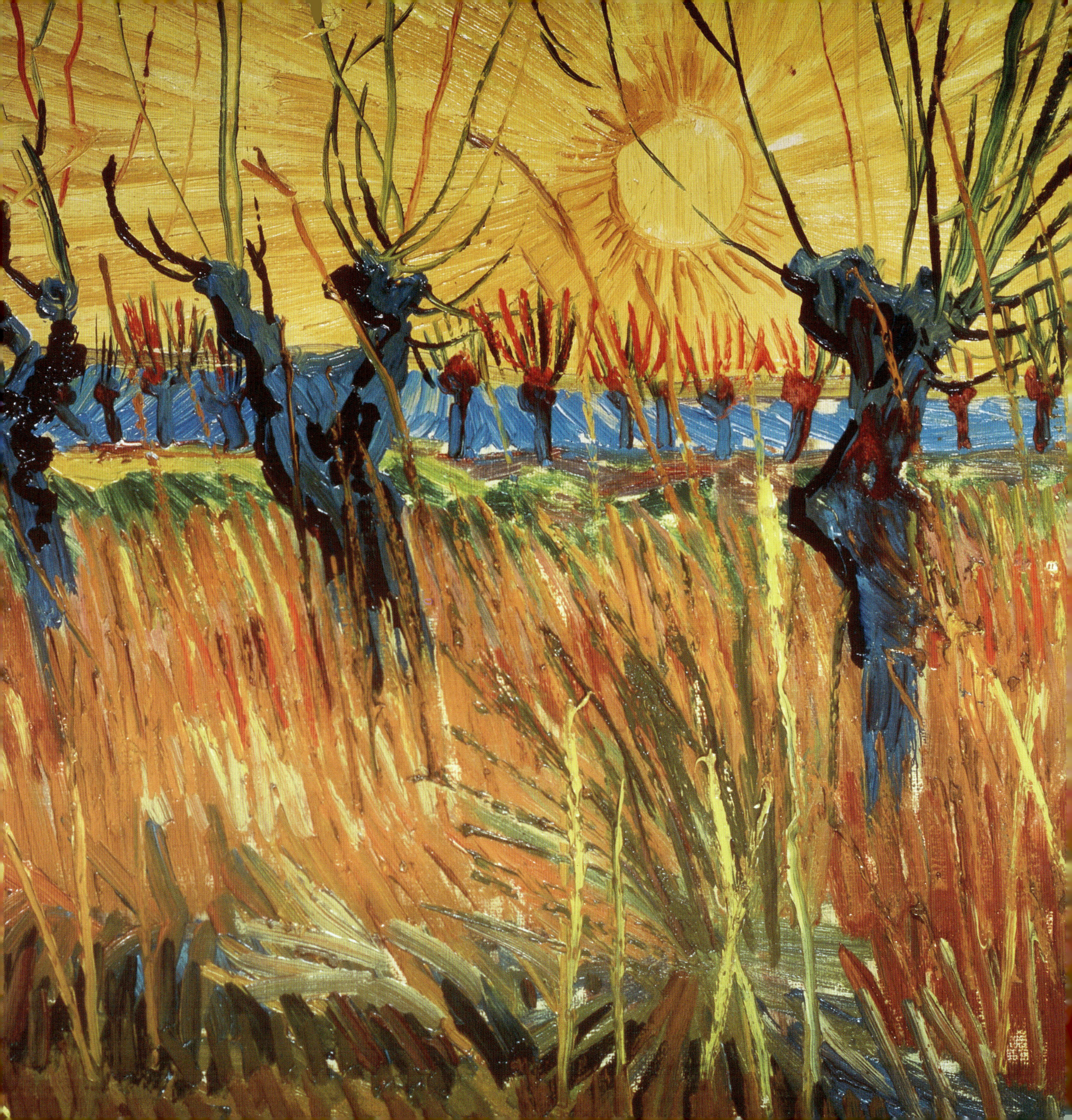

WHAT WE SAY WITH THE BRUSH

"Old Gauguin and I understand each other basically, and if we are a bit mad, what of it? Aren't we also so thoroughly artists enough to contradict suspicions on that score by what we say with the brush?"

VINCENT TO THEO, JANUARY 1889, FROM ARLES

*D*URING HIS FIRST MONTHS in Arles, Vincent followed a regular routine. In the morning, he would leave his rented room and set out for the fields to paint. Burdened with his equipment and dressed in spattered and increasingly ragged clothes, Vincent made an odd impression on the residents of Arles, who generally regarded him with suspicion. He developed a strong relationship with the town's postman, Joseph Roulin, but otherwise spent most of his time alone. He wrote to Theo that often he would pass several days without exchanging a word with another person, aside from ordering his dinner at the café. He had hoped to meet other artists but had little success, lamenting, "I haven't made the least progress in people's affections." Although Vincent denied feeling lonely, insisting that he was fully absorbed in his painting, he clearly longed for sympathetic companionship. His letters to Theo, as well as those to his friends, frequently extended an invitation to travel south and stay with him in Arles.

In May 1888, Vincent leased four rooms in a two-story building on the *Place Lamartine*. At first he planned to use the space as a studio, but in July, when Theo shared a family inheritance with him, Vincent made plans to move into the house. He called it the Yellow House, after the warm, buttery color of paint on the exterior walls. On the ground floor, two rooms served as a studio and a kitchen. Two smaller rooms could be reached by climbing a narrow stairway. These were well-lit during the day, and Vincent decided to furnish them as bedrooms. In one, he placed a

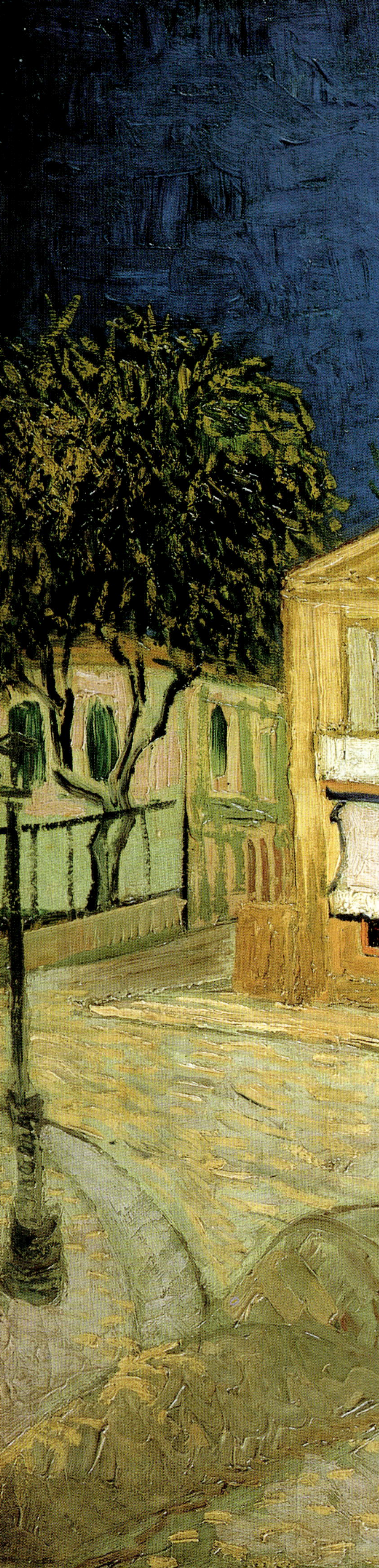

The Yellow House *(1888). The palette of yellow and blue—Vincent's signature colors—expressed his deep feelings for his little house and the fellowship of artists that he hoped would gather there. The exterior of the house was, in fact, painted a yellow that he associated with the pale, fresh hue of butter, but he intensified its hue and depicted it against a bright cerulean sky. He often commented on the sunny quality of the surrounding square, and the bright yellow tones he used enforce this sensation.*

VAN GOGH MUSEUM, AMSTERDAM. OIL ON CANVAS (28¼×36 INCHES).

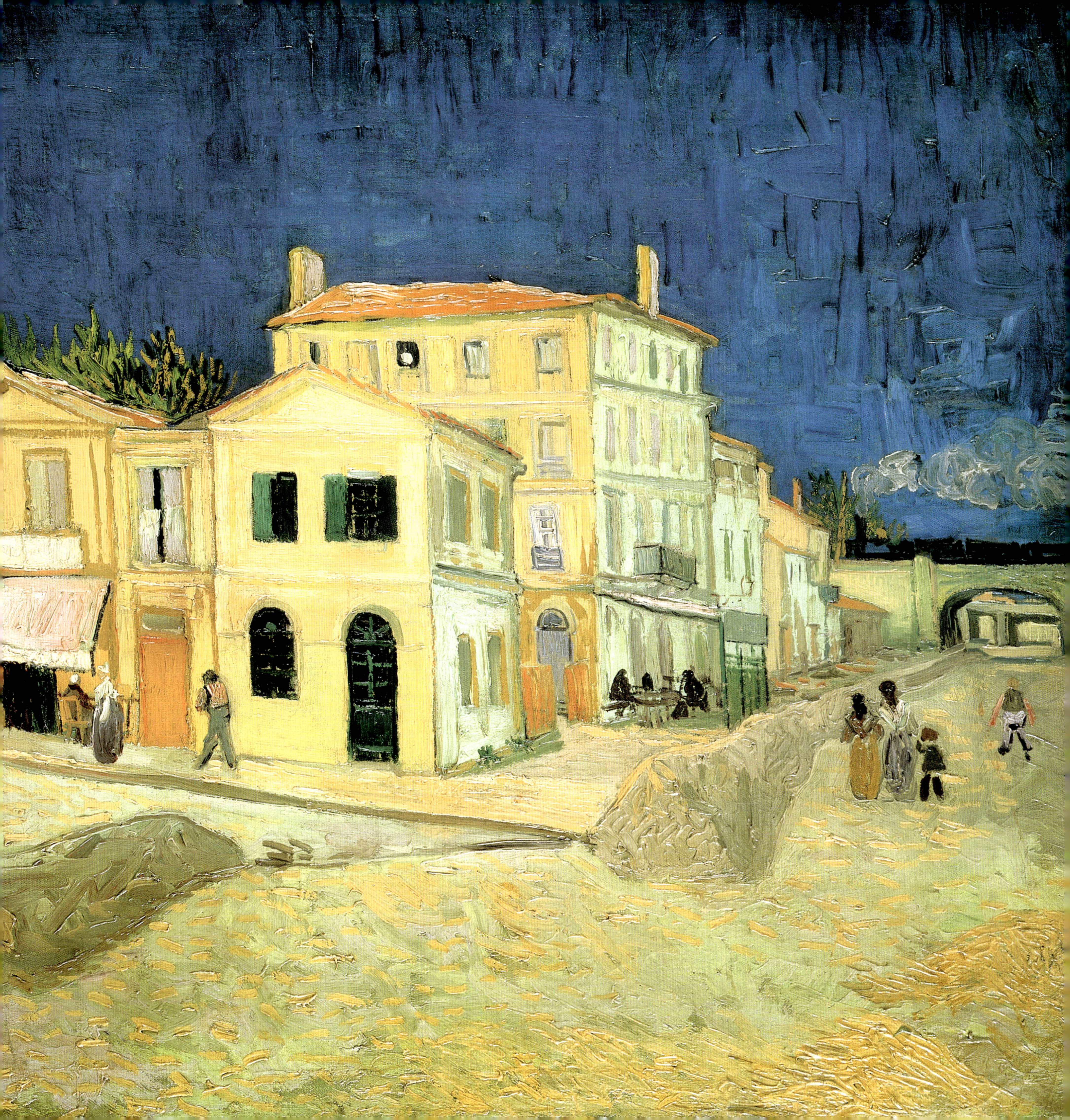

What We Say with the Brush

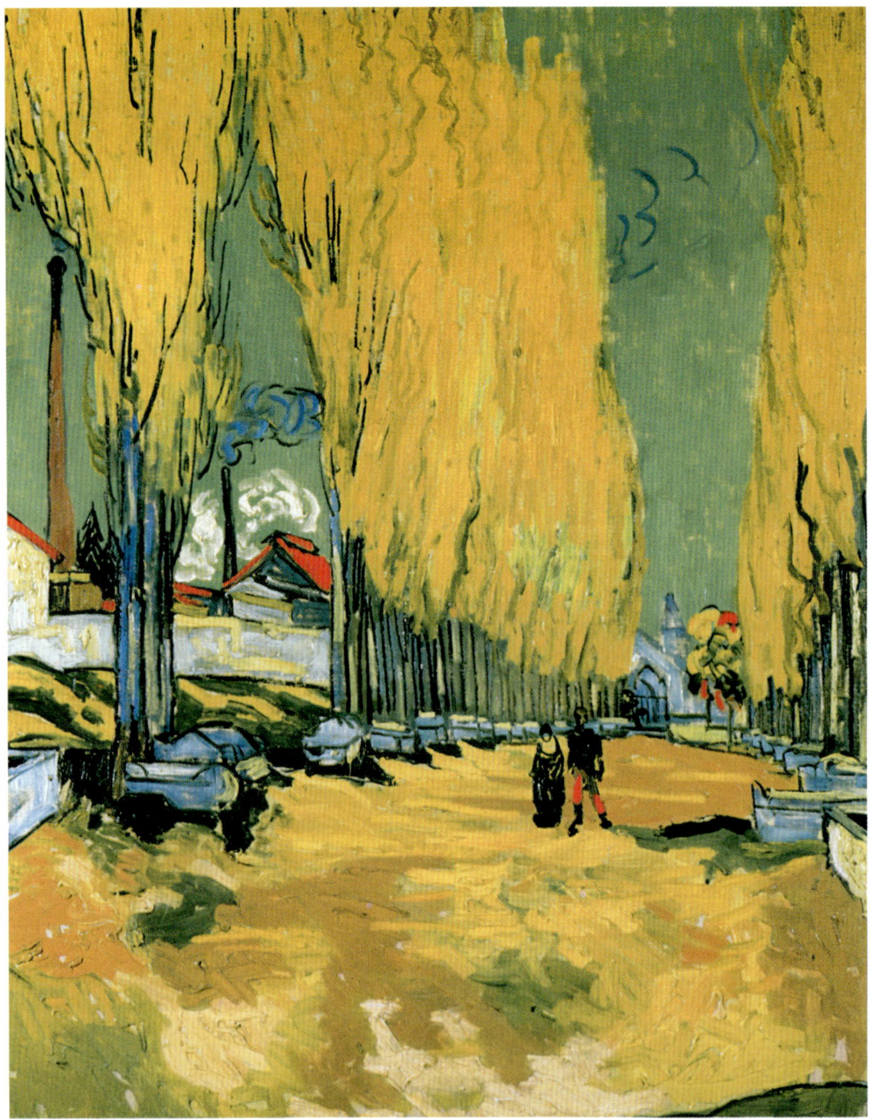

Les Alyscamps (1888). In a view down the Allee des Tombeaux, the poplar-flanked path between rows of ancient sarcophagi, Vincent portrayed two lovers taking a stroll. The woman wears the distinctive local costume, while the man's uniform identifies him as a Zouave whose regiment was temporarily billeted in Arles. This adds a poignant note to Vincent's favorite motif of companionship. Soon the soldier would move on, and the relationship would end.

plain, unpainted bed; a simple table; and some rustic chairs with woven rush seats. For the other, he planned a more elegant scheme: fine furniture, including a walnut bedstead with a fine coverlet and a dressing table with a matching cupboard. In a letter to his sister Wil, he explained that he would use the first room as his own bedroom, but the second would always be ready for a guest. By autumn, the house was ready to be occupied. Vincent moved in alone and painted a portrait of the house, in the tones of yellow that he now

regarded as his signature color, against a bright blue sky. He also painted his bedroom, writing to Theo that with its pale violet walls, red tile floor, and wooden furnishings "the yellow of fresh butter," the room, as he rendered it, "ought to rest the brain" with its simple color scheme.

Just a month earlier, Vincent wrote to Emile Bernard about his plan to cover the interior walls of the Yellow House with a special set of paintings. "I am thinking of decorating my studio with half a dozen pictures of 'Sunflowers,' a decoration in which the raw or broken chrome yellow will blaze forth on various backgrounds— blue, from the palest malachite green to royal blue, framed in thin strips of wood painted with orange lead." Vincent worked on his sunflower bouquets through September, painting at a frenetic pace with the knowledge that the flowers would soon be out of season. He piled the paint on his canvas and shaped it with his palette knife, carving the petals and stems in thick impasto. He worked the background and the table in short interlocking strokes resembling a woven basket. He was pleased with his new floral paintings and hung them on the walls of his guest room, writing to Theo that he would see "these great pictures of the sunflowers, 12 to 14 to the bunch, crammed into this tiny boudoir with its pretty bed and everything else dainty" when he came to visit, and he assured his brother that the effect would "not be commonplace."

But even more than a visit from Theo, Vincent keenly anticipated the arrival of Paul Gauguin. Vincent had asked Theo to extend an invitation to the painter as early as June. After many delays and excuses, Gauguin arrived at Vincent's door on October 23, 1888. Eager to be working with his new companion, Vincent immediately escorted his guest to his favorite locations, and they set up their easels together in the ancient and picturesque cemetery *Les Alyscamps* (Elysian Fields). They invited a local innkeeper, Madame Ginoux, to pose in the studio in the Yellow House, but soon their conflicting attitudes toward art led to heated debates. While Vincent believed that he needed to work fast, in the open air in front of his subject, Gauguin advocated a slower approach, urging Vincent to rely more upon his memory and imagination. That December, Vincent painted a pair of symbolic portraits using chairs to reflect their individual characters and their differences. For Gauguin, he chose an upholstered armchair with two contemporary French novels and an illuminated candle placed on the

seat. For himself, Vincent chose a plain rustic chair with a woven rush seat standing on the tile floor of the kitchen in front of a box of sprouting onions. Although their friendship was increasingly strained, Gauguin responded to Vincent's tribute, depicting Vincent at his easel in *Van Gogh Painting Sunflowers* (1888).

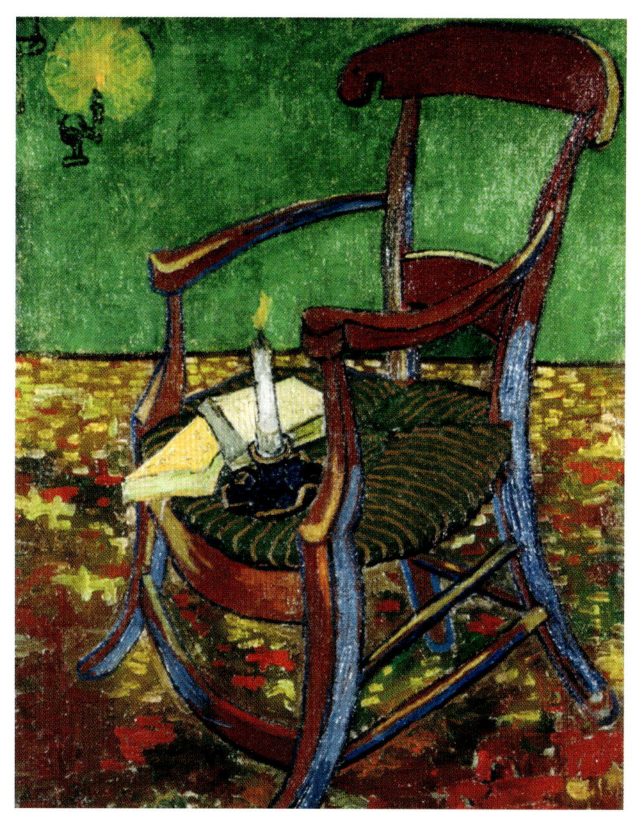

In the aftermath of Vincent's self-mutilation and Gauguin's hasty departure from Arles, Vincent became convinced that if he could return to his painting he could also regain his stability and his health. On January 4, 1889, Vincent left the hospital and returned to the Yellow House. Shortly after, he painted a simple still life of onions and a lit candle, recalling the symbolic portraits he had made of himself and Gauguin. He painted two self-portraits in his winter clothing, his lacerated ear hidden behind a large surgical dressing. Vincent also made copies of his own sunflower bouquets, using the paintings as his model, for the flowers were long out of season. Through these familiar images, Vincent reflected on his brief but life-changing encounter with Gauguin, and he wrote to Theo they should be judged only "on that score by what we say with the brush."

What We Say with the Brush

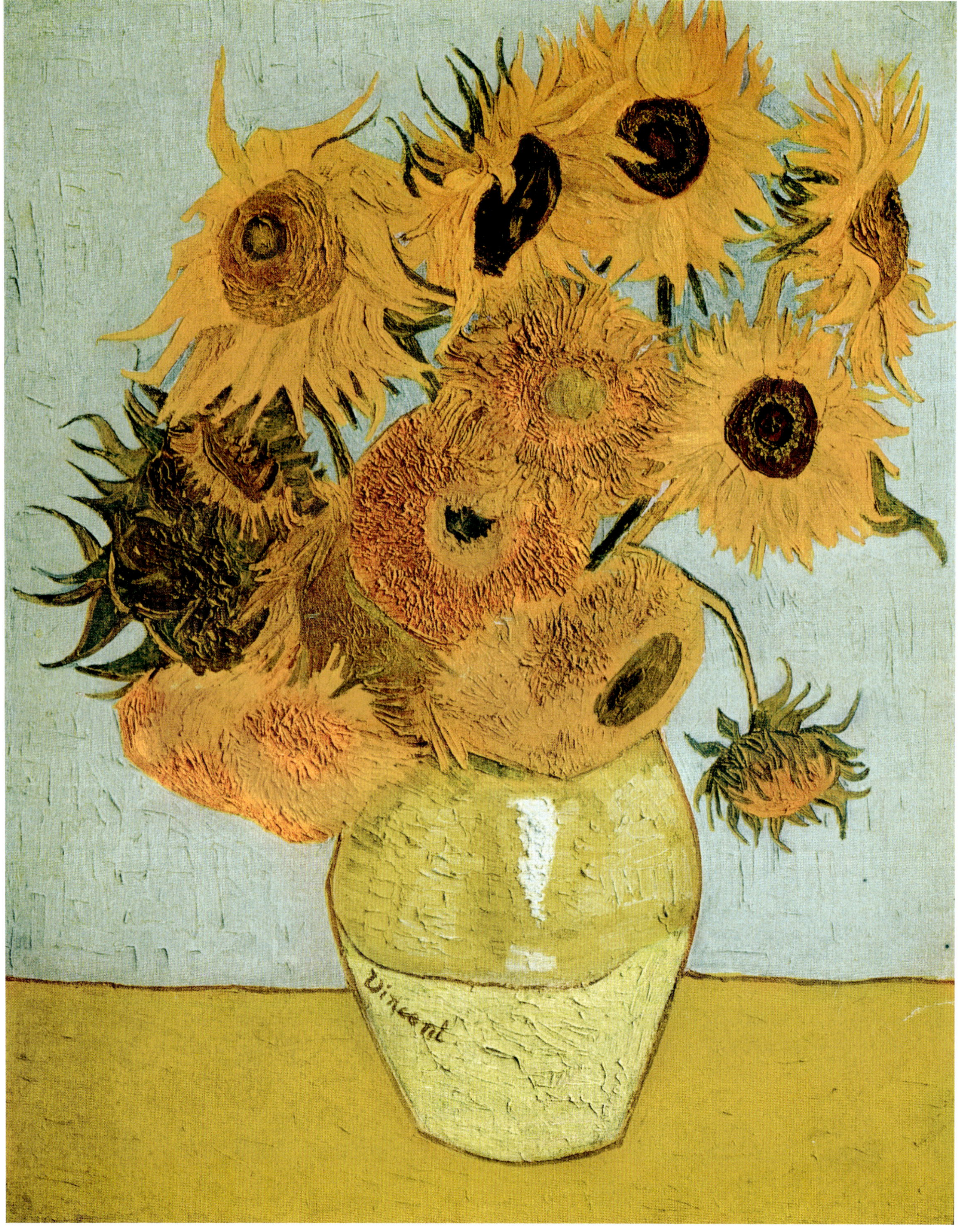

Still Life: Vase with Twelve Sunflowers *(1888). In mid-August, Vincent wrote to his friend Emile Bernard that he was painting canvases of sunflowers to brighten the walls of his studio. He described the vivid colors he was using—chrome yellow and royal blue—and compared the effect to stained-glass windows. The thickly worked paint, which sculpts the flower petals and creates a basket-weave pattern on the table's surface and the curve of the vase, heightens the color effects.*

Bayerische Staatsgemaldesammlungen, Neue Pinakothek, Munich. Oil on canvas (35¾×28¼ inches).

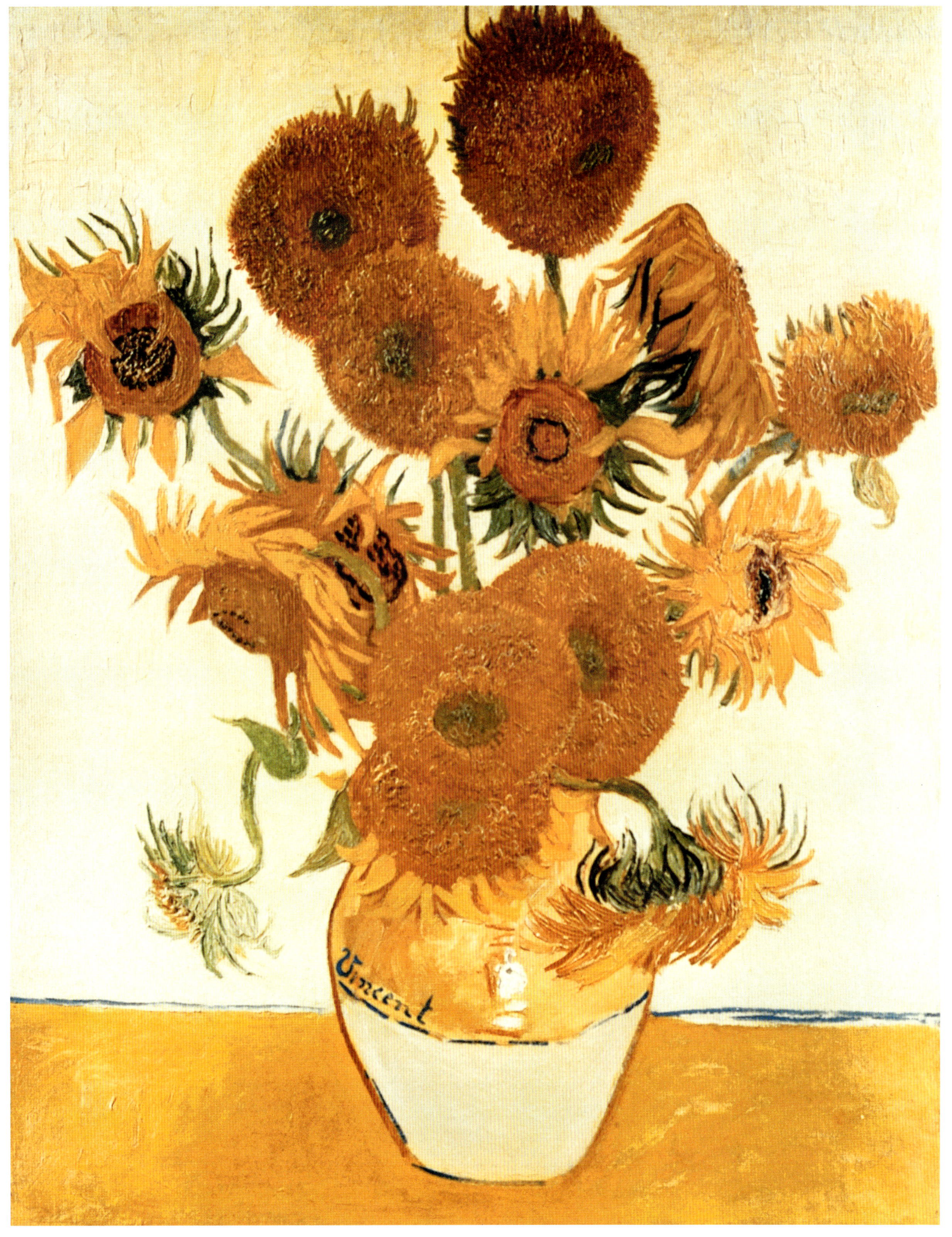

Sunflowers *(1888).
Sunflowers were more
than a mere decorative
scheme for Vincent. As a
floral emblem, the sun-
flower was traditionally
associated with worship
and constant devotion. To
Vincent, their vibrant
colors and radiant forms
represented the vitalizing
power of the sun. He
regarded this painting as
his best, and aside from a
few touches of green in
the stems and the blue
contour lines, Vincent
worked in a restricted
palette of yellow, from a
pale, sunstruck tone to a
ruddy ocher.*

National Gallery, London. Oil
on canvas (36½×28¾ inches).

WHAT WE SAY WITH THE BRUSH

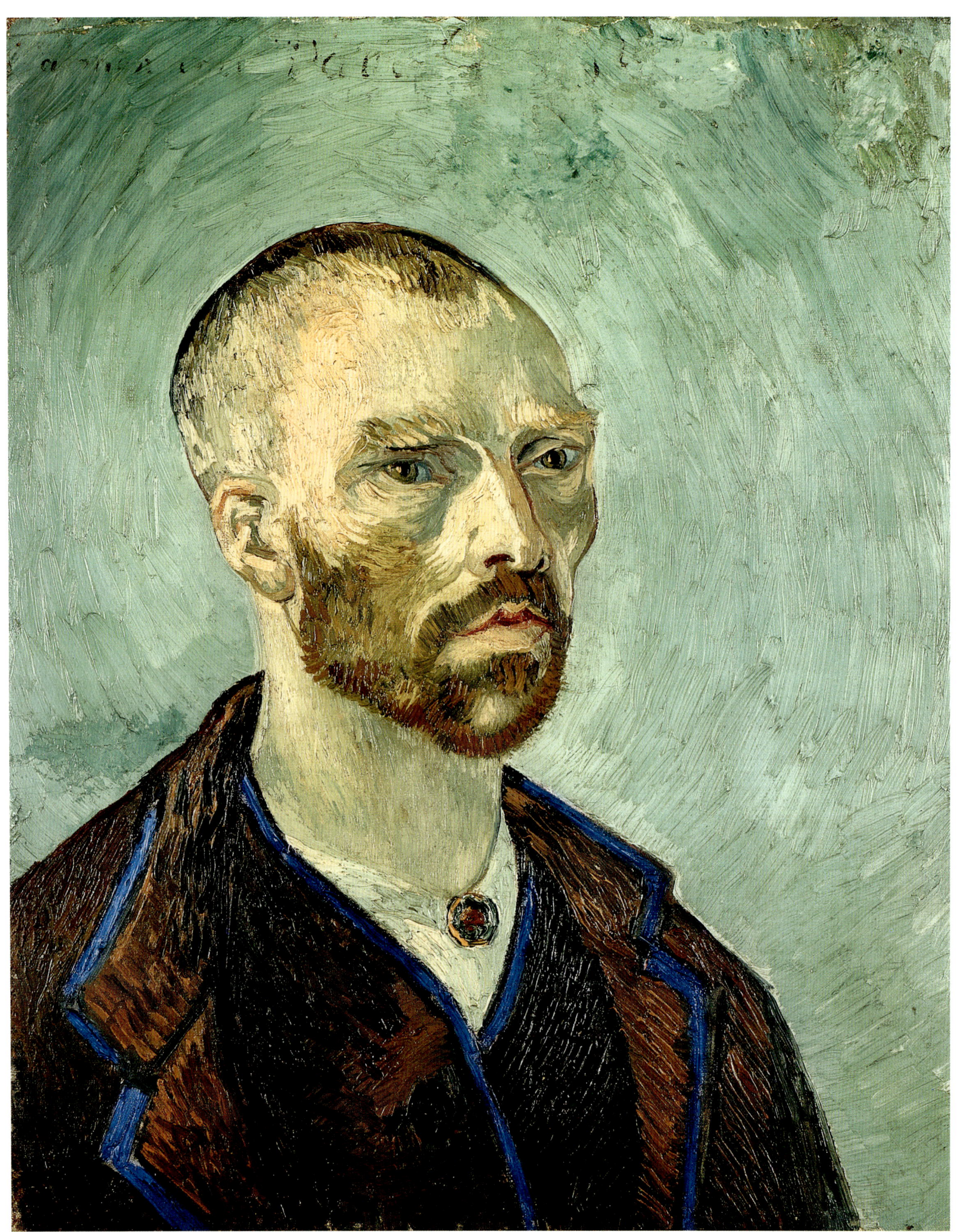

Self-Portrait Dedicated to Paul Gauguin (Bonze) *(1888). Vincent painted this stark self-portrait in anticipation of Gauguin's arrival in Arles. Gaunt, with close-clipped hair, he portrayed himself as a counterpart to a Japanese* bonze, *a simple follower of the Buddha. He hoped that a circle of like-minded artists would gather in Arles, and he envisioned Gauguin as the head of the fellowship. With this modest presentation, dedicated to the older painter, Vincent expressed his intense desire to follow Gauguin's bold direction in art.*

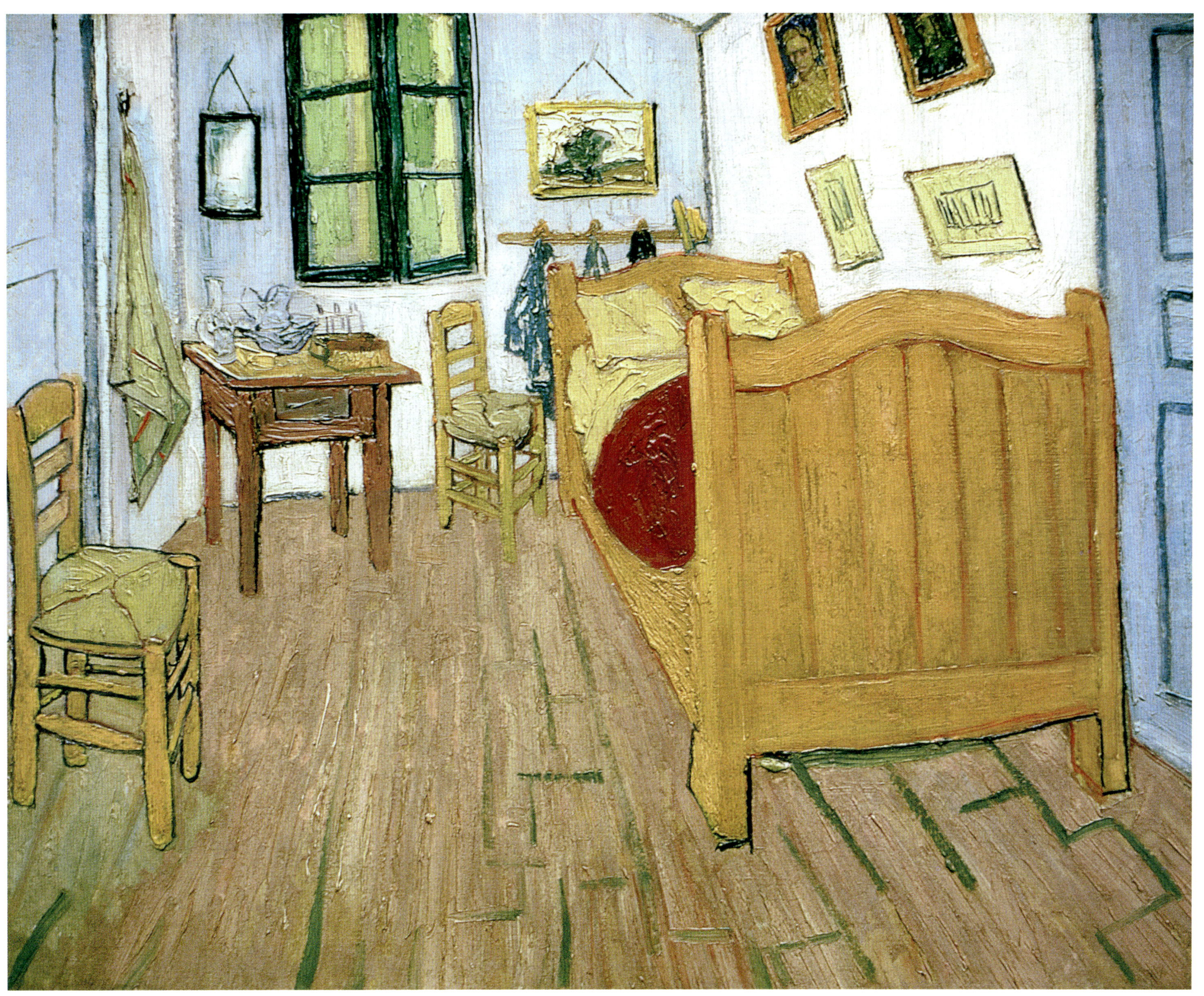

The Bedroom *(1888). Vincent sent a sketch of the way he furnished his own bedroom to Theo. A letter accompanying the sketch described the contents of the room in detail. While Vincent hoped his plans would convince Theo that he was making practical use of the funds he received, he also wanted to convey his progress on a painting of the subject of his room. He defined his approach as simple, intended to give weight and gravity to the subject while evoking the sense of restful sleep.*

Van Gogh Museum, Amsterdam. Oil on canvas (28¼×35½ inches).

WHAT WE SAY WITH THE BRUSH

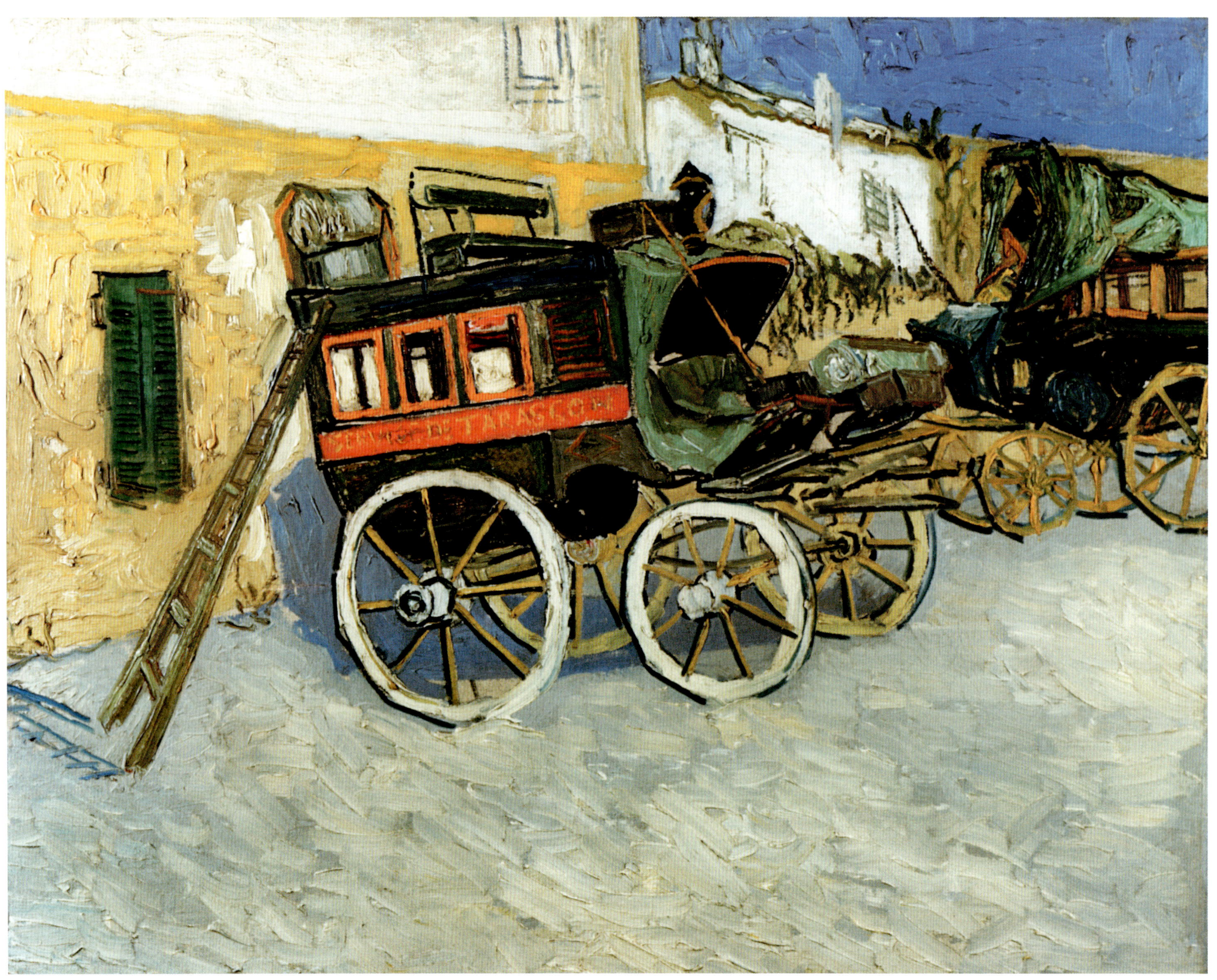

Tarascon Dilegence *(1888). As he waited for Gauguin to come to Arles, Vincent*
continued his investigation of intense and expressive color. The red panels of this car-
riage, taken in ensemble with its green cab, represent the chromatic vitality he sought in
his painting. But the heavy application of paint—the sweeping strokes on the ground
and the interlocking strokes on the wall—reveal his deepening immersion in the act of
painting on a surface that records every movement of his brush.

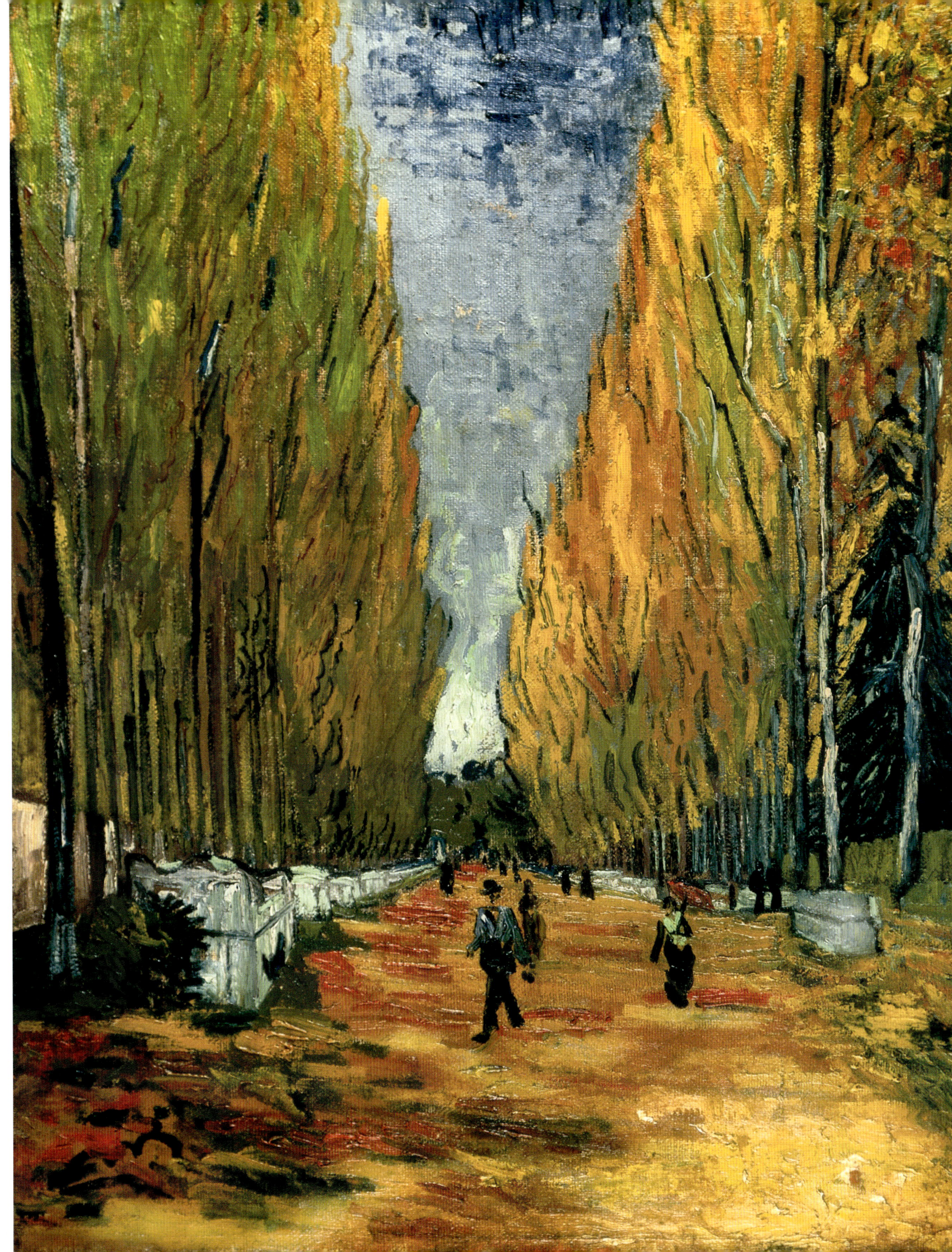

Les Alyscamps *(1888).*
Shortly after Gauguin
arrived in Arles, Vincent
took him to his favorite
places to paint. They set up
their easels together in the
ancient cemetery known as
Les Alyscamps *(Elysian*
Fields). In contrast to
Gauguin's slow and delib-
erate process, Vincent
painted quickly, slashing
his pigment on the canvas
with thick, broad strokes.
This difference became a
point of contention
between the painters;
Vincent worked in a rush
of emotional energy in
opposition to Gauguin's
cerebral, considered
approach.

What We Say with the Brush

The Red Vineyard (1888). As the weeks passed, Gauguin moved his easel out into the fields surrounding Arles, and Vincent followed. The Red Vineyard combines his efforts to learn from Gauguin's example with his own enduring interest in color and motif. The bold diagonal axes that sweep across the foreground to meet the high horizon reflect Gauguin's formal approach to composition, but the thickly worked surface illuminated by a yellow sun in a yellow sky mark Vincent's own aesthetic concerns.

PUSHKIN MUSEUM OF FINE ARTS, MOSCOW. OIL ON CANVAS (29½×36½ INCHES).

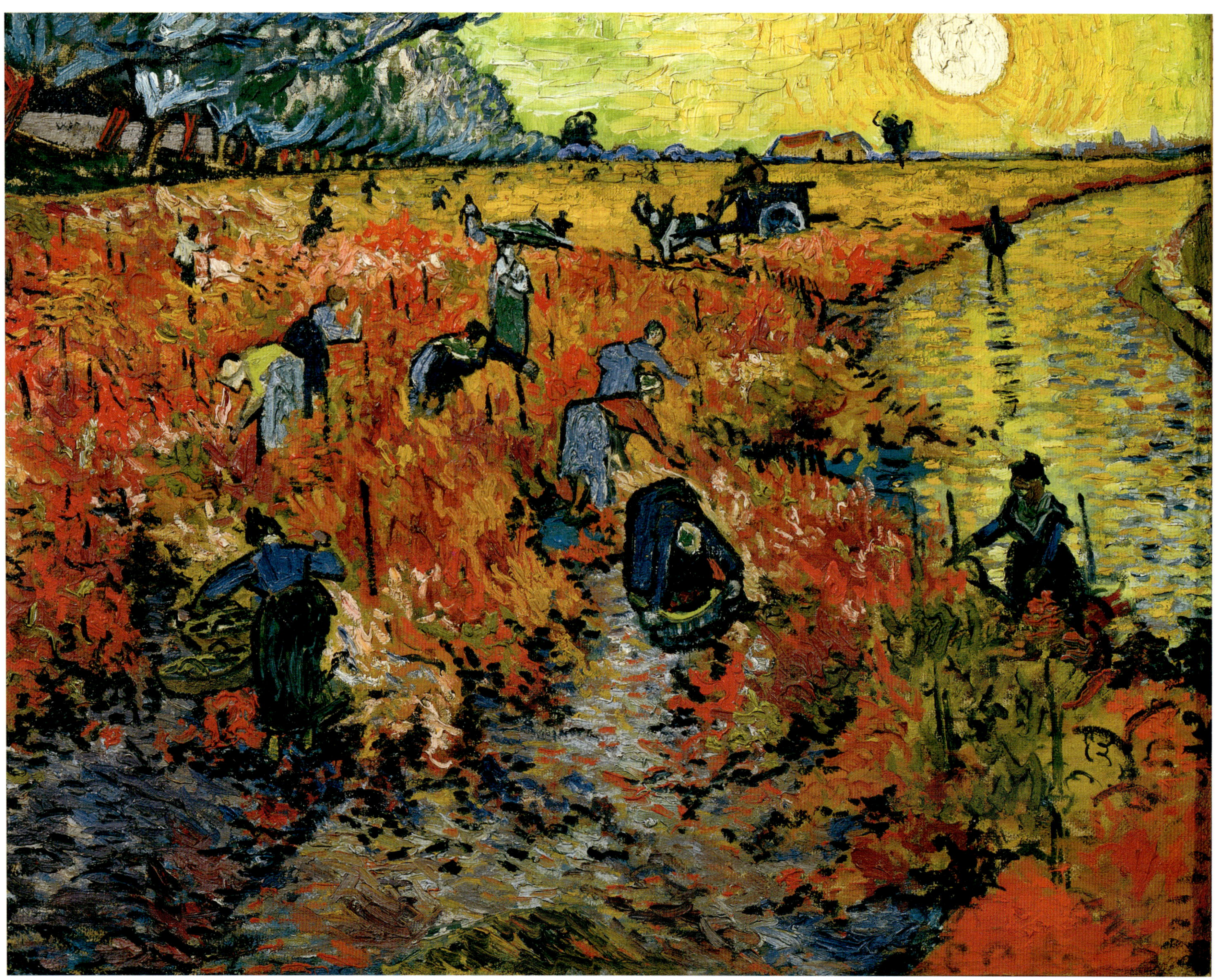

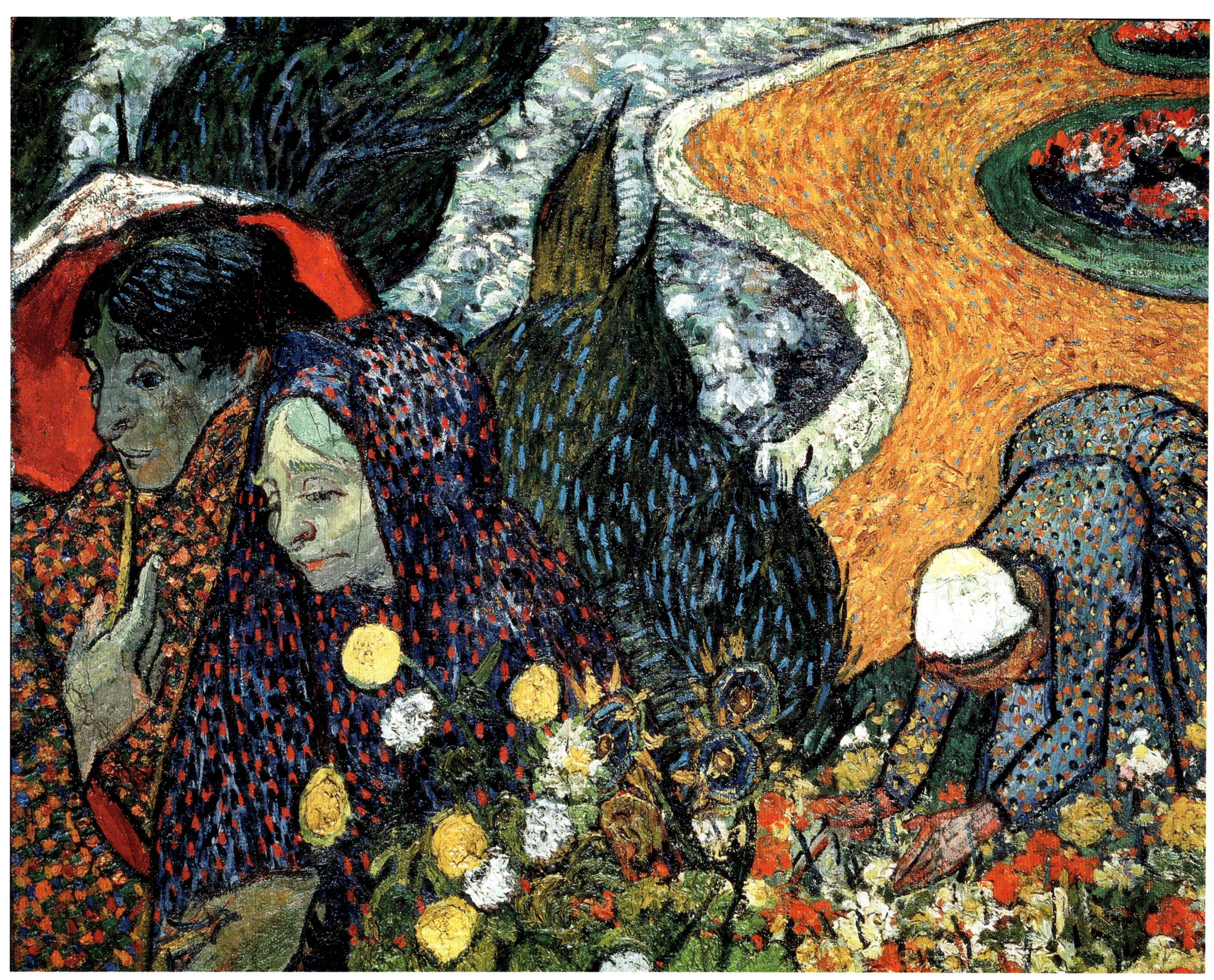

A Memory of the Garden at Etten *(1888). In response to Gauguin's advice that he work
more from imagination and less from nature, Vincent painted a recollection of his mother
and his sister walking through a garden in his boyhood village. In a letter to his sister he
explained that the motifs and the colors carried specific meanings. The "somber violet
violently stained by the citron yellow of the dahlias" suggested their mother's personality,
whereas the red and green presented Wil as a character out of a Dickens novel.*

Hermitage, Leningrad. Oil on canvas (29×36½ inches).

What We Say with the Brush

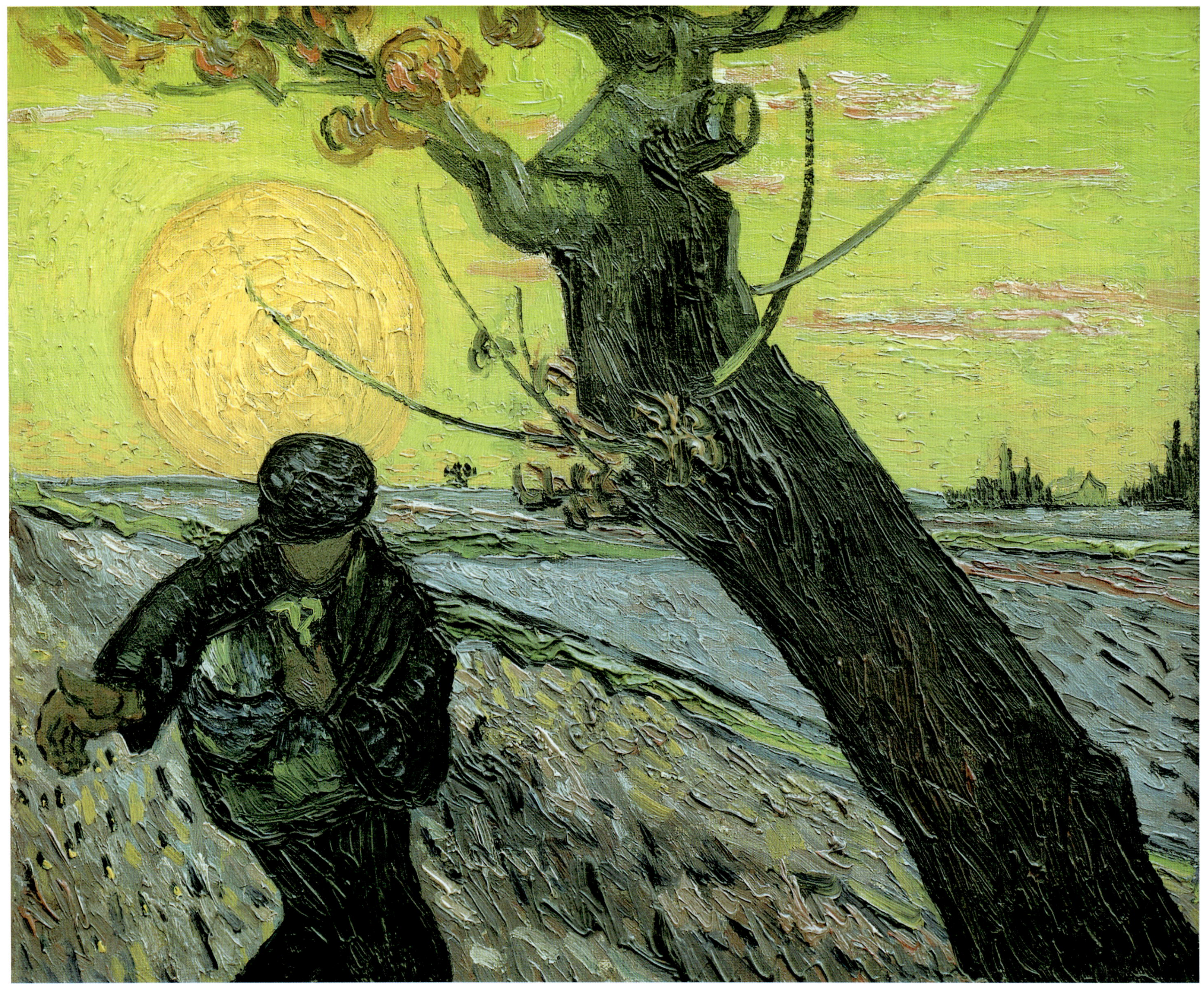

The Sower *(1888). The bright color contrasts and the articulation of the tree trunk mark Vincent's return to the spirit of the Japanese print. The vast, burning sun, painted with concentric impasto strokes, hovers above the head of the sower whose simple yet essential gesture—casting the seed with his outstretched hand—embodies the parallel Vincent saw between artistic and agricultural endeavor. The germination of ideas seemed as natural and necessary to Vincent as the cultivation of the land.*

Van Gogh Museum, Amsterdam. Oil on canvas (12½×15¾ inches).

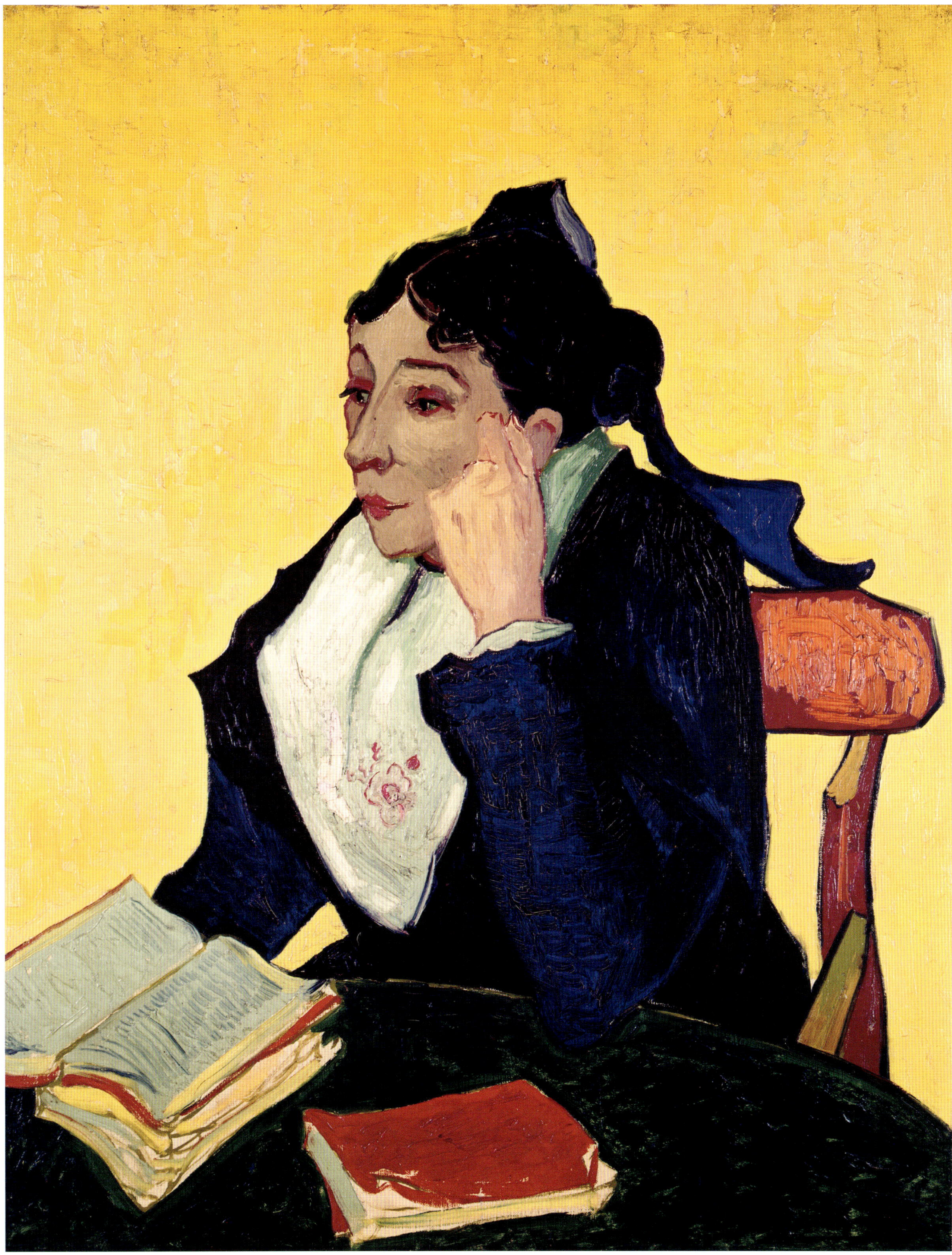

L'Arlesienne: Madame Joseph-Michel Ginoux *(1888). Marie Ginoux, proprietress of the Café de la Gare on the Place Lamartine, came to the Yellow House to sit for the two painters in early November. She wore traditional Arlesienne costume and posed with an umbrella on the table before her. Vincent completed one painting during the hour-long session, while Gauguin worked on a drawing. Vincent later made this version of his portrait, replacing the umbrella with a pile of books.*

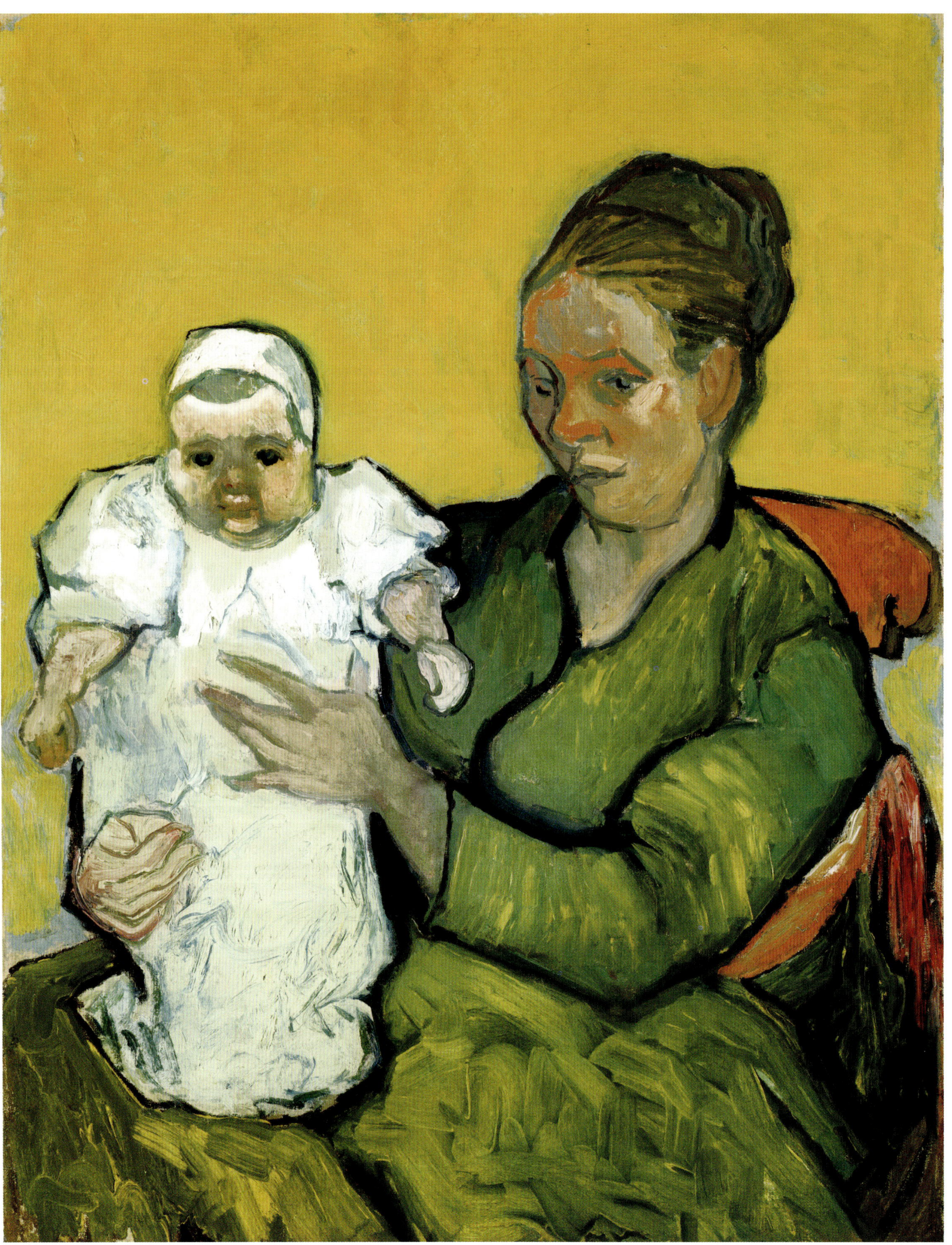

Madame Roulin with her Baby
Marcelle *(1888). At the end of
November, the bitter north wind
and the freezing rain forced Vincent to work indoors. Vincent
turned his energy to portrait
painting, and he convinced his
friend Joseph Roulin and his family
to sit for him. He long believed
that portraiture was the premier
subject of painting, and his repeti-
tion of subjects, such as Augustine
Roulin holding her youngest child,
reveals how he was striving to
improve.*

PHILADELPHIA MUSEUM OF ART. OIL ON CANVAS
(36¼×29 INCHES).

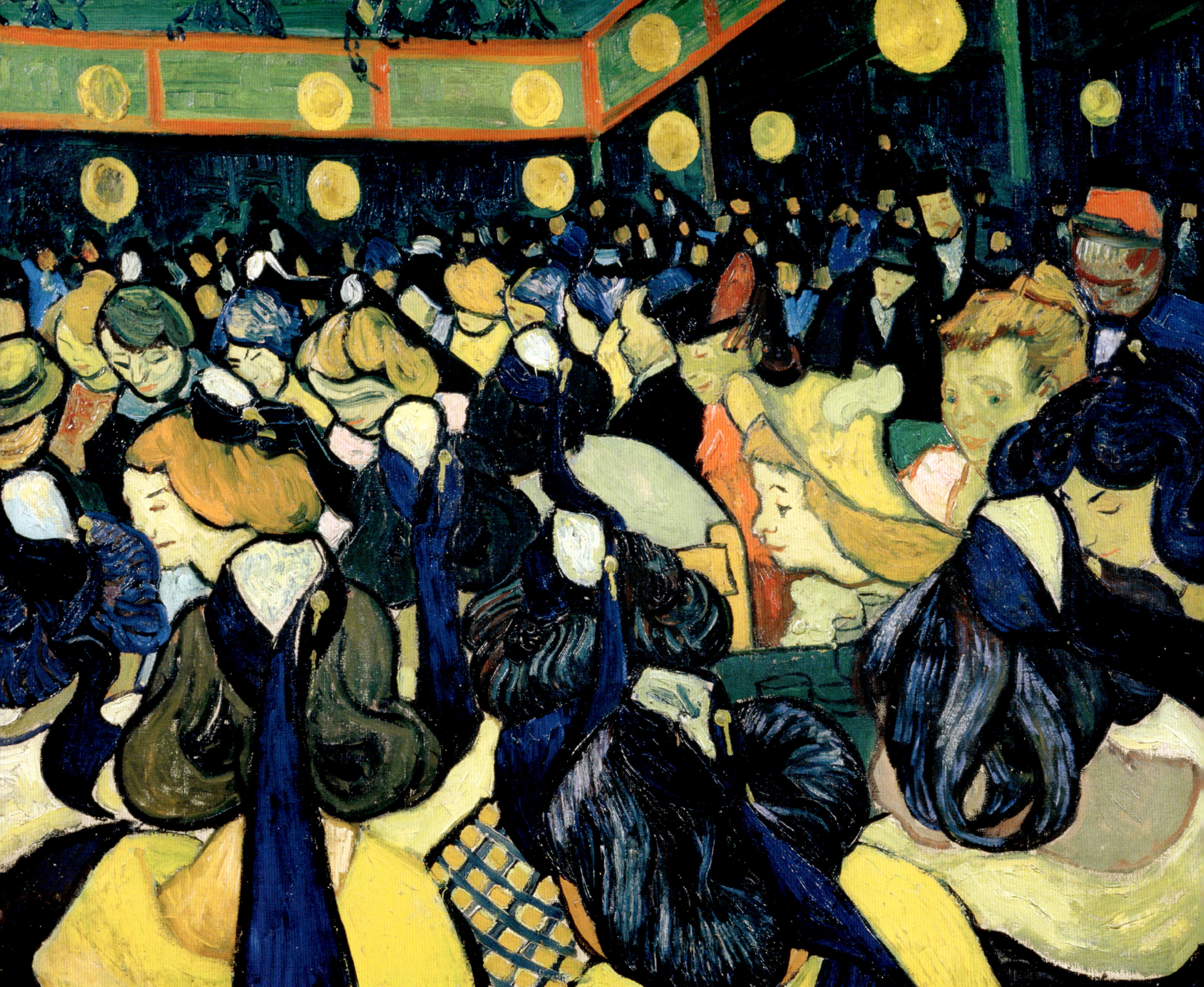

The Dance Hall *(1888). In a letter to Theo, Vincent expressed a discomfort at the profound influence Gauguin was having on his art but admitted that he was considering the older painter's advice. Vincent remained profoundly attached to his need for firsthand observation of nature, but in* The Dance Hall *he demonstrated his ability to assimilate new aesthetic ideas. By employing a sinuous contour line that isolates each hue into a separate cell of color, Vincent created a flat decorative effect in the synthetic manner favored by Gauguin's young followers.*

Musée d'Orsay, Paris. Oil on canvas (25½×32 inches).

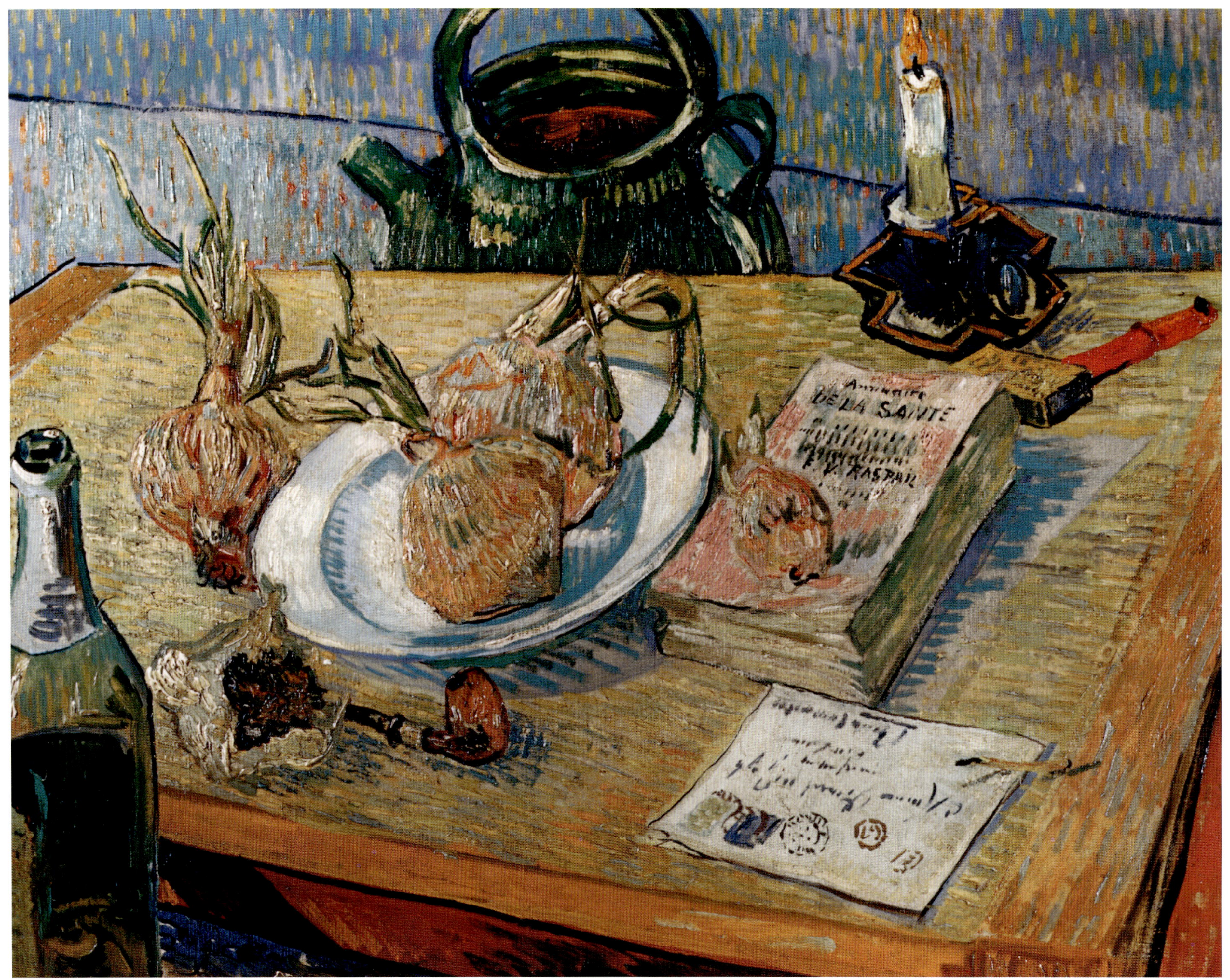

Still Life: Drawing Board, Pipe, Onions and Sealing Wax *(1888). Vincent returned to the Yellow House after a two-week stay in the hospital. Weak from loss of blood and shaken from what he called his "artist's fit," he immediately set to painting, as if to prove to himself and others that he would recover his mental, as well as his physical, health through work. He began as if reviewing his skills, with a few still-life compositions, using the symbols from his chair portrait to reaffirm his identity.*

KRÖLLER-MÜLLER MUSEUM, OTTERLO, NETHERLANDS. OIL ON CANVAS (19¾×25¼ INCHES).

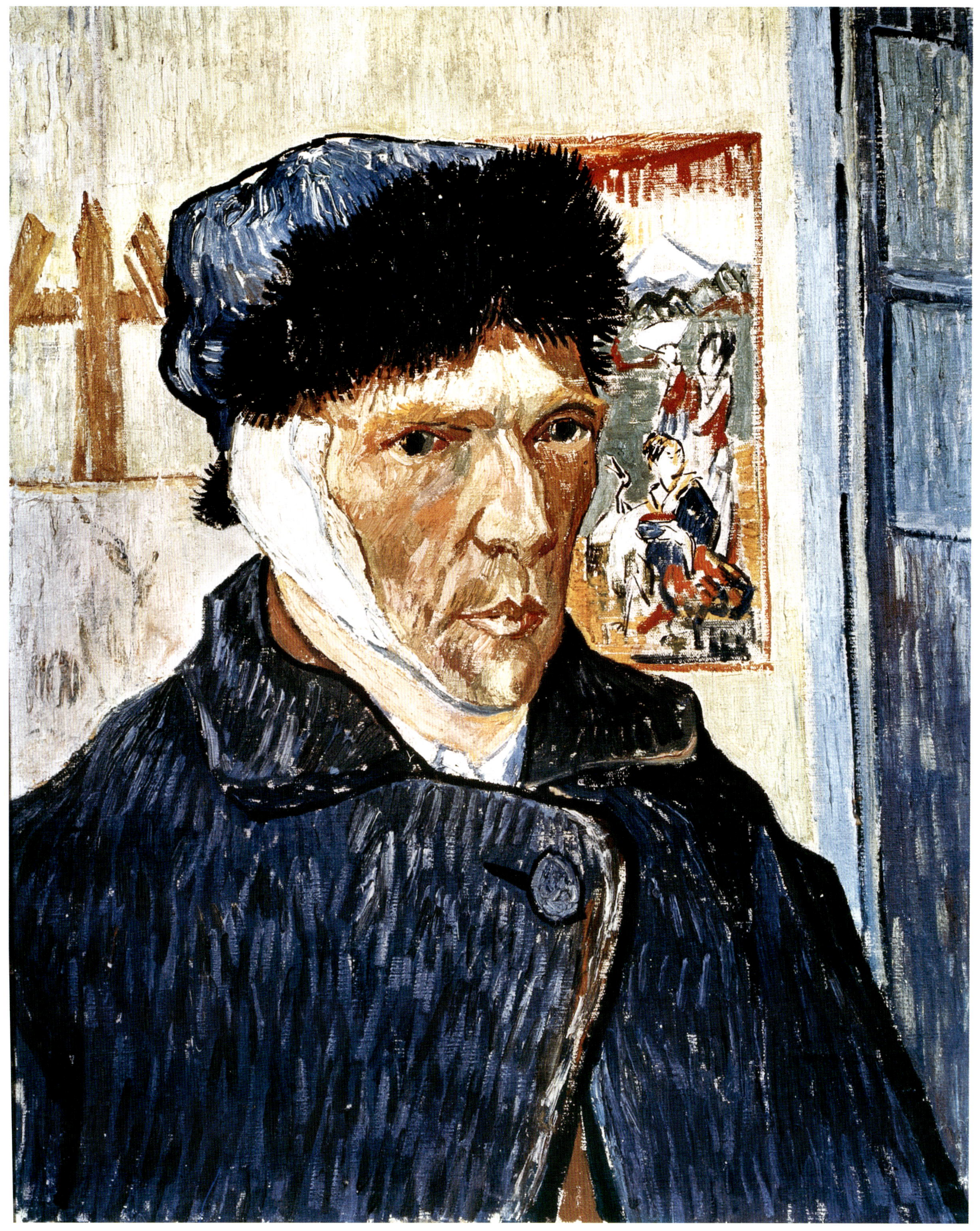

Self-Portrait with Bandaged Ear *(1888). Vincent painted two self-portraits while recovering from his self-inflicted wound. He was bundled up in a heavy winter coat and large fur hat, but he did not attempt to hide the heavy dressing on his ear. He wrote to Theo that his seizure and its aftermath ended his dream of organizing an artists' community in Arles. He asked why he had not heard from Gaugin: "Have I scared him?"*

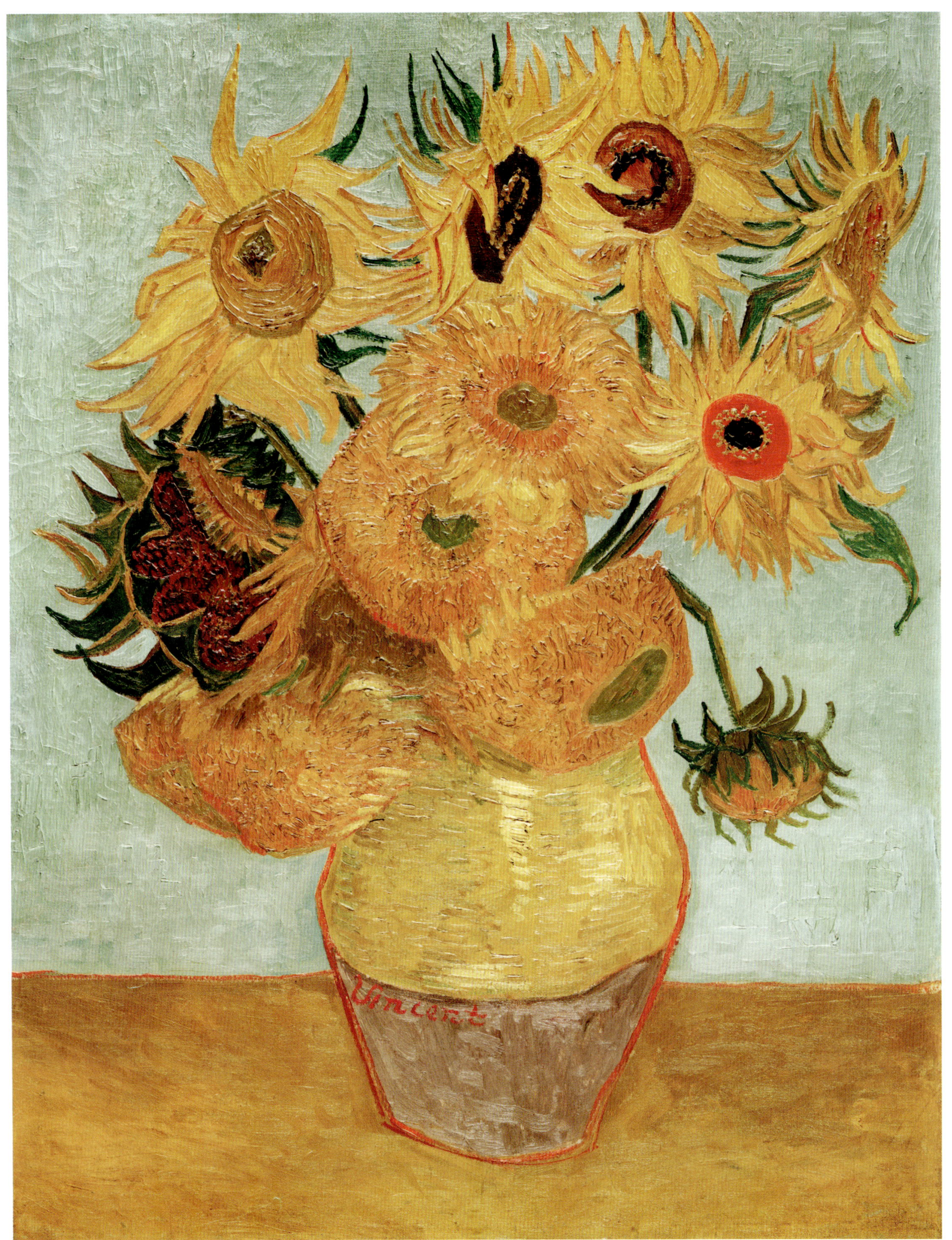

Still Life: Vase with Twelve Sun-flowers *(1888). Vincent used his own paintings as models as he resumed his work in January. His sunflower still lifes became a source of consolation as well as inspiration. He urged Theo to send Gauguin one of the paintings, remarking that his former housemate always liked them. In the sunflower, Vincent forged his own emblem, and he reflected that just as other artists were linked with specific flowers, "the sunflower is mine in a way."*

PHILADELPHIA MUSEUM OF ART. OIL ON CANVAS ($36\frac{1}{4} \times 28\frac{1}{2}$ INCHES).

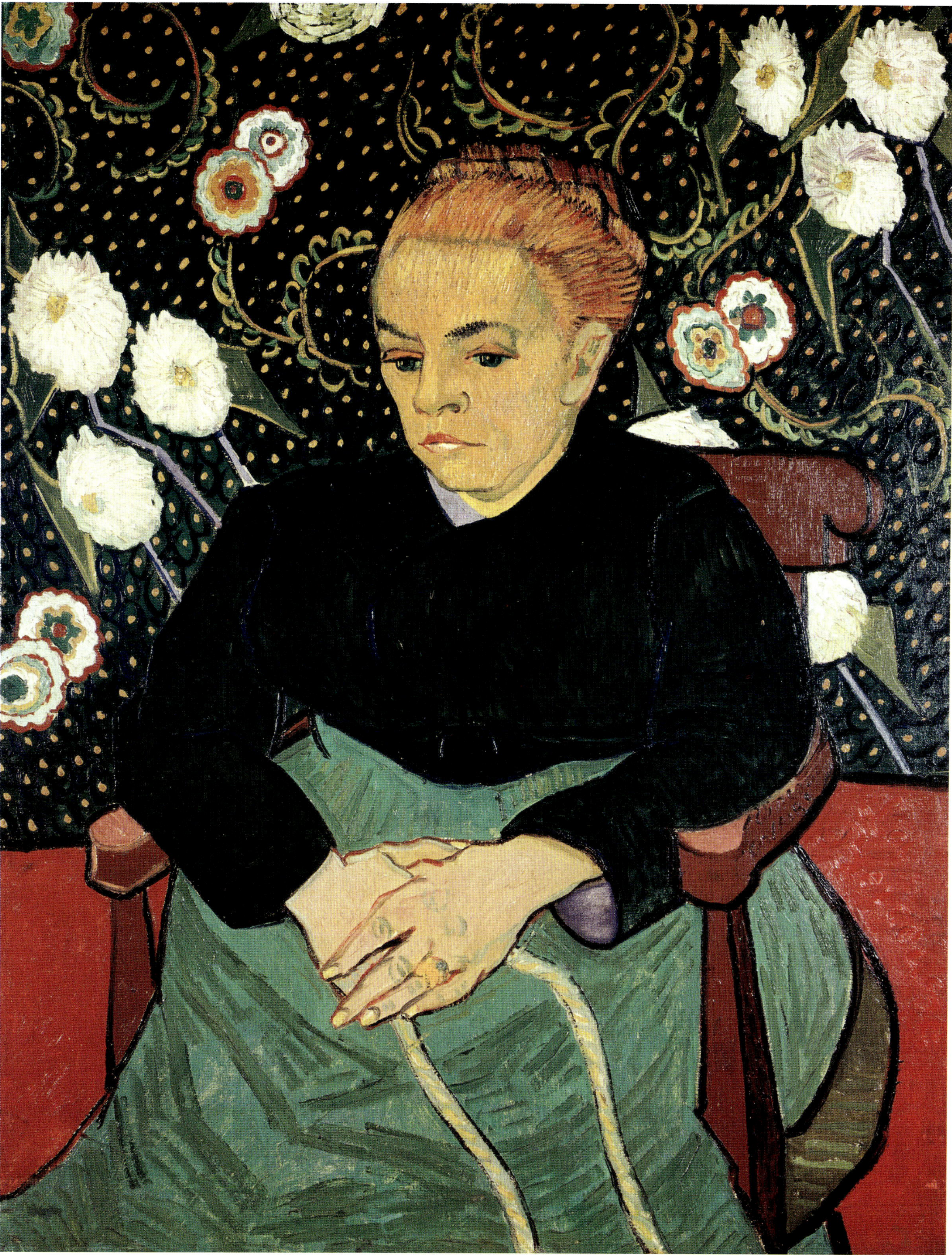

Madame Roulin Rock-
ing the Cradle (La
Berceuse) *(1889). Vin-
cent found a nearly
finished portrait of the
postman's wife in his
studio. Seated in the
armchair, holding a rope
that was attached to her
infant's cradle, Vincent
regarded the work as
soothing, a "lullaby in
colors." In the form of the
caring mother, Vincent
saw the embodiment of
consolation, and he
imagined* La Berceuse
(The Lullaby) *presented
as a triptych with a
sunflower still life on
either side.*

To Give Consolation

"Gauguin, Bernard, and I may... not conquer, but neither shall we be conquered; perhaps we exist neither for the one thing nor for the other, but to give consolation or prepare the way for a painting that will give even greater consolation."

VINCENT TO THEO, BETWEEN JUNE 17–19, 1889, FROM SAINT-RÉMY

UNABLE TO LIVE securely on his own in Arles, Vincent voluntarily entered Saint-Paul-de-Mausole, a psychiatric asylum in nearby Saint-Rémy-de-Provence. There, he found a protective and sympathetic environment where he believed he could regain his health as well as his strength of purpose. Although aware of his condition and the possibility that the seizures might return, Vincent held a powerful conviction that work would restore his emotional balance. Even before he made the decision to commit himself, he wrote to Theo: "As far as I can judge, I am not properly speaking a madman. You will see that the canvases I have done in the intervals are steady and not inferior to the others. I miss the work more than it tired me." When Vincent entered the asylum on May 8, 1889, his condition was diagnosed as a form of epilepsy. As long as he remained stable, the doctors allowed Vincent to paint, though for the first weeks of his

residence, he was confined to the hospital for supervision. It was high spring, and he longed to take his easel outdoors. Instead, Theo arranged for Vincent to set up a studio in an empty ground-floor room adjacent to the neglected hospital garden, which was filled with wild irises pushing up above a tangle of weeds. From there, he painted the irises with their vivid blue petals swaying like pennants on their tall green stalks.

From the window of his hospital room, Vincent could see groves of olive and cypress trees with the Alpilles hills rising in the distance. Making the most of his limited view, he painted the twisting

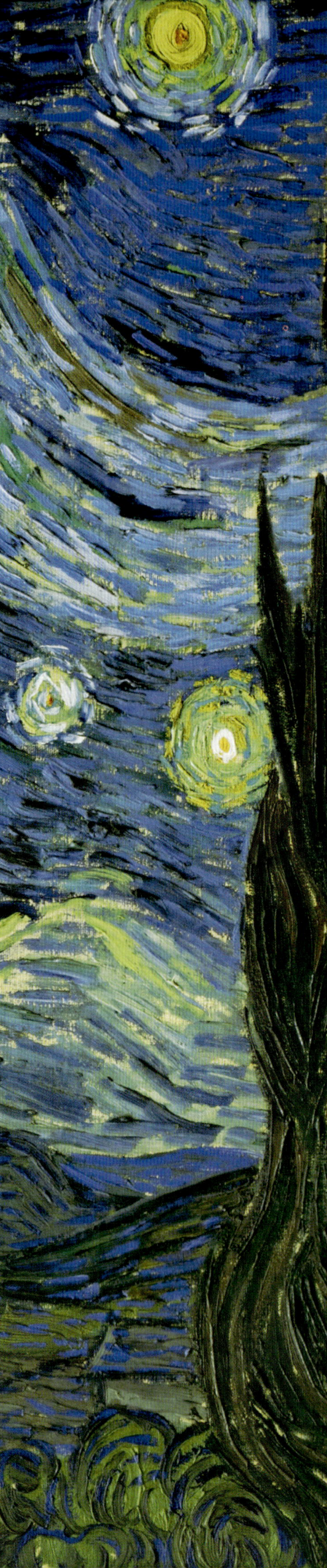

The Starry Night (1889). Vincent's room in the Saint-Rémy asylum looked out on the eastern sky. He painted the view as a panoramic vista spreading out into an almost infinite distance under a tumultuous sky ablaze with stars. The writhing branches of the cypress in the foreground are carved, like the stars, in thick impasto, and the tree vibrates with the rhythms of nature's divinity. The orange-yellow crescent moon makes a stark contrast to the vivid blue firmament, recalling Vincent's belief that arbitrary color allowed him to express himself "more forcefully."

MUSEUM OF MODERN ART, NEW YORK. OIL ON CANVAS (29×36¼ INCHES).

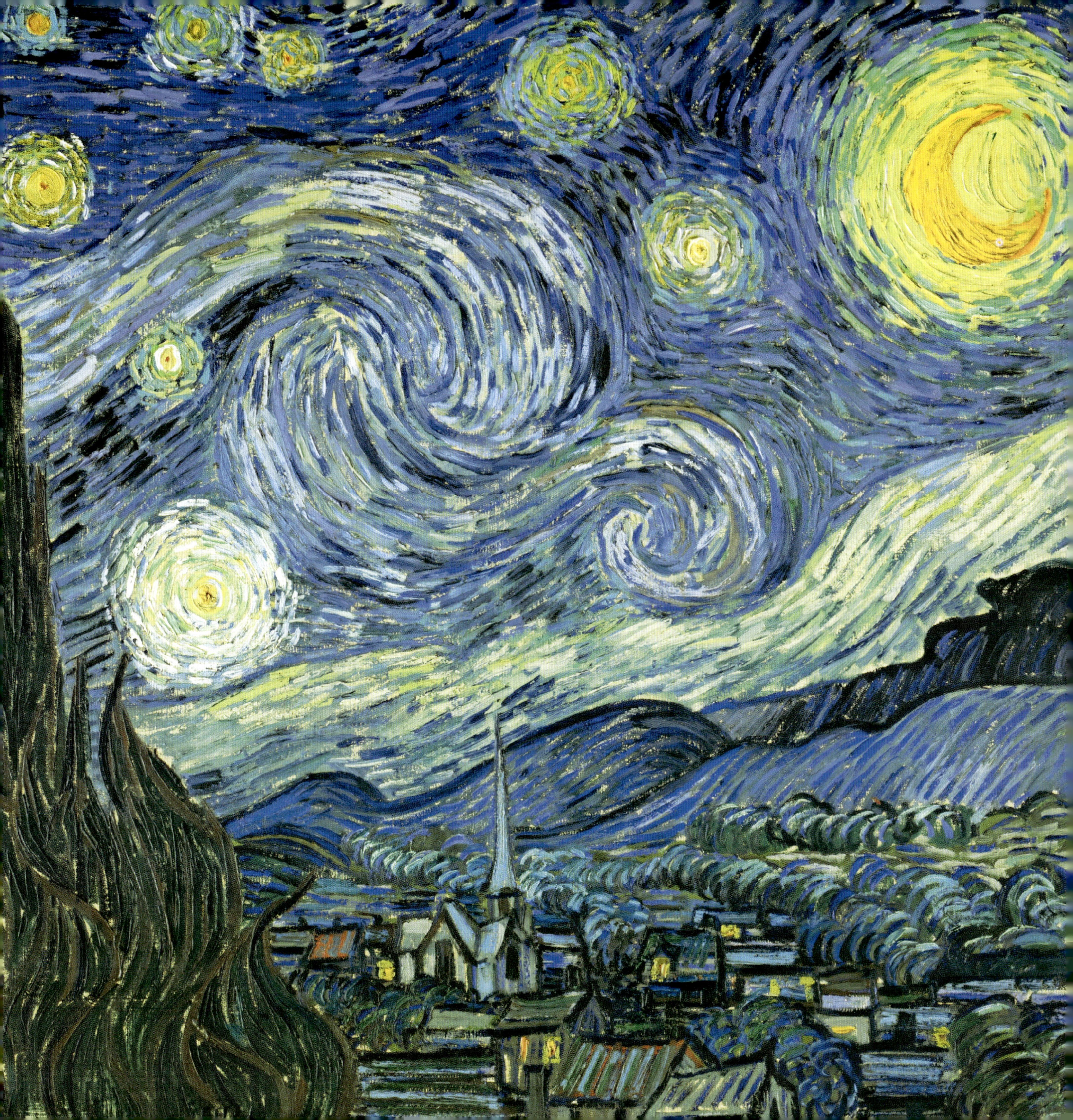

TO GIVE CONSOLATION

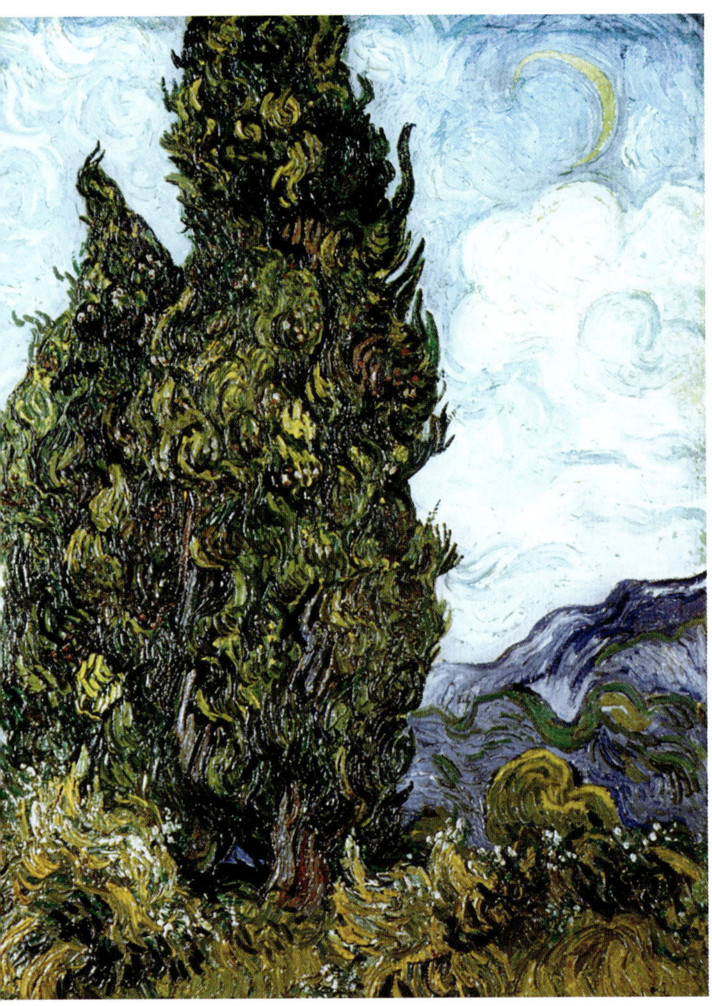

Cypresses *(1889). Within a month of his arrival at the mental asylum, Vincent gained permission to paint in the open air. He ventured just beyond the grounds of the hospital into the groves of cypress trees that he could see from his window. He observed them closely, explaining to Theo that the trees were constantly on his mind and that as a motif they reminded him of sunflowers, "because it astonishes me that they have not been done as I see them."*

branches of the cypress trees writhing around their trunks as if to chart the vigor of their growth. He used heavy paint, building his surface with thick impasto that emphasized the contrast between the dark stand of trees and the pale but volatile sky. He described the effect—"a splash of black in a sunny background"—as difficult to capture. In June, while still under confined observation, Vincent painted *The Starry Night* (1889). During the previous year in Arles, he had taken his paints outside on an autumn night to view the stars that illuminated the sky over the Rhône. The resulting painting, *Starry Night over the Rhône* (1888), proclaimed his exhilaration as well as his anxiety. He portrayed the stars as dabs of gold, casting their hazy auras over a deep blue night sky. Black silhouettes of boats bobbed off the dock in the foreground, where an anonymous pair of lovers strolled arm in arm. In contrast, the panoramic terrain of *The Starry Night* appears to undulate back into the distance under a chaotic sky. Magnified many times in size, the auras of the stars swirl around their hot, glowing centers while comets flash shimmering trails of light. The vivid crescent moon radiates like the sun, and the whole sky is charged with an energy that Vincent depicted in sweeping, energetic strokes. The sinuous form of a cypress tree punctures the foreground, and deep in the middle distance, tiny buildings cluster around a fragile-looking church and its slender spire. Although based upon the reality of the view out of his window, *The Starry Night* proclaims the power Vincent sensed in the universe, a power he revered and embraced but could not fully comprehend.

In his letters to Theo, Vincent repeatedly expressed his frustration at not being allowed to work outdoors. But by mid-June, he was permitted to paint in the fields surrounding Saint-Rémy in the company of an attendant. Although he alluded to the expense of remaining in the asylum, Vincent never curtailed his requests for more canvas and more paint. He was also eager for news of the art world in Paris and urged Theo to extend his regards to his friends Paul Gauguin and Emile Bernard. Many of his letters from Saint-Rémy-de-Provence reflect upon the pictures he had painted in Arles. Isolated from the energetic exchange of ideas that he had experienced in Paris, as well as when living with Gauguin, his concern marked an attempt to position his own work in a realm that he feared was becoming increasingly distant and out of his reach. To bridge that growing chasm, Vincent reflected upon artists and writers—such

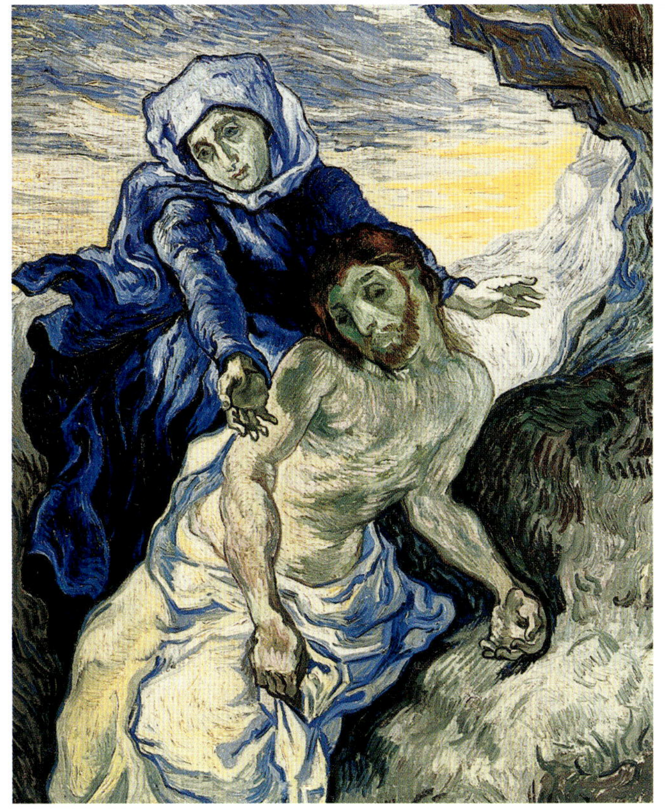

Pietà (After Delacroix) *(1889). In his return to work, Vincent resumed his old habit of making oil copies of black and white reproductions of the works of art he admired. Eugène Delacroix's color theory had shaped his own ideas about color from his earliest reflections on painting. The resonant contrast of blue and yellow—broken only by Christ's red hair and beard—heightens the emotional power as well as his personal connection to the art of Delacroix.*

as Honoré Daumier and Émile Zola—who articulated a deep and empathetic understanding of current human conditions. It was Vincent's hope that his own art could do the same. He worried little about professional success or failure, suggesting, "Perhaps we exist neither for the one thing or the other, but to give consolation or prepare the way" for an art that would salve the anguish of the modern soul.

During the first week of July, Vincent visited Arles to retrieve some of the paintings he had left in his studio. Shortly after, while painting in the fields on the outskirts of Saint-Rémy, he suffered a severe seizure that left him debilitated for more than five weeks. By September, his condition had stabilized, and he cautiously returned to work by painting familiar subjects. He painted two self-portraits that revived his favorite contrast of colors, with yellow for his pallid complexion and rich ultramarine blue for his jacket and the swirling color field behind him. He made replicas of some of his Arles paintings, including the view of his bedroom. But he longed to take his paints

outdoors and work in front of the example of nature. He complained to Theo that he felt "like a fool going and asking doctors permission to make pictures," but he fully grasped the seriousness of his condition, realizing that "a more violent attack may forever destroy my power to paint." With a lack of models, he returned to the practice of copying reproductions. He made a replica of Eugène Delacroix's *Pietà* and, using a set of prints after Jean-François Millet's *Labors of the Field,* he revived the spirit of consolation and solace he had found before in nature. The inherent order of rural work, sowing and reaping in a never-ending cycle, reassured him. He had long associated the sower with the burgeoning of ideas, but now the reaper rose in his regard.

He described them to Theo as opposites—the sower bringing new life and the reaper bringing death—but he found consolation in his grim reflection: "I see in this reaper… the image of death…. But there's nothing sad in this death; it goes its way in broad daylight with a sun flooding everything with a light of pure gold."

Self-Portrait (1889). Vincent had painted at least 40 self-portraits over the course of his career. To render his own image, Vincent faced the challenge of confronting his own identity and emotional condition, and he subjected himself to uncompromising scrutiny. In one of his last attempts to express his own image through his art, Vincent employs a vigorous brush stroke and a nearly monochrome palette for his jacket as well as the background, creating an emotionally charged atmosphere from which he warily gazes back at the viewer.

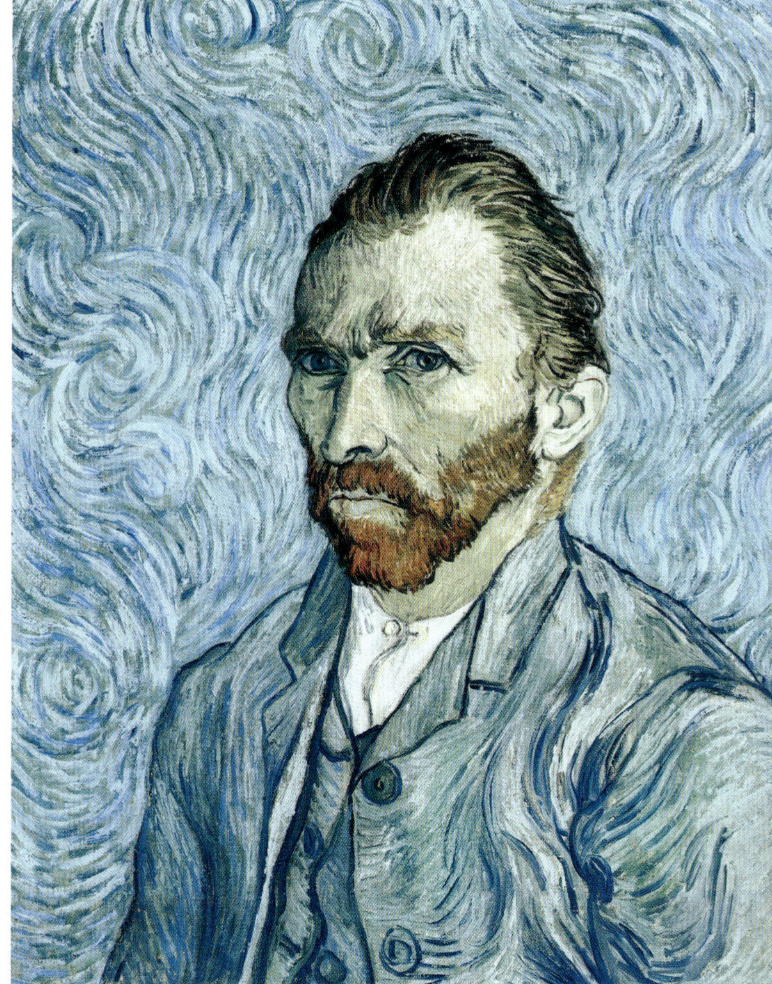

To Give Consolation

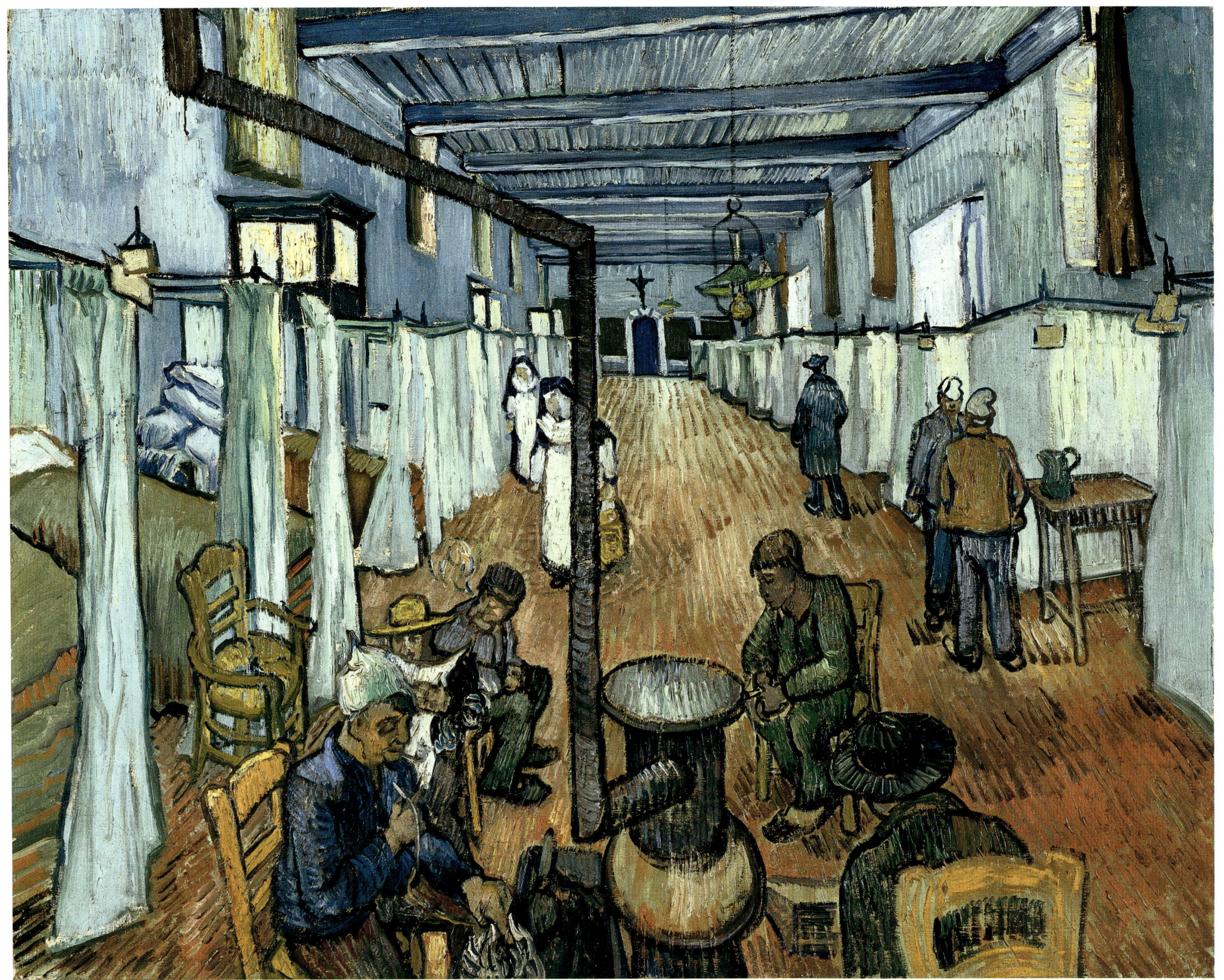

Ward of Arles Hospital (1889). *Vincent spent his last months in Arles living in the hospital. When his health permitted, he left the premises to paint in the fields. He also painted the scenes outside his window. He felt more secure living with medical supervision, but in his painting of the men's ward of the hospital, the exaggerated length of the corridor and the nervous contours that delineate the figures of the patients express the emotional weight of his isolation and confinement.*

Collection Oskar Reinhart 'Am Römerholz,' Winterthur, Switzerland. Oil on canvas (28¼×35¼ inches).

Orchard in Blossom with View of Arles *(1889). In* Orchard in Blossom with View
of Arles, *Vincent returned to the subject that gave him inspiration after his arrival in
Arles. The lighter, silvery character of his blue and green palette conveyed the sense of
nature's fresh renewal, and his deft even stroke, which evokes a gentle breeze stirring the
grasses, conveys the tranquility and promise Vincent associated with the spring season.
But the twisted trunk of the tree recalls the intensity he infused into the motif of the
sower the previous year.*

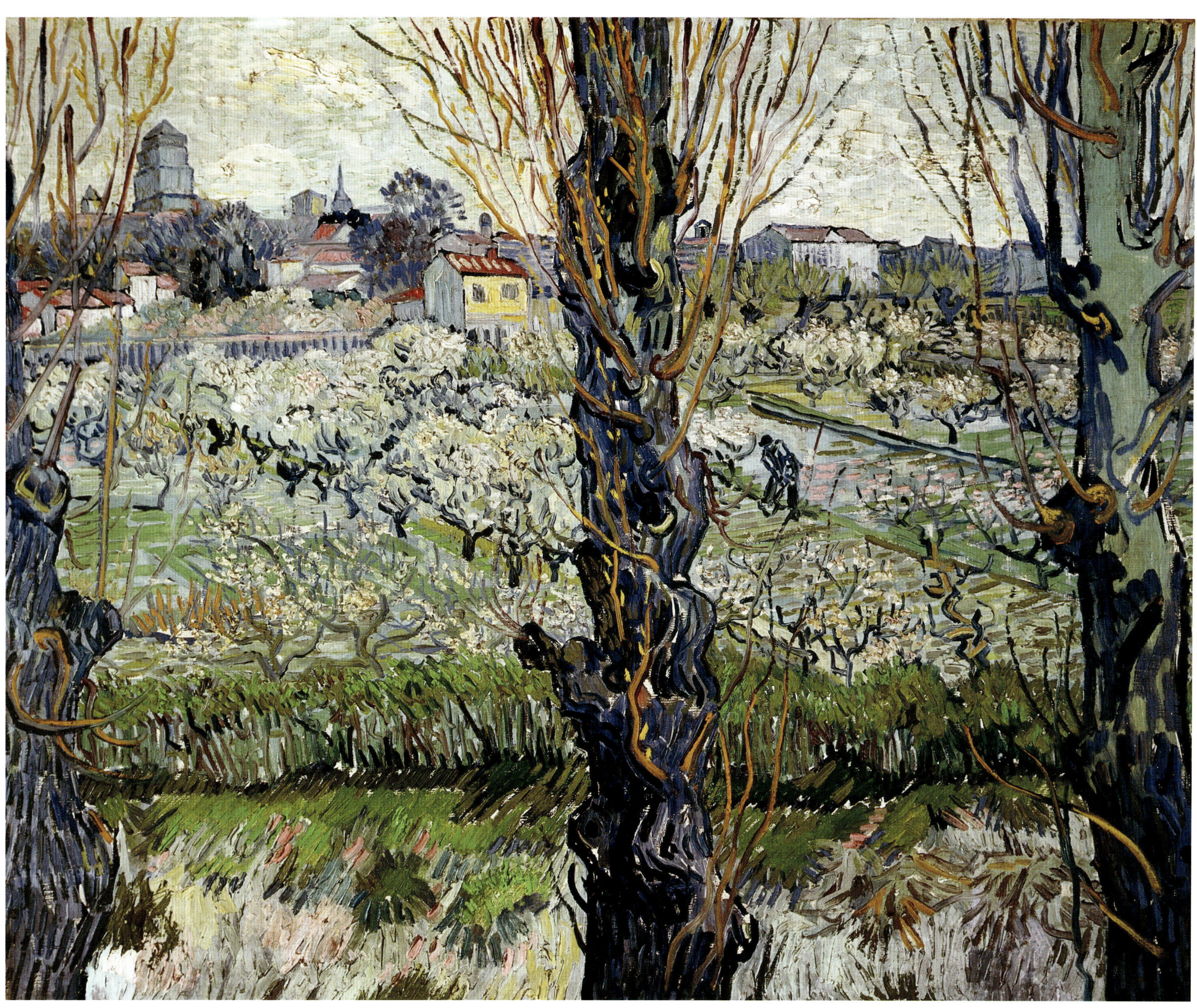

To Give Consolation

Le Crau with Peach Trees in Blossom *(1889). Vincent moved to Provence for the restorative warmth of the sun and picturesque tranquility of the rural location. The blue sky, verdant fields, and blooming fruit trees sparked a vitality in his art that freed him to experiment with a lighter palette and varied brush strokes. In nuanced tones and with a delicate touch, he painted the fields a last time, asserting that his physical and emotional trials were justified by his artistic development.*

COURTAULD INSTITUTE GALLERY, LONDON. OIL ON CANVAS (25¾×32 INCHES).

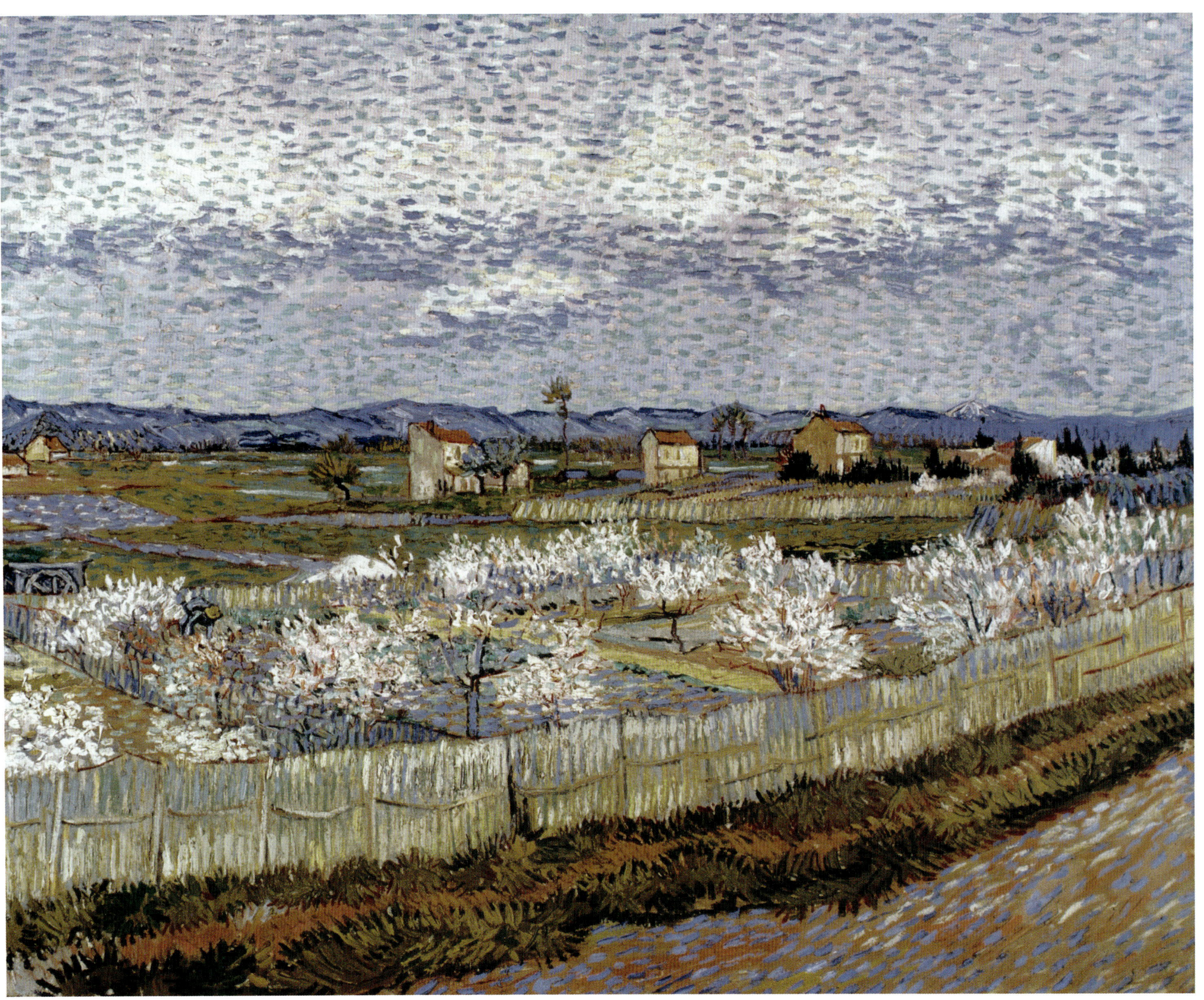

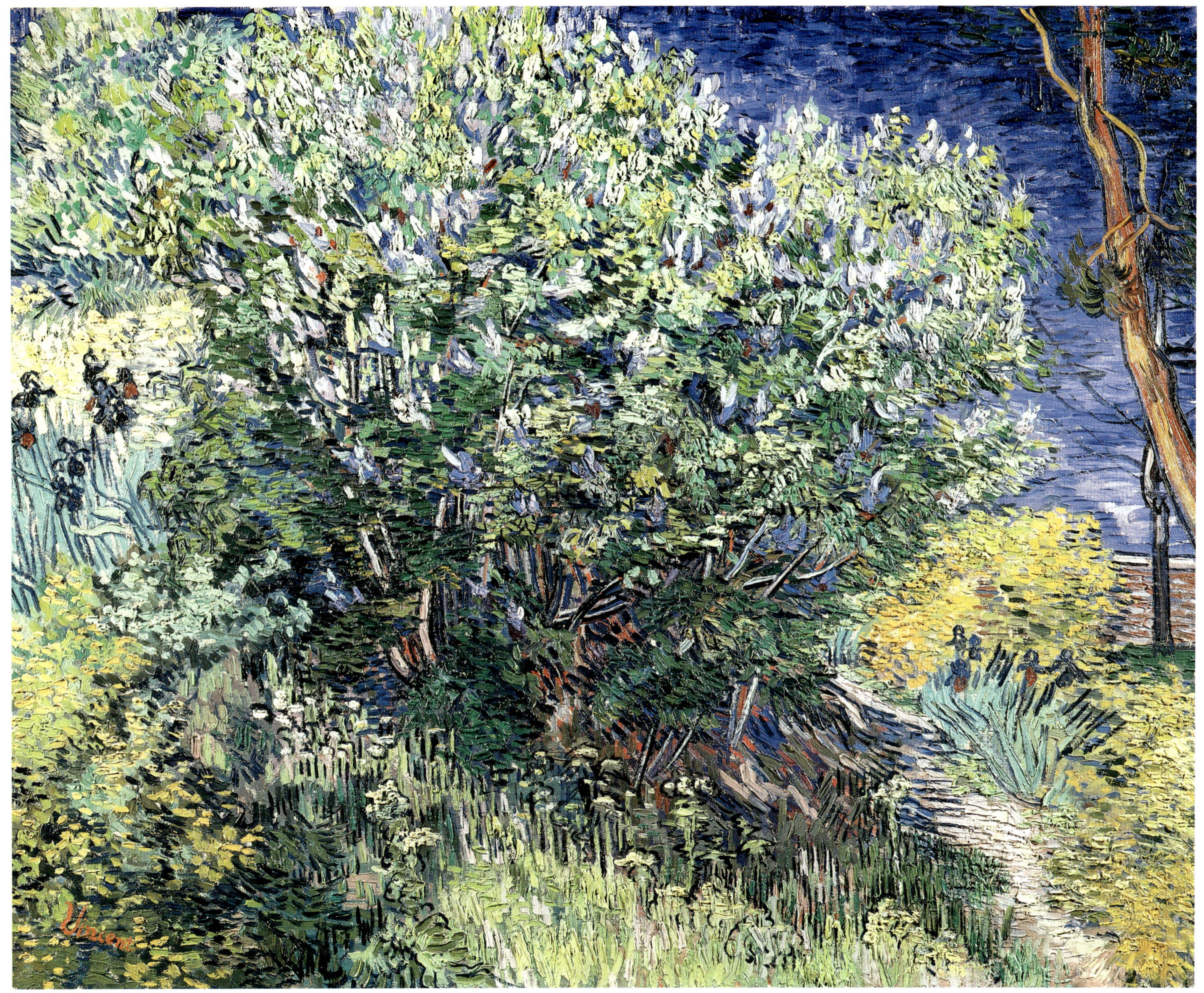

Lilacs *(1889). Living in constant fear of the return of his seizures, Vincent voluntarily entered the mental asylum of Saint-Paul-de-Mausole. While his condition was assessed, Vincent considered the potential subjects available to him in confinement. These included an unkempt garden and the view out his window, but he longed to take his easel to the countryside. The leafy lilac trees, just coming into their pale blooms, gave him a subject to paint on the grounds of the asylum.*

Hermitage, Leningrad. Oil on canvas (28¾×36¼ inches).

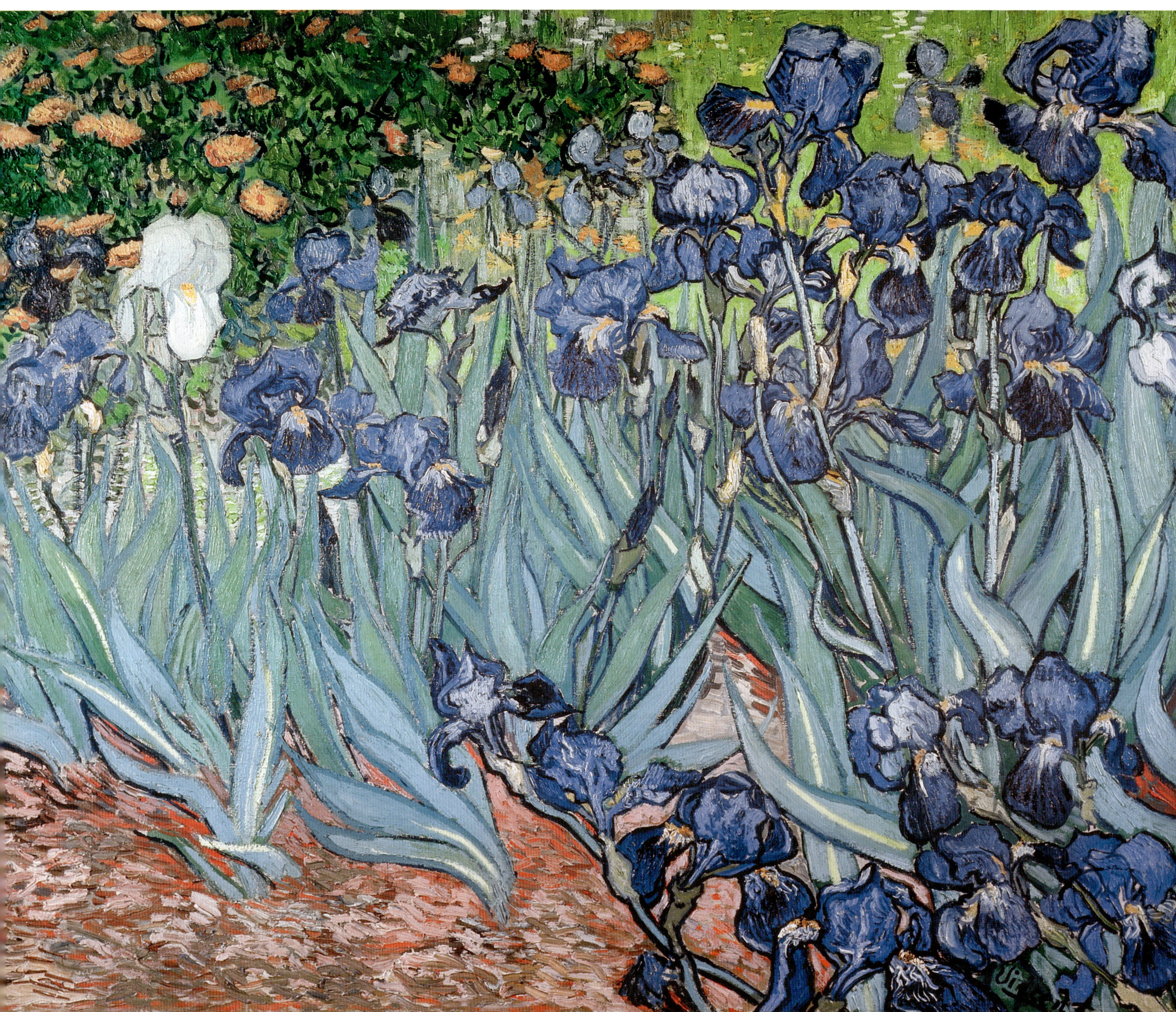

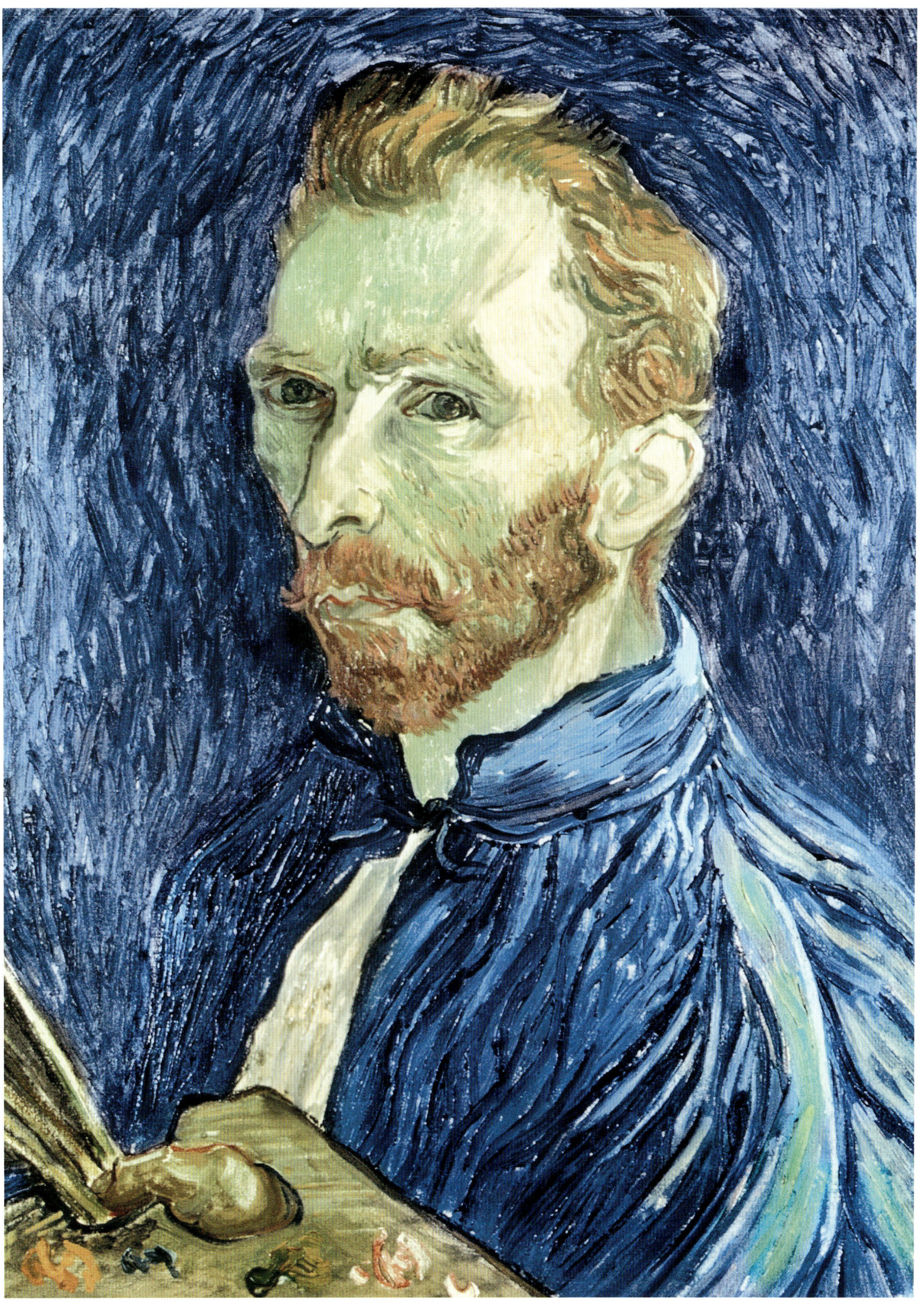

Irises *(1889). During his first month in the asylum in Saint-Rémy under the care of a sympathetic staff, Vincent's fears abated. His doctors recognized his need to work, and by the end of May, Vincent found it necessary to ask Theo to send him more canvas and paint. He painted the irises that grew on the hospital grounds, and he assured Theo, "When you receive the canvases I have done in the garden, you will see I am not too melancholy here."*

Self-Portrait *(1889). The violence of the seizures Vincent suffered in the summer left him debilitated. To prevent him from ingesting more turpentine, his doctors confiscated his painting materials. When he recovered sufficient calm and strength, he was able to return to painting. His first self-portrait of this time shows him haggard, and he described his appearance as "lean and pale, a poor devil," but he positioned himself to hide his maimed ear.*

A Corridor in the Asylum *(1889). Vincent painted the corridors of the asylum, just as he had painted the men's ward at the hospital in Arles. Here, only a single figure can be seen, passing from the seemingly endless hall into one of the anonymous rooms that stretch along the length of the corridor. The long, narrow hall, penetrating into the deep distance, conveys the sense of futility he experienced in confinement. His letters also reveal an increasing discontent, and he began to propose the possibility of leaving the asylum and living with supervision.*

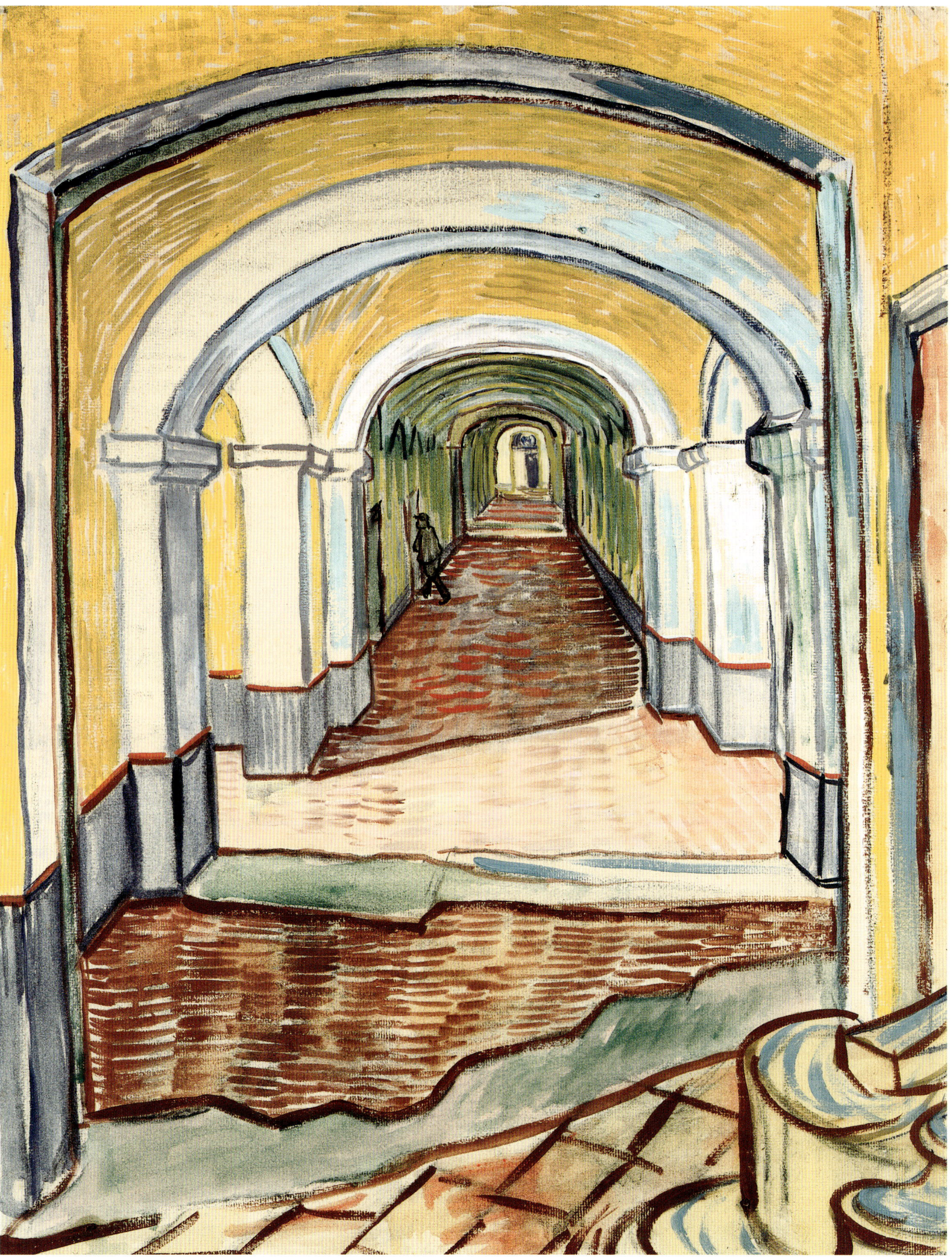

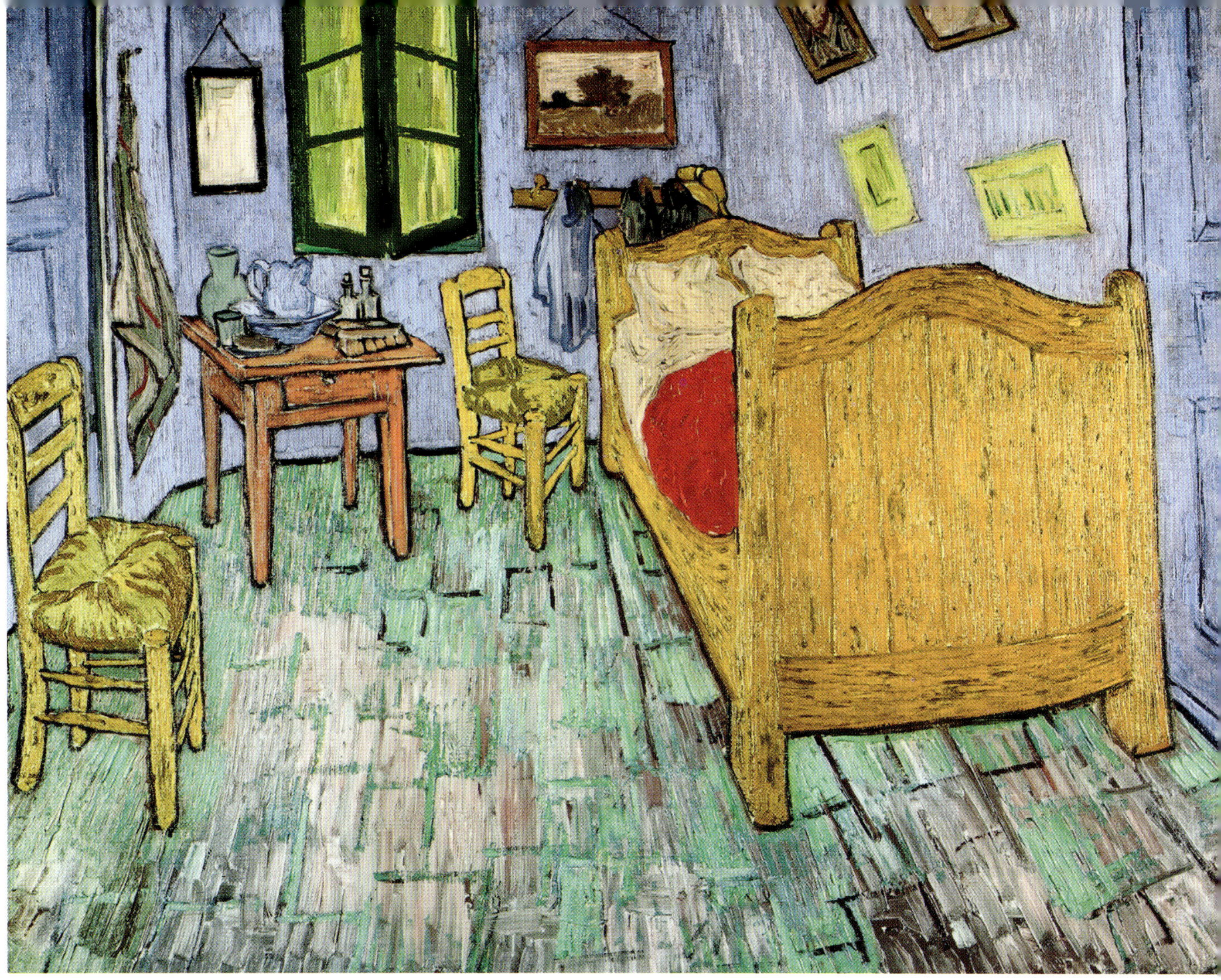

The Bedroom *(1889). Just as Vincent revived his motif of sunflowers as he recovered from his self-mutilation, he returned to the images of the Yellow House as he recuperated in Saint-Rémy. He reprised the painting of his bedroom, intensifying the colors and sharpening the details of the pictures on the wall. When his thoughts strayed back to his life in Arles, he was filled with wistful regret, telling his brother, "I still think that Gauguin and I will perhaps work together again."*

Art Institute of Chicago. Oil on canvas (28¾×36¼ inches).

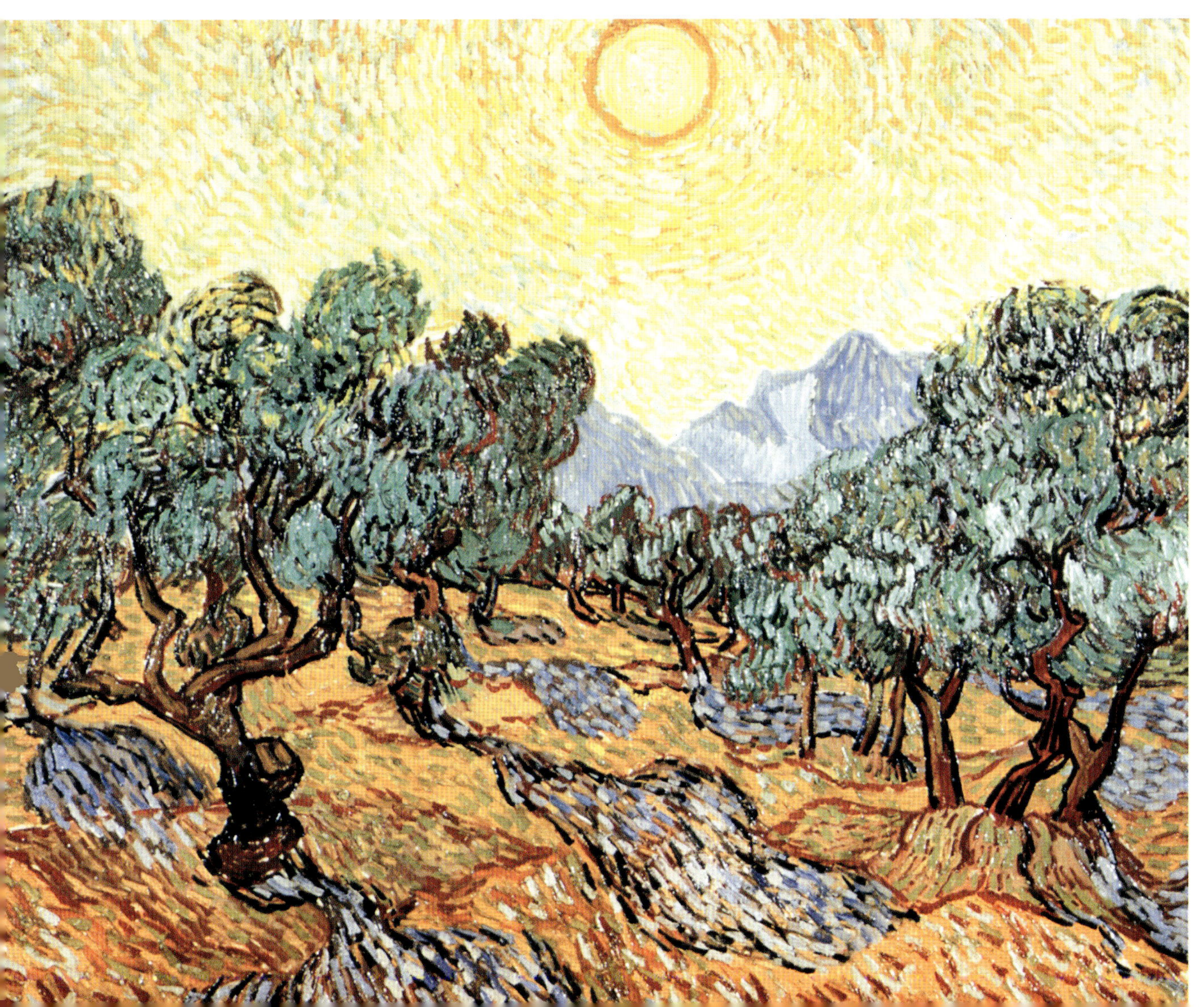

The Olive Trees *(1889). When Vincent was finally allowed to leave the premises of the asylum to paint, the surrounding olive groves drew his interest. Always believing that work in nature restored and consoled him, Vincent painted the twisting trunks of the trees with dense green foliage under a yellow sun in a yellow sky, recalling the landscapes he had painted the previous year in Arles.*

Minneapolis Institute of Arts. Oil on canvas (29×36½ inches).

103

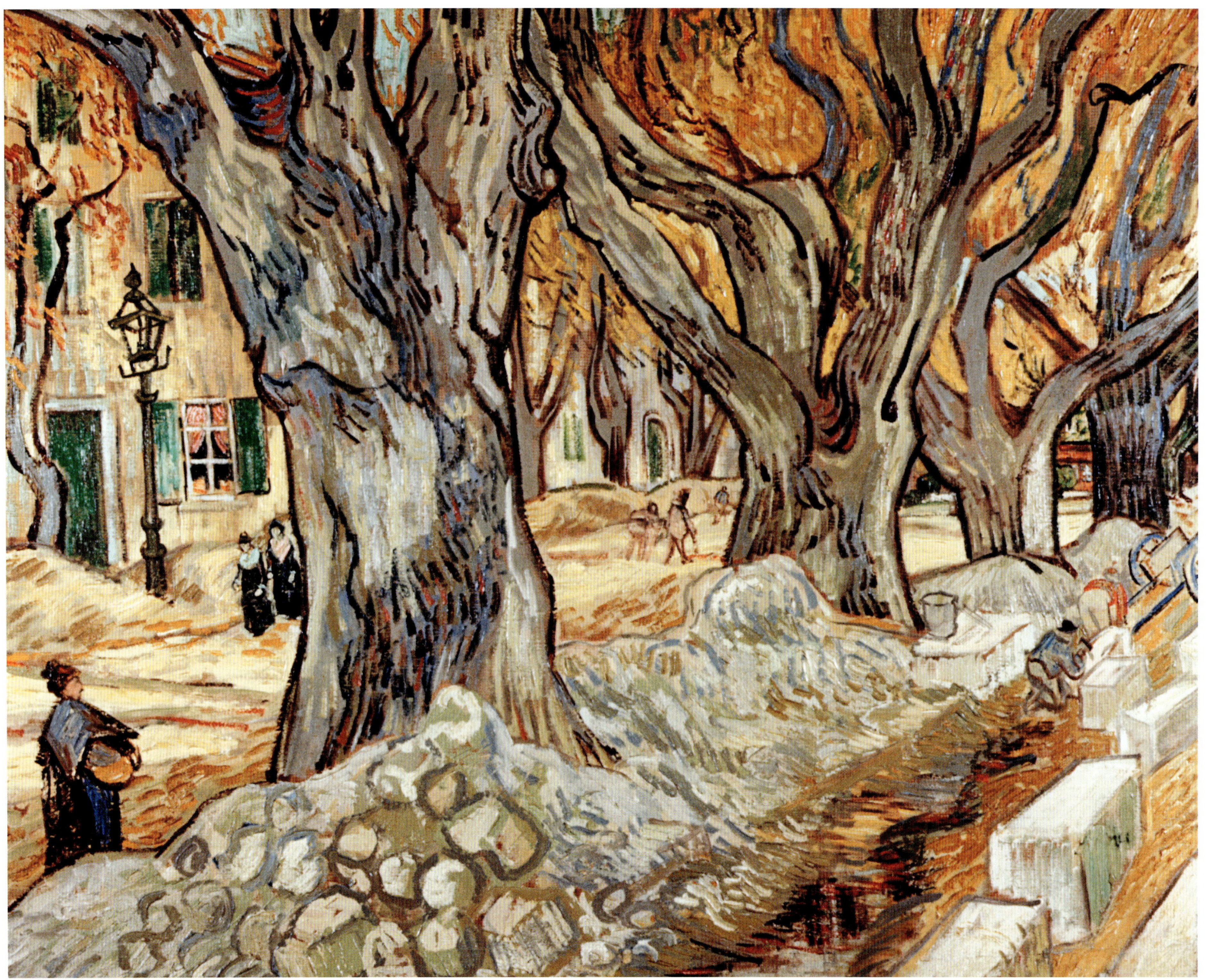

The Large Plane Trees *(1889). Here, Vincent restricted his palette to shades of yellow, recalling the chromatic experiments of the sunflowers. Hints of green on the ground and in the tree trunks cool the tonality, while the branches in the right distance flame brightly in autumnal orange. These color modifications and the expressive contours of the twisting branches indicate the overwhelming energy of nature, in contrast to the static blocks of masonry that line the road.*

CLEVELAND MUSEUM OF ART. OIL ON CANVAS (29×36¼ INCHES).

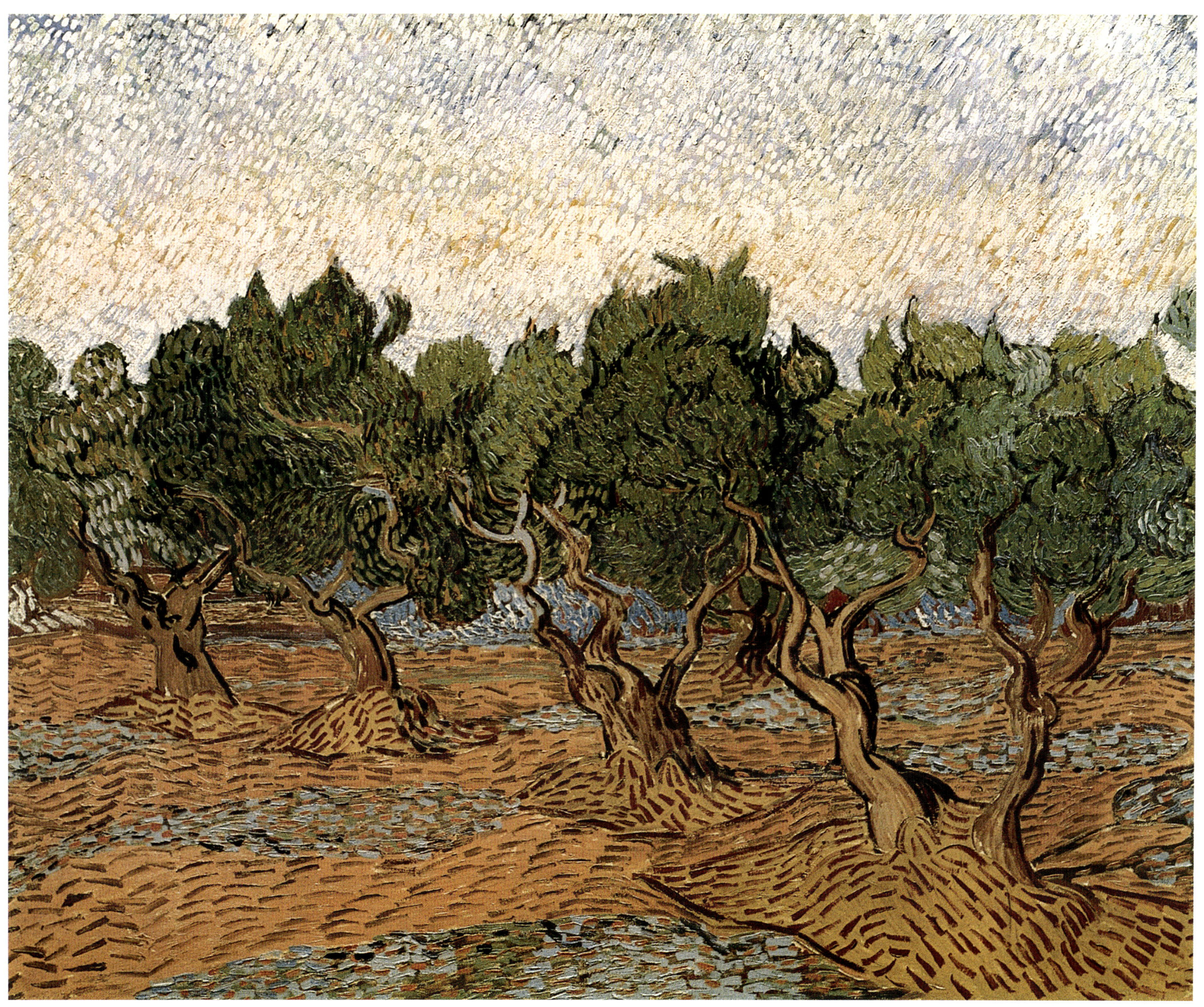

Olive Grove (1889). When Vincent first arrived in Saint-Rémy, he wrote to Theo that the olive groves reminded him of the heightened colors he had sought when he moved to the south. The leaves appeared like "old silver… turning to green against the blue," and the "orange-colored plowed earth" suggested nature's fecundity. After more than six months in confinement, this vision remained; only the sky has changed to a cooler greenish blue.

Van Gogh Museum, Amsterdam. Oil on canvas (28¾×36¼ inches).

To Give Consolation

Noon: Rest from Work (After Millet) (1890). *Vincent suffered another severe attack in December, but his recovery was rapid. Two more attacks followed in January and February requiring an extended convalescence. When he was able to paint, he again turned to the works of Millet to find consolation. The clear pure hues of blue and yellow, as well as the thick application of paint, reveal no diminishment of his power or of his identification with the honesty of agricultural toil.*

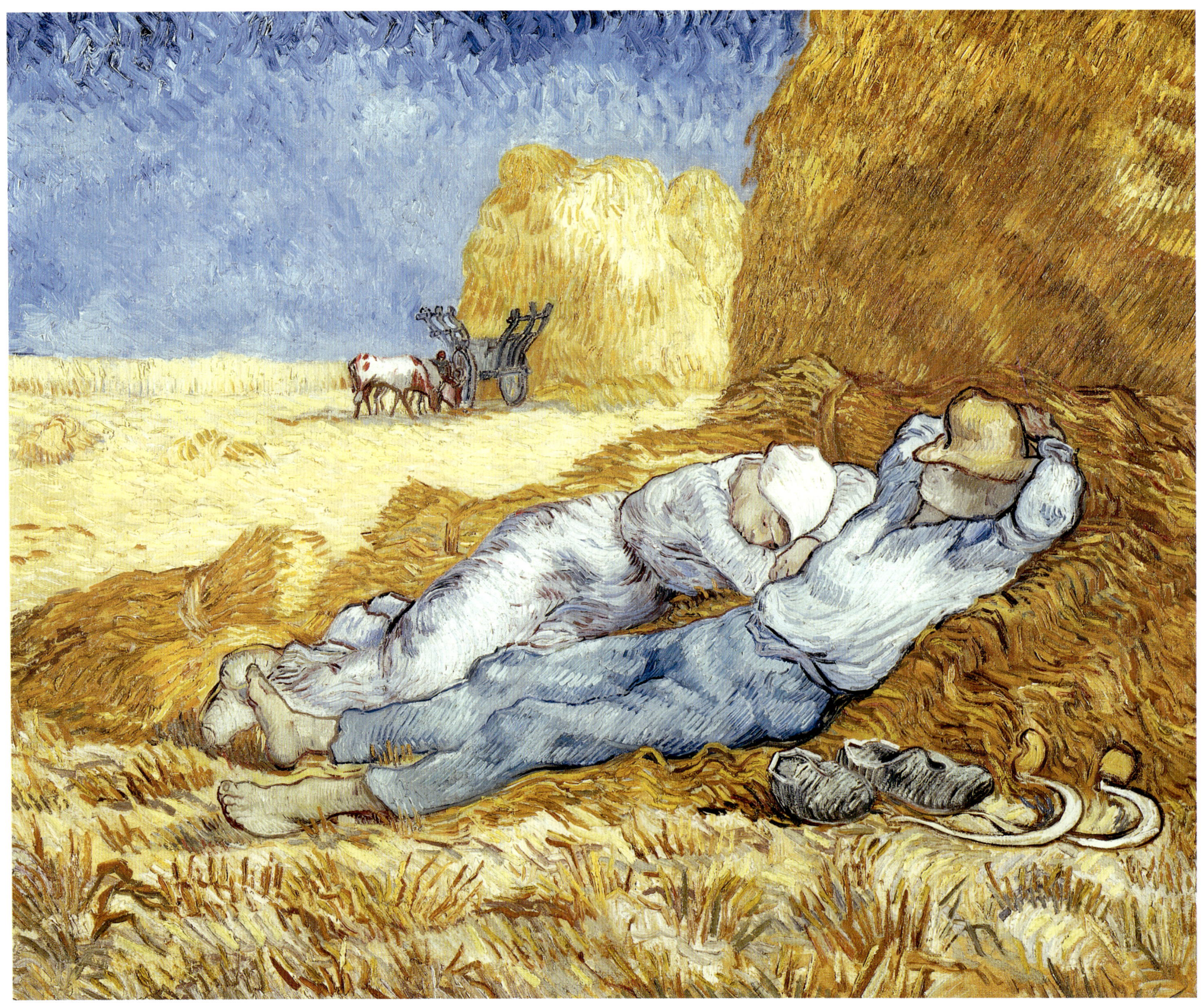

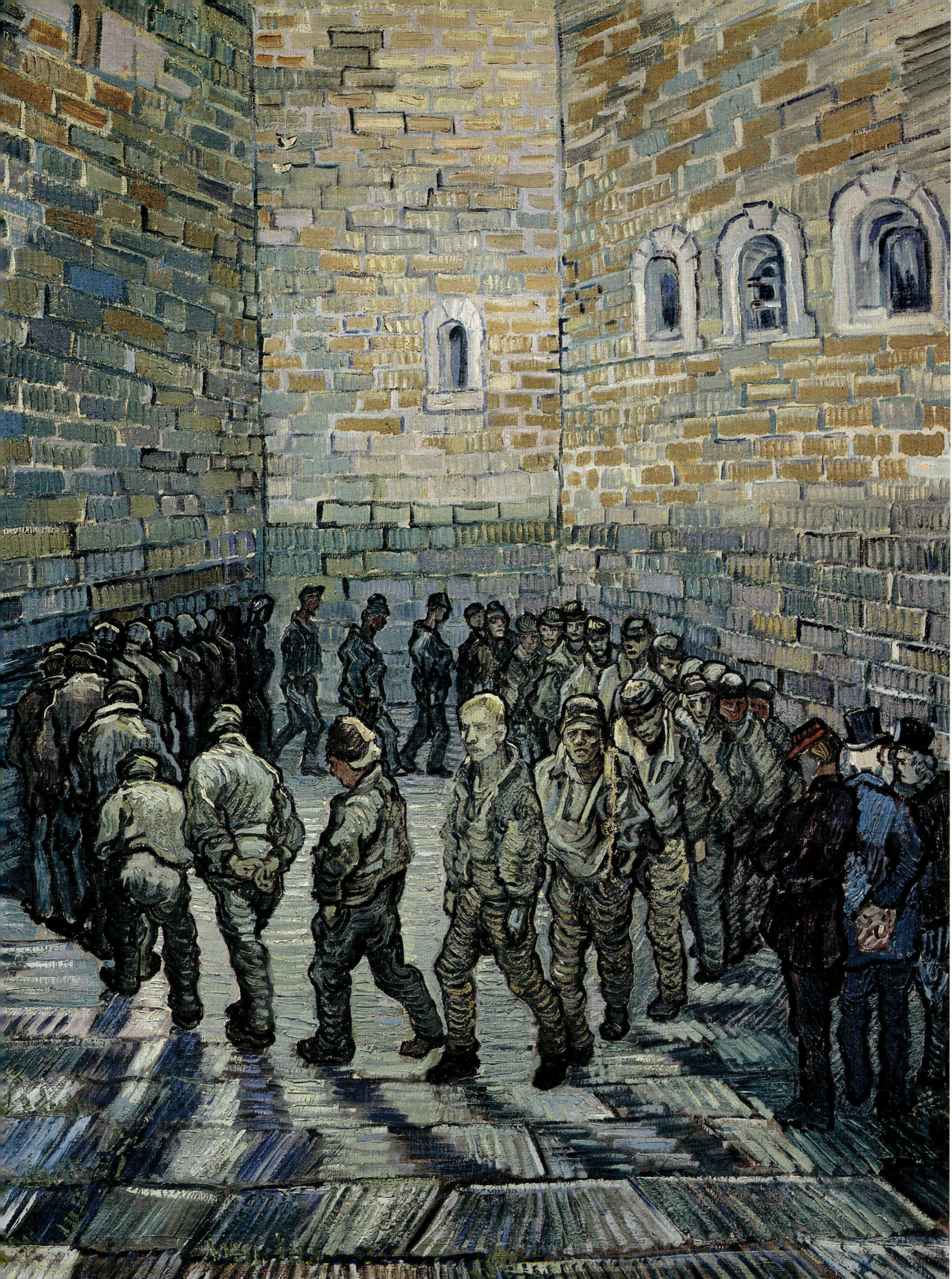

Prisoners Exercising (After Doré) *(1890). As Vincent regained his strength, his desire to leave Saint-Rémy intensified. He made an oil copy of Gustave Doré's print of life in prison, portraying the inmates marching slowly in an endless circle, exercising their stiff limbs. The nearly monochromatic palette and the sense of confinement created by the splayed walls heighten the monotony of the image of futile activity, reflecting Vincent's own frustration and discontent.*

PUSHKIN MUSEUM OF FINE ART, MOSCOW. OIL ON CANVAS (31½×25¼ INCHES).